PENGUIN BOOKS

CHAPTER AND VERSE

Mike Bryan is a native Texan. He has been, among other things, a newspaper reporter, magazine editor, construction superintendent, counselor in a drug treatment program, and story analyst in the movie business. His previous books include *If at First* (with Keith Hernandez), *Dogleg Madness*, and *Baseball Lives*.

MIKE BRYAN

CHAPTER AND VERSE

A Skeptic Revisits Christianity

PENGUIN BOOKS

PENGUIN BOOKS
Published by the Penguin Group
Viking Penguin, a division of Penguin Books USA Inc., 375 Hudson Street,
New York, New York 10014, U.S.A.
Penguin Books Ltd, 27 Wrights Lane, London W8 5TZ, England
Penguin Books Australia Ltd, Ringwood, Victoria, Australia
Penguin Books Canada Ltd, 10 Alcorn Avenue,
Suite 300, Toronto, Ontario, Canada M4V 3B2
Penguin Books (N.Z.) Ltd, 182-190 Wairau Road,
Auckland 10, New Zealand

Penguin Books Ltd, Registered Offices: Harmondsworth, Middlesex, England

First published in the United States of America by
Random House, Inc., 1991
Published by arrangement with Random House, Inc.
This edition with a new afterword published in Penguin Books 1992

1 3 5 7 9 10 8 6 4 2

THE LIBRARY OF CONGRESS HAS CATALOGUED THE HARDCOVER AS FOLLOWS:
Bryan, Mike.
Chapter and verse : a skeptic revisits Christianity / by Mike Bryan
p. cm.
ISBN 0-394-57509-1 (hc.)
ISBN 0 14 01.7194 0 (pbk.)
1. Fundamentalism. 2. Evangelicalism—United States. 3. Bryan, Mike.
4. Criswell College. 5. First Baptist Church of Dallas. 6. Dallas (Tex.)—
Church history. I. Title.
BT82.2.2B78 1991
277.3´0829—dc20´— 90-53532

Printed in the United States of America
Designed by J. K. Lambert

For my family and friends
and their many disparate beliefs

CHAPTER AND VERSE

CHAPTER 1

For a couple of months I had been looking for a friendly venue for a book about a shaky atheist who revisits the faith of the forefathers, if not his own father, a story about Christians who actually believe the Bible versus all the other kinds. Family and friends thought I was crazy or, worse, on the brink myself. My oldest friend surreptitiously told my wife (I found out later) I'd either quit the project after a big waste of time or I'd be born again, and that latter possibility scared the hell out of him. New York book editors weren't all that excited with the idea, either. Christians? Who cares? People who buy books are only interested in Swaggart and the Bakkers, the ones they can dismiss as hypocrites, the ones they can laugh at. I wasn't convinced. If there are only a dozen genuine evangelical Protestants remaining, so much the better, as long as I could find a couple of them. The paucity of Tibetan gurus and Trappist monks doesn't lessen their credibility with the outside world, but strengthens it. The novelist Flannery

O'Connor still sells pretty well in the secular market, and she was a devout Catholic: if the faith is just symbols and so on, she said, forget it. Audiences with the Lubavitcher Rebbe, old and venerable head of that very orthodox Hasidic sect in Brooklyn, are prized by Christians and Jews alike. Perhaps evangelicalism will acquire such a patina of respect over the coming decades, should the scourge of the televangelists wither. It might happen.

I rejected the suggestion that I approach some highly esteemed conservative Protestant seminary. That was a plausible idea—they do exist—but I didn't want to retreat to the ivory tower. I needed intellectually respectable Christianity (granted, a contradiction in terms to many minds), but also one that has manifestations good and bad in the real world where the faith is practiced by the millions. It's said all the time, in reference to the issue of hypocrisy, that the main problem with Christianity is Christians. Apparently Gandhi shared this opinion. Perhaps a Bible-based Protestantism does always degenerate into the embarrassment we see on TV. I wanted to find out.

That was my thinking when, in my local newspaper in Houston, where I lived at the time, I read a profile of Criswell College and its president, Dr. Paige Patterson. The college was founded in 1970 as the baccalaureate wing, in effect, of the First Baptist Church of Dallas, a mega-church pastored by the famous Southern Baptist preacher W. A. Criswell. (In December 1990 the church announced the appointment of a successor to the eighty-year-old preacher.) Criswell College was described as a bulwark of the conservative movement within the Southern Baptist Convention, a group of 38,000 congregations that is, with more than fourteen million worshipers, the largest non-Catholic denomination in the United States. Patterson was portrayed as an enthusiastic lightning rod for controversy within the rowdy—some say self-destructive—politics of his denomination and as, all in all, considerably more iconoclastic and freewheeling than my notion of a Baptist preacher allowed for. So I called Patterson's office and asked his secretary

Sherry Poe if her boss would have time to talk with me. A few days later I had the appointment.

At that time the college was housed on the ninth and tenth floors of a downtown building owned by First Baptist Dallas, right across Ervay Street from the main church auditorium; the students sometimes made derisive remarks about their urban "campus." The school has since moved to the more spacious grounds of a church a few miles to the east, purchased and renovated with a $3.5 million donation from Mrs. Ruth Ray Hunt, the last wife of H. L. Hunt (who was himself baptized late in life by W. A. Criswell) and one of the wealthier members of the congregation.

Although I wasn't expecting an unctuous soul-saver as I walked into Patterson's office, I was surprised that the man who came around his big desk to greet me with a grin was wearing wrinkled chinos and a worn tweed jacket—an outfit, I surmised, that was intentionally *not* the shiny worsteds of the televangelists. The cowboy boots I might have expected. Patterson is a stocky, puckish redhead who could have afforded to lose a little weight (and did, in the following months), a man with a clearly irrepressible streak of mischievousness who on first impression struck me as more like a professor of behavioral psychology than as a man who believes the Bible is the true and uncorrupted Word of God. His wry smile didn't evaporate as I introduced my somewhat vaguely formed notion for this book: not another cold-blooded piece of sociology on the religious right, certainly not another snappy book about the charlatans on television, but something a little different. I don't assume that all conservative Protestants are hypocrites, shysters, or their pathetic dupes. I'm not convinced by my friends who find nothing ultimate, immutable, or even clearly defined to worship—certainly not the God of the Judeo-Christian tradition—but who seem compelled to *believe* in some way and therefore dream up debased mysticisms that are just as farfetched as the old-time religions they reject for their implausibility: for every Oral Roberts there's a Shirley MacLaine; Christ is washed up but Seth lives; if

John Denver had been on board the *Challenger* shuttle flight (as originally planned, he claims) the tragedy would not have happened, because, Denver said later, "It's not my karma." I told Paige Patterson I wouldn't be afraid to get down in the trenches to find out whether we—almost everyone I know; the secular world—have been a little rash in consigning a biblical Christian faith to the same fate as Zoroastrianism.

My riff concluded, Patterson eyed me carefully, with amusement, and then asked, "Now tell me, what exactly do *you* believe?" I said that if he wanted to define God as "the Ground of our Being" or some equivalent dodge designed mainly (or so I thought at the time) to get people of a secular mind to say yes, I believe, then yes, I believe. But, no, Patterson doesn't view God that way. Do I have any concept of his own transcendent, personal God of redemption and salvation? Any belief at all that Jesus Christ might really have been God incarnate? No, I replied, I'd never had the slightest inkling. I looked him right in the eye when I said it because I wanted him to understand clearly that I would not be attending the Criswell classes on some kind of undercover operation. I didn't believe what he believed, but—if this would help my application—I didn't believe anything else, either.

From the neck up, the subject of theology has always fascinated me, but I also scribbled years ago in the margin of my *Portable Nietzsche*, "If life *had* 'meaning' it would drive me crazy." That's a belligerent thing to say, and a good churchman could be forgiven for suspecting that I was protesting too much. C. S. Lewis, one of the best-selling Christian apologists of this century and far and away the finest writer among them, would harumph knowingly and declare that the hound of heaven was after me and therefore still is, because that beast is relentless. There's some documentation for that suspicion, which I shall reveal, but there's also much earlier evidence that I'm a pagan bred in the bone.

Church was dutifully attended by my family, prayers were uttered at the dinner table at the grandparents' homes, but nominal Protestants, that's what we were, just like almost everyone else we knew. I was baptized in the Methodist church we attended in San Angelo, Texas, and I still have the inscribed Revised Standard Version of the Bible to prove it. The year was 1956. The next year we moved to Houston, and that's when I began badgering my parents about coercing me to go to church; it was a battle every Sunday. My parents liked the preacher, a man named Don Pevey, and I recall enjoying his oratory also, but for me it was just that. His message of Christian faith, the rest of the service, the Sunday school, the Boy Scout troop that met in the adjacent building—it was all lost on me.

One morning in Sunday school when I was eleven or twelve years old I had the anti-epiphany that settled the matter for many years, perhaps forever. I can still picture the scene: windows on the south side of the room, my chair facing west, the sun shining on my left. I don't recall the point of theology or the story from the Bible (probably the latter) that the teacher, a woman, was presenting, but quite precise in my memory are the seven words that flashed through my mind: I don't believe a word of this.

I was way too young to have based that conclusion on any careful assessment of the options. I could not have heard of everyday Christian liberalism, much less existentialism, agnosticism, or atheism, Feuerbach, Freud, or Nietzsche. And I was way too ordinary for that rejection to have been the telltale evidence of a precocious rejection of all the world, signaling big trouble ahead. No. My assessment of the historical truth of Christianity just came from my intuition as a kid, and it was not all that big a deal. In my mind the subject of Jesus Christ must have fit right in with, say, Santa Claus, whom I had already given up. It was ten years later, maybe even more, before I realized that unbelief in God is the somewhat weightier matter. Another twenty years and I was sitting in the president's office at Criswell College. Patterson smiled and invited me into his school, his church, and his home.

"But you don't know me from Adam—excuse the phrase."

"No, but I've met you. And you could write one of two books. You could write a hatchet job about evangelicals. Well, so what if you did? Everyone would recognize it as such, and that would be an old story, anyway. Or you could write an honest book, and if you do that, we'll take our chances."

Then he added, "Sure, you'll write things we disagree with, but if it comes down to your interpretation versus ours, well, let the good Lord decide."

He opened the doors of the school, no strings attached. I could attend classes, trustee meetings, prayer meetings, go out with students and professors on their evangelizing assignments, catch a mission trip overseas. "I'll just make the announcement during a faculty meeting that you'll be around," he said. But there was a catch of sorts. Patterson confided that I would inevitably become a project at the school, "prime meat for the headhunters," as he phrased it with zest. He warned that I would find the four-hundred-strong student body at Criswell somewhat more overbearing than himself and the rest of the faculty in their demeanor and proselytizing. "We have some Green Berets around here," he announced gleefully. Then he asked with a disarming smile, "How will you handle it when you walk into a prayer meeting and twenty people are on their knees praying for your everlasting soul?"

"I don't know," I said, and murmured to myself that I hoped it happened. I asked him a question in reply: "How will the students react when word spreads that this fellow writing the book and asking questions all over the place isn't one of them?"

Patterson replied quickly, "Hey, if our ideas can't stand up to your questions and ideas, then *we* as believers have a problem, don't we? We can learn from you. Our feet are clay, too." I appreciated that attitude, although I didn't imagine for a moment that Patterson really believed he and his people could learn anything about God from me. What they might hope to learn was more about how to handle people like me.

After our lengthy conversation Patterson walked me down the hallway to the other offices on the tenth floor and introduced me to a couple of Criswell professors, who also found my story amusing and my agenda perhaps a bit curious. I didn't see any Elmer

Gantry types on that first visit to the college, no holy rollers, and this was encouraging. Oh, Paige Patterson was ready to get down and save me (when I left his office with a promise to let him know how the book idea was coming, he replied, "Come back again whatever happens, and let's talk about the Lord"), but he wears lightly his mantle of blessedness, far more lightly than, say, William Buckley, Jr., who isn't even ordained, as far as I know.

Patterson, like Buckley, is a conservative Christian with dogmatic views, certainly, but as I quickly learned he and everyone else at Criswell bristle at any suggestion that their belief automatically classifies them as some kind of psychologically crippled obscurantist reactionary Neanderthal losers—one long harangue, no commas. They've heard themselves labeled all that and more. In 1924, H. L. Mencken referred to the fundamentalist plaintiffs at the Scopes monkey trial as "gaping primates" who believed in "degraded nonsense." Now we have the Bakker and Swaggart scandals, the Second Coming date-setters who will no doubt prosper as the millennium approaches, the Armageddon gangs already heading for Montana, the mini-Armageddon at Jonestown.

Conservative Christians often complain of a conspiracy against them in the secular press. A poll commissioned by one of their groups revealed that fewer than 25 percent of active journalists working for major newspapers, magazines, and television stations and networks had attended church in the past year. I hope that wasn't news to anyone. The press does stories on Christians like Pat Robertson and Jim Bakker mainly in order to denigrate them and, by extension, their beliefs. A true biblical Christianity that means what it says, as opposed to the vestigial and harmless cultural observance that most of us grew up with and many still observe, is a faith based on ignorance and, even more damning, dependent on such ignorance for its survival: sixty-five years after the Scopes trial, that connotation of the pejorative term "fundamentalism" hasn't changed in the popular press.

Orthodox Christianity is a dead letter to the secular world. We accept this fact and go our diverse ways, looking back with sympathetic or derisive condescension on Bible-believing Christians whose quaint picture of the world is simply not correct. We don't call them gaping primates, of course. We can afford to be magnanimous. We've won.

~~~~~~~

Now that almost all higher education in this country with the exception of the postgraduate seminaries is thoroughly secular, it's easy to forget (and easier yet not to know) that many of the most famous American universities didn't start out that way. They were Bible colleges of sorts. Harvard was financed with public money and dedicated to the education of Puritan ministers. Princeton, Dartmouth, and Brown were founded during the Great Awakening, a series of Christian revivals in the mid-1700s, by evangelical denominations with sectarian goals. Columbia, my alma mater, established with a grant from King George II, was in essence a religious institution: its first president was an Episcopalian clergyman, and classes were held in the schoolhouse of Trinity Church on Wall Street.

Tempus fugit. It's a safe bet that almost any remaining Christians on these campuses today will be of the liberal or unabashedly nominal variety who are as puzzled as frank unbelievers by conservative Christians' continued belief in the inerrant historicity of the book of Genesis, the Fall, incarnation, resurrection, blood atonement, heaven and hell. How, in their hearts, in their *minds,* in this pagan Western culture, do they pull it off?

Dietrich Bonhoeffer, the martyred Protestant theologian and pastor who died in a Nazi prison camp, wrote in one of his famous last letters from prison, "Man is challenged to participate in the sufferings of God at the hands of a godless world." This epigram, as convoluted as a drawing by Escher, is worth a few moments' consideration by skeptics and faithful alike. Even if evangelical Southern Baptists, in league with other Bible-believing Christians, elect every politician, mandate school prayer, outlaw abortion, pornography, and anything else they disapprove of, this will *still* be a godless, post-Christian world. Contrary to the wisdom of the old phrase, we can legislate morality, and do so all the time with some effectiveness, but we (they) will never be able to legislate faith. A majority of Americans tell pollsters they believe in God, Jesus Christ, an afterlife, and the Last Judgment. We're supposed to be a deeply religious culture—but where are the manifestations of all this belief? Walking into a church twice a year hardly counts—a thesis with which evangelicals agree, a subject for much future discussion. I say you need only read Benvenuto Cellini's autobiography, to pick one of a hundred books, to understand that the sculptor's world of the Renaissance was a *truly* godly world, even given the budding humanism that would turn out to be the beginning of the end for widespread orthodox faith. Cellini may not have been an orthodoxly pious man, but the world he portrays was one in which belief in God was the oxygen breathed by almost every man and woman and, like oxygen, was inhaled without pause for deliberation. Paige Patterson may be a chosen soul, but he wouldn't deny that such orthodox belief requires a determined effort for many Christians today, precisely because belief is no longer orthodox. Thus the post-Christian cultural context dictates the forms of belief as well as the forms of doubt. They are the two sides of the same cultural coin: as the secular world becomes ever more skeptical, traditional belief is perceived to be and perhaps is, as a matter of self-defense, ever more dogmatic and defensive.

Paige Patterson and the people at Criswell College acknowledge that their Christian beliefs are out of sync with the times—this is too obvious to dispute—but they propose that this asymmetry is not a reflection on that faith but a condemnation of these times. They don't appreciate being painted with the same broad brush that smears their infamous fellow believers from the world of television and newspaper headlines. They believe the conservative, informed Christian worldview can indeed tolerate the light of day, and they educate themselves with this idea in mind before going forth to spread the good news. Hoping to establish doctrinal as well as public relations distance between themselves and their embarrassing brethren, the people at the college and other conservative Christians who aspire to being taken seriously by the outside world now prefer to be called evangelicals rather than fundamentalists. This is solid strategy, PR-wise, but the press has caught up with the tactic and now uses the terms interchangeably.

Modern Protestant evangelicalism is often dated from 1947, when Fuller Theological Seminary was founded in Pasadena, California. As the joke goes, evangelicals are fundamentalists with *earned* Ph.D.'s. Indeed, the professors at Criswell College have their doctorates or they are obtaining them, in some cases from strictly secular programs, and they have these aspirations for their best students. Their school was originally named the Criswell Bible Institute, but the trustees soon enough dropped "Bible" and changed "Institute" to "College." Of about 500 generic Bible colleges in the United States today, only 130 are accredited as reputable degree-granting institutions, and many of these schools have dropped, or never had, "Bible" in their name. In the context of higher education the word is a stigma; too many Bible colleges are academically a joke. Even the faithful are embarrassed at what sometimes passes for Christian learning. The school in Dallas is now named the Criswell College and Graduate School of the Bible; it has the standard accreditation from the Southern Association of Colleges and Schools, as well as from the American Association of Bible Colleges. Among the requirements for the undergraduate degree, even for those students whose high school preparation is minimal and whose goal is to be a plain country preacher, are one-year courses in Hebrew and Greek.

CHAPTER 2

Only once in the New Testament is Jesus Christ seen in a vision of heaven as standing at the right hand of God; all other times He's sitting. Professor Danny Akin noted in passing this peculiarity about Acts 7:56 in his initial lecture to a large class of freshmen and sophomores at Criswell College. It was the spring term 1989—my period of residency at the school. I had accepted Paige Patterson's invitation to Bible college.

Akin's fine point of biblical exegesis isn't included in the voluminous notes in my own Oxford Annotated Bible, perhaps because the editors of that liberal piece of work, left over on my bookshelf from a couple of religion classes in college, attach no special significance to the language: left, right, standing, sitting—these descriptions shouldn't be taken all that seriously, and certainly not literally. But evangelical Christians like Paige Patterson, Danny Akin, and their students at Criswell do take Scripture seriously, and usually literally. So does Charles Ryrie, a teacher for many years at Dallas Theological Seminary, a member of First Baptist Dallas, and editor of the Ryrie Study Bible, a popular edition (but perhaps less so, in the opinion of some at Criswell, following Ryrie's recent divorce). His footnote to Acts 7:56 explains that Jesus Christ was seen in other heavenly visions as sitting beside God (Mark 16:19, Heb. 1:3) as a sign that His act of atonement for our sins was indeed completed on the cross, but Christ is also sustaining His people in their times of need on earth, and therefore the vision of His standing is also accurate and appropriate. It certainly is appropriate in this episode from Acts, in which the disciple Stephen challenges a mob of stiff-necked, teeth-gnashing Jews for rejecting the good news of the Righteous One. Stephen gazes intently into heaven, sees Christ *standing* in concern for the situation He witnesses below, and proclaims his vision to the mob. The Jews, infuriated all the more at this fresh blasphemy against their monotheistic God who shares His throne with no one, stone Stephen and he dies, the first martyr of the new church.

Almost two thousand years later, sixty Criswell students—sixty Christians and me, the stranger, the pagan in their midst—were gathered at seven-thirty in the morning to hear their professor's lecture on Acts. Arriving early for my first class, I took a seat at one of the round tables near the door and greeted students Amy Ker and Perri Wade. I fudged a little with the introductions, acknowledging that I wasn't a student, admitting I was writing a book about the school and other Christian matters, omitting my status among the unsaved. I didn't see any reason to bring that up in the first thirty seconds.

Perri Wade rummaged through her bag of books. Finally she looked up and grinned, "This is a Bible college and I forgot my Bible!" As our table filled up, I shook hands all around. Schedules and part-time jobs were compared and analyzed. The discussion turned to the parking situation, which everyone agreed was terrible. Students (including myself in the honorary category) got a discount from downtown rates at a high-rise garage but were left with a walk of four or five blocks to the school. We agreed this was a bit much on a cold winter morning in the Car Belt.

Someone mentioned a visitation the previous night: "We saved three people, so we did good." The salvation of three souls would be good cause, I surmised, for some kind of appraisal or discussion, but no one said anything in response. The other tables slowly filled with young people, for the most part, but quite a few folks in their thirties. At forty-one I was a senior citizen. Dress was casual, very casual: women in pants; women in designer jeans; one kid with a semipunk haircut, white turtleneck, and sharp black sweater; another who looked sixteen and wore a mod Christian T-shirt. The few guys in ties looked square as could be and, because I had been cautious on my first day, their number included me, a mistake I would not repeat. My conclusion from this initial and cursory appraisal of the student body was a relief: whatever I was in for at Criswell College, it would not be the revenge of the nerds.

Our professor used to lift weights. A short, muscular man, Danny Akin is proud of the 310 pounds he once bench-pressed and the marathons he has completed. A dedicated jock in high school, his academic preparation was exceedingly minimal—an SAT score of 910 ("On my second try! The first time was 870")—when he moved to Dallas from the suburbs of Atlanta in 1977 to enroll at Criswell. He hadn't even read the entire Bible. Ten years later Akin was the newest teacher in the Department of Theology, and he was just completing the dissertation for his doctorate in the thoroughly secular humanities program at the nearby University of Texas at Arlington. His subject for that paper was the soteriology of Bernard of Clairvaux, a twelfth-century Cistercian monk. (Soteriology is the theory of Christian salvation.)

Akin and his wife Charlotte have four young boys. He's an associate pastor at a large Southern Baptist church in Dallas. During the 1989 spring term he would be appointed dean of students at Criswell. He has pink cheeks, a baby face, and a telltale

Southern accent delivered in a high voice. In short, he didn't look or sound much like a college professor as he strode into the large ninth-floor classroom carrying his trademark can of diet soda. For one thing, he had way too much *energy*.

Akin whipped through all the pro forma explanations of attendance, papers, tests, and quizzes. He said he'd be happy to work with folks in an emergency "unless you're a sorry good-for-nothin'," in which case he claimed he'd have no sympathy for you at all. I didn't believe him. You could probably work it out with Akin, about whom I could discern nothing pedantic or sanctimonious. He might refer to Jesus' apostles as "those guys" or "the gang." Many of the students addressed him as Danny. I'll stick with Akin.

Unlike some of his students, Akin's own journey into faith had not been a particularly difficult one. He did not come to hold his beliefs as the result of a profound spiritual crisis or bitter experiences with everyday life, but rather as an acceptance of the truth and value of his family's tradition. He was born in 1957 in Atlanta, where his father installed draperies for a major department store, doing the work for the governor's mansion, Hank Aaron, Coretta Scott King. His father was a good churchman, Akin told me in the course of several conversations during the term, but his mother was special: if the family attended church on Sunday mornings *only*, she was disenchanted. Akin has a clear memory of a winter evening when he was about seven years old, holding on to the door frame and leaning back over the floor furnace after the family had arrived home from church, saying to his parents with a heavy heart that he needed to talk with the pastor about being baptized and coming forward to make public that he loved Jesus Christ, who was to be the Lord of his life. He did that, but then as a teenager he wandered away from the commitment.

"Sports were all I lived for," he told me. "They were my God, in a sense. However, if you had asked me if I knew I would go to heaven when I died, I would have said yes. I had committed my life to Jesus Christ. But I wasn't *living* for him and it bothered me—but not enough to do anything about it."

He compared this fairly typical teenage scenario with the story of his mother's brother, who left the church as a teenager but never came back before dying of a massive heart attack. "I don't know that he was a believer," Akin concluded. "My mother wants to say that he was because he made a profession of faith when he was a little boy and walked down the aisle, but he gave no evidence from the time he was fifteen. Zero evidence. It was bizarre that he turned out that way and my mother exactly the opposite. You wonder what was the difference. That's something only God knows."

In high school Akin's promising baseball career was hampered by injuries. After graduation his jock friends went off to college on athletic scholarships, leaving him behind in Atlanta, living at home, working part time, going to junior college, and staring down the barrel of a career as a P.E. coach. Not bad, but not what he had wanted, which was a professional baseball career, or at least a fair shot at one. Then one Saturday night some kids invited him to a Hawaiian luau.

"The minute I got there I thought, What am I doing! They were playing Hawaiian music and wearing grass skirts. Normally I listened to the usual rock music; I didn't listen to *luau* music. I almost left, but then I really had a great time. This confused me. These were Christian kids playing these silly games, singing these silly songs. I wasn't cussing or trying to take a girl to bed or listening to an acid rock band or watching a movie where they were killing somebody. And you have to understand, most of those kids I had treated really bad in high school. I was a jock, very popular, big man on campus, and these were all *church kids.* I used to ridicule them. But there I was, having a good time. It messed up my . . . paradigm."

He went to more of those parties. Some of the kids were just going along, he knew, but some were "sold-out storm troopers: they really loved the Lord." He began going to church more often.

When he heard about tithing as a Christian obligation, he did that. When he found out he could exceed the ten percent standard, he emptied his savings account of three or four hundred dollars.

"*Happy* to do it."

Tuesday night visitation? That's the Southern Baptist tradition of evangelizing the backslid in their homes. Akin began going without fail and was startled to realize that fewer people show up for evangelizing on Tuesday than for the social functions on Wednesday. Many times on those home visits Akin had to apologize to former classmates for the way he had acted in high school, but not everyone wanted to hear about it. One particular friend was never home.

"God just changed my life in a really radical way." Akin summarized that year of his life. "I was a *babe* who walked by faith." When he arrived at Criswell the following year he was still naïve, as well as underprepared. "I came here strictly to study and prepare to go wherever God wanted me to go. No second thoughts. No ulterior motives. I've learned since how the religious game can be played, but I didn't know about such stuff. This sports fanatic didn't even watch the World Series. I didn't watch the Saturday or Sunday football games; before, I would never miss them. I studied ten hours every Saturday and six hours every Sunday. God gave me the ability to start studying."

After his freshman year he returned to Atlanta to marry Charlotte. A week later he was back in Dallas in summer school. Charlotte took a job and her husband worked as a janitor for First Baptist Dallas. He graduated in 1980. "That graduating class was an amazing one. There were only about thirty of us, but twelve or fourteen are making very significant contributions to Southern Baptist work and the kingdom of God."

~~~~~

In the Akin class I was attending nine years later, he announced that surveys had revealed a problem with a Criswell education: lack of scriptural content.

"Imagine!" he exclaimed to general laughter. "Graduates of Criswell College!"

I was certainly surprised. The school has the reputation within the Southern Baptist Convention for turning out those sold-out storm troopers for the Lord. The great majority of the almost four hundred students at Criswell hoped to become Southern Baptist preachers, missionaries, or evangelists. Others, including many of the fifty or so women at the school, would major in counseling (women cannot preach in conservative Christian churches), and a few students were already thinking of an academic career. All were supposed to be serious Christians, and all should know their Scripture, and thus the biblical studies requirement had been expanded to include six one-semester courses, three each in Old and New Testament, and a seventh requiring the intensive study of one book in its original language.

Akin paused for procedural questions, sipped his soda, and began informing us about the Acts of the Apostles, as the book is officially named. I had not read Acts in twenty-five years, if ever, but I now believe it's the best place to begin for someone revisiting the faith. Almost everyone in the Western world has some idea of the material of the Gospels of Matthew, Mark, Luke, and John—the events of Jesus' brief career on earth—but Jesus did not really establish what became the Christian church. He was the charismatic, perhaps divine, founder of that faith, but the transformation of what was first a Jewish sect into a worldwide religion was a task for lesser men, and the earliest episodes of political and theological discord are the subject of Acts. This book is fresher material.

The physician Luke picks up the story in Acts where he had left off the account in his Gospel, with Christ's post-Resurrection appearance at Emmaus, where He charged His disciples to witness for the faith in all Judea and Samaria and to the ends of the earth. Then, Luke writes, "As they were looking on, he was lifted up, and a cloud took him out of their sight" (Acts 1:9).

That sentence is the only verse of the Bible that explicitly describes the Ascension; it is thus weighty with theological significance. Did Luke and his contemporaries believe that Christ rose up into outer space, from where He now looks down on us, or was Luke invoking as a metaphor the imagery of the three-tiered universe, the accepted norm of the ancient world? More important, was this event the subjective experience of believers *only,* proof of the presence within them of the Holy Spirit, or was it a public event in the material world? Could a bystander have recorded the Ascension on videocam?

"No," Danny Akin said, "the passage doesn't mean that early Christians thought Christ rose up into outer space somewhere. The three-tier universe is a metaphor. You can be *too* literal." However, Akin went on, the verse also means what it says, and he quoted Jerry Vines, president of the Southern Baptist Convention at the time, to the effect that if you had been standing there with a Polaroid, yes, you could have captured the scene on film. That's the evangelical position. Many liberal Christians reject all the bodily post-Resurrection appearances of Christ, including this one at the Ascension, and assert instead that these witnesses were experiencing a truth revealed through the eye of faith, as the phrase often goes, not one that has or requires photographic proof. The skeptic or unbeliever dismisses all such episodes as ecstatic visions of the generic sort, hallucinations, or simply fiction. "What is truth?" queried Pontius Pilate when Jesus, soon to be crucified, told him that he had come into the world to bear witness to that elusive concept. The footnote to John 18:38 in the Ryrie Bible states that Pilate was not being philosophical but was merely expressing frustration with the prisoner's evasive answers. I'm not so sure. I like to believe Pilate was a precocious man, in this respect, caught up in questions of twentieth-century epistemology.

In any event, Luke certainly isn't drawn into these modern-day musings, embedded as they are in doubt; perhaps he had no way of knowing they would even be asked. His main purpose in Acts is to demonstrate the progress of the good news he believed to be true, so he moves quickly to the story of the church in Jerusalem, beginning with the pivotal visitation of the Holy Spirit on Pentecost and the apostle Peter's sermon to the Jews on that same day.

These curious Jews had been drawn to the Pentecostal scene by a sound come from heaven "like the rush of a mighty wind." They saw the new converts speaking in other tongues and assumed they were drunk with new wine. Peter points out that this is unlikely because it's only nine o'clock in the morning. He directs the crowd to consider instead the prophecy of Joel in the Old Testament, wherein God declares that in the last days He will pour forth the Spirit and show wonders in the heavens above. Repent in the name of "this Jesus whom you crucified," Peter urges the Jews, and you, too, will receive the gift of the Holy Spirit you have witnessed today. Pentecost was the traditional day for celebrating the delivery of the Law to Moses on Mount Sinai, seven weeks after Passover, which itself commemorates the liberation of the chosen people from bondage in Egypt. It stands to reason that the Jews attracted by the ruckus in Peter's congregation would have been prone to consider any unusual events on Pentecost as relevant to their tradition. Three thousand of them were quickly baptized.

Acts records the most famous conversion in the Christian tradition. Saul of Tarsus was a consenting bystander at the stoning of Stephen—that episode in which the martyr sees Jesus Christ standing at the right hand of God. Saul was a radical, dogmatic Jew—a Pharisee—who delighted in persecuting Christians. Two chapters after the stoning, Saul is on his way to Damascus to find Jews who had converted to the Way (one of the earliest names for the new sect) in order to bring them to Jerusalem for punishment—an arbitrary extradition proceeding, in effect, a right granted to the Jews by the Roman Empire for dealing with their defectors. Then something happened that changed the world, literally. Luke writes:

Suddenly a light from heaven flashed about him. And he fell to the ground and heard a voice saying to him, "Saul, Saul, why do you persecute me?" And he said, "Who are you, Lord?" And he said, "I am Jesus, whom you are persecuting; but rise and enter the city, and you will be told what you are to do." (Acts 9:3–6)

A corollary to the question what would we have witnessed at the Ascension is what would we have seen and heard on that desert road. Luke says that the men with Saul heard the voice but saw no one. For three days in Damascus, Saul is sightless. He neither eats nor drinks. Then the Lord sends to him the disciple Ananias and "something like scales" fall from his eyes, and his sight returns. The man who had gone to Damascus with the intention of persecuting the Christians converts to their new faith instead. Luke now refers to Saul by the Roman name Paul, whose story now becomes the focus of Acts and whose subsequent New Testament letters to the Romans, Corinthians, Galatians, Ephesians, and others are the backbone of Christian apologetics and doctrine.

Many Christians have equally pivotal moments in their lives, but few hear voices. Danny Akin was called into the ministry during an evangelizing mission to an Indian reservation in Arizona the summer before he entered Criswell College. In order to go, he turned down a chance to tour Latin America with his junior college baseball team—a highly regarded nine. The injuries that had initially kept him off the team were healed, the coach was impressed by his workouts, but Akin declined the invitation.

"A year before, why, touring with a baseball team would have been my life's ambition," he told me. "But now I told the coach I was honored but couldn't go. I said I had made a commitment to go on a summer mission trip to Arizona to talk to little kids about Jesus Christ. He looked at me like I was crazy. 'Are you *religious* or something?' That was his attitude. I said, 'Well, no, not really, but this is important to me.' "

One night, tired, bitten by fire ants, annoyed with the lackadaisical attitude of some of the other kids on the trip, Akin decided not to go to the church service, but at the last minute changed his mind. "And for whatever reason," he told me, "that particular night I felt that God was calling me into the ministry. I'd never been more sure of anything in my life. The pastor thought he was preaching to the Indians, but he was preaching to me. I was literally gripping the pew, saying, 'God, is this really what you want me to do?' I had been thinking about that decision for several months, but I certainly didn't go to Arizona with any such intent. I have since been told that many times people are called in such situations, but I didn't know that at the time. At any rate, I was *convinced*—but no audible voices, nothing like that. I went forward to make public that I was surrendering my life to full-time Christian service."

The first recorded meeting of men committed to full-time Christian service was the apostolic council held at Jerusalem in A.D. 48–49. In Acts Luke describes the scene, a monumental event because it was then that Peter and Paul and other contentious advocates of the new faith—all of them Jews, probably—agreed that gentiles did not have to be circumcised (as commanded of all Jewish males in God's covenant with Abraham, Gen. 17:10) before they could become Christians. Thus the new faith would not be just another Jewish sect. However, the split between the two religions was not yet complete: gentiles were advised to avoid eating meat that wasn't kosher, and also to avoid unchastity. These early Christians may have worn yarmulkes and prayer shawls.

Luke's agenda in Acts, Danny Akin told the class, is to elevate the ministry of Paul among the gentiles of the eastern Mediterranean and Rome to the apostolic status of Peter's work among the Jews of Jerusalem, which had been highlighted by the triumph of the Holy Spirit on Pentecost. Luke documents Jewish resistance to Paul's mission at every turn; only once, in the sixteenth chapter of Acts, does he attribute persecution directly to gentiles. By the time Paul arrived in Corinth during the second of his three missionary journeys through the lands of the eastern Mediterranean, he had had enough of the reviling Jews. He "shook out his garments and said to them, 'Your blood be upon your heads! I am innocent. From now on I will go to the Gentiles' " (Acts 18:6).

Luke is careful to assure his readers that his story is *not* what it might otherwise appear to be, an issue of church politics and his own personal pride (Luke traveled with Paul, as indicated by his sudden switch in the sixteenth chapter to the first person plural "we"). Rather, he attributes this turn of events in the focus of the early church to the intervention of the Holy Spirit, whose sanction is invoked over one hundred times early in the book.

Unlike Danny Akin, some contemporary scholars don't accept this explanation. They see, instead, a concerted effort by New Testament authors operating under Greek and Roman influence to absolve those cultures of any guilt for the death of Jesus and the troubles of the early church. All the blame was directed at the Jews instead. A prime exhibit in this argument is Matt. 27:24–25, in which Pontius Pilate washes his hands of any responsibility for the impending crucifixion of Jesus, and the mob of Jews enthusiastically agrees, crying out, "His blood be on us and on our children!"

Way too pat, these New Testament authorities argue: this passage and many others were later additions to the story for the transparent purpose of fixing the blame on the Jews.

~~~~~~

All this and more about Acts I learned or was directed toward in just the first thirty minutes of Danny Akin's first lecture. In his opening remarks Akin had urged the students to purchase the voluminous notes and references he had prepared for the course (and for each course he teaches), available at cost in the bookstore. The notes for the New Testament course ran to three hundred pages. Now I understood the necessity of that study aid. Akin fires out information, opinion, exhortation, and provocative remarks of all kinds at a breakneck pace impossible to record with pen and paper. Some students bring tape recorders to his classes.

After Akin takes a question from a student, he looks around for more, answers those, barks "all *right!*" and launches into another subject. You have missed your chance on the previous one. He has a propensity and talent for chasing rabbits, as he phrases it, and his students have an equivalent talent for raising the game in the first place. The Xeroxed notes for the lectures allow them the freedom to do so. Among the remarks Akin brought forth that first morning was a quick discussion of the "mesmerizing power of the ancient world, more so than any other, to grip the imagination." I agreed with him, but we were dealing with two different ancient worlds. My reading had been in the Greek and Roman cultures, by and large. The scene in Palestine, although part of the Roman Empire, was out of the purview of my education. One reason the book of Acts is an entrancing re-introduction to the New Testament is that the scene in that book moves all around the Mediterranean area. We are not stuck in Jerusalem, Galilee, and thereabouts.

In retrospect I see a couple of reasons for my bias against the culture of the Bible. First, the literature from Palestine is for all practical purposes limited to that one volume, with its single subject and viewpoint; whatever its greatness, it lacks the scope of the vast literature of Greece and Rome. Second, and more important, I and the secular education establishment are in active or passive rebellion against the religion espoused in the Bible. The Scriptures are for Sunday school.

At Columbia I took a class on the Old Testament, while in another we studied a different ancient quasi-religious text, the Iliad. The religion described in that book is dead, of course, but unlike Judaism and Christianity it doesn't claim to be alive. Therefore The Iliad is free to live in the secular universities as an amalgam of history, myth, and literature, unmolested by belief, while the Old and New Testaments, still suffering the sincerest assaults of religious faith, are trapped in limbo, no longer the liturgy they once were but not yet the pure history and literature they will presumably become when belief dies for good. So the Bible is mainly *quaint.* Of course, this attitude is seldom if ever stated explicitly. It was not at Columbia, where the Old Testament professor's attitude was nevertheless just about the opposite of Danny Akin's: the words in his Bible very seldom meant what they said.

His Bible was my Bible, but from those first days in Dallas I realized that, while I didn't believe I would ever believe that Moses drew water from the rock or Jonah survived in the great fish (whale is an incorrect translation) or the eyewitnesses at the Ascension saw Jesus lifted up on an actual cumulus cloud, the people at Criswell consider the most bizarre episodes from the Bible to be just as credible as the police blotter in *The Dallas Morning News* — no, *more so.*

CHAPTER 3

~~~~~~

Few pastors have ever matched W. A. Criswell's feat of preaching on absolutely every verse of the Bible, Old and New Testaments, in order (although not with equal emphasis: the Song of Solomon merited one Sunday, Revelation three and a half years). The pastor accomplished this over a seventeen-year period beginning shortly after he arrived at First Baptist Dallas from Oklahoma in 1944. Criswell was one of the more famous fundamentalist preachers of that pretelevangelical era. Because he eschewed TV, however, he was left behind as a celebrity when Billy Graham (a member of Criswell's church) and then all the others mastered the airwaves. But Criswell's church became a Dallas and Southern Baptist institution. It has an active membership in residency of 16,000 to 18,000 (but boasts of 28,000, a highly inflated figure) served by over 30 ordained associate pastors (including Paige Patterson) and a full-time staff of about 300. Over 7,000 people attend one or more of the 100 Sunday school classes every week, so the streets around the church are more crowded on Sunday than on the other days of the week, when they are almost deserted because the office workers use underground tunnels. The church has its own Christian academy that grants a high school diploma, and some of those students proceed to Criswell College. It owns a Christian radio station with a new 100,000-watt tower, a health club, and downtown real estate worth many tens of millions, minimum. The whole operation has been referred to as the Baptist Vatican.

Criswell is now a revered if somewhat outmoded emeritus figure within the conservative Christian movement—outmoded to the point of embarrassing. His remark before the Southern Baptist Convention in San Antonio in 1988 is infamous in these circles: "We're trying to rescue the convention from the leprous hands of the liberals! Don't believe a word of the lying liberals! They call themselves moderates—but a skunk by any other name still stinks."

Asked in a television interview that same year about the history of segregation within his denomination, he explained in purest innocence that "birds of a feather flock together." Paige Patterson, also a guest on the show, had to bail him out on that one. Some of the evangelicals at the school named after Criswell recall these episodes with chagrin. But the man can preach: eighty years old, he is still a potent force behind his pulpit and preaches at the 8:15 and 10:50 A.M. services most Sundays of the year. Nor is he a stranger on Sunday and Wednesday night.

The first sermon I heard on my mission to Dallas—the first I had heard on other than ceremonial occasions in over twenty-five years—was delivered by Criswell, and his subject was seminal. Posted on the marquee outside the First Baptist Dallas auditorium was this question: "Who Can Raise Lazarus from the Dead?"

At 10:50 A.M. I joined the full house of 2,400 Southern Baptists in the red brick sanctuary that is usually referred to (prosaically, I thought) as the auditorium. Indeed, the small, square-shaped 100-year-old building in the middle of downtown is a straightforward structure, with flagrantly ordinary stained-glass windows, red carpet over linoleum, and a flat ceiling of acoustical tiles. This unpretentious Protestant homeliness might stand in intentional contrast to the aspiring steeples and soaring ceilings of so many Catholic churches and a good many Methodist, Presbyterian, and Episcopalian domiciles, too. Conservative Protestants consider those architectural refinements as little more than the trickery of a bogus religiosity whose refined atmosphere and beautiful protocols serve only to distract the worshiper from the burden of acknowledging his only true means of saving grace, in their opinion: a personal relationship with the Lord and Savior Jesus Christ.

Criswell wore a business suit. Conservative pastors would not be caught dead in vestments—another way of setting apart their faith and their calling from the ecclesiastical confusions and ceremonial religions down the street. It is not much of an exaggeration to assert that evangelical Protestants define their belief in terms of its conflict with two other groups: unbelievers of all sorts (including the patently false religions of Hinduism, Islam, etc.) and Catholics. It is not unusual to hear someone at Criswell doubt the saved status of a Catholic.

Protestants reject the idea that merely performing any of the seven sacraments of the Catholic faith (baptism, confirmation, penance, the Eucharist or mass, extreme unction, marriage, and holy orders) grants a measure of divine grace to the worshiper, regardless of his spiritual state. Likewise, they reject the idea of purgatory as being unscriptural and an extension of the idea that you can somehow work out your problems with God even after death. They frown upon what they see as the syncretism of Catholicism, the "keep what you've got but add this to it" evangelizing technique that Danny Akin first encountered on that trip to Arizona; he was shocked to see a totem pole right next to a shrine to Mary. And of course Baptists spurn what they consider this cult of the Virgin, in any of its manifestations. Baptists don't go to Mary. They go to Christ as the only true source of a saving grace.

Martin Luther found this principle in Paul's epistle to the Romans (apparently the moment of insight was just as instantaneous as the conversion of Saul on the Damascus road) and his enunciation of it lies at the heart of the Protestant Reformation: Protestants reject Catholicism because they believe Catholicism has rejected the plain teachings of the Bible. Luther, an Augustinian monk before he quit in order to marry, was obsessed by feelings of his own guilt in the eyes of God, and he was convinced that no man on his own could approach God and have any hope of reconciliation: we are all wickedly sinful and heaven is too far away. No works, penances, sacraments, indulgences, or church dispensations—the trappings of Catholicism in that day—could possibly earn the forgiveness of a just and righteous God. Such beneficence could only be God's freely given gift, grace, and mercy, and could only be bestowed upon those who have faith in the work of His Son.

The ensuing "works versus faith" contretemps—mere *hope* for salvation based on problematic works versus *assurance* of salvation based solely on faith—remains for conservative Protestants today the chief demarcation between themselves and Catholics. Evangelicals consider themselves the most loyal heirs to the spirit of Luther. They point out that ancient Judaism, too, had disintegrated into an elaborate "works religion"—specifically, the legalism of the Pharisees whom Jesus rebelled against. Jesus, they say, was the Luther of his own time and his was the Jewish Reformation, declaring dead the old religion with its politics and legalism, proclaiming the new covenant of personal salvation for all mankind.

Conservative Protestants wonder why anyone would choose the works formula with its built-in contingency—how would you ever know you had performed enough penances?—especially because the faith hypothesis has substantial, even overwhelming, grounding in the letters of the Apostle Paul. Classic is Paul's formulation in Eph. 2:8: "For by grace you have been saved through faith; and this is not your doing, it is the gift of God—not because of works, lest any man should boast."

That seems clear, but as with so many biblical issues, other verses imply that good works are indeed part of the package. Evangelicals reply that they are saved not *by* good works, but *unto* them: the saved Christian will naturally seek to help his fellow man.

First Baptist Dallas does retain from Catholicism two of the seven sacraments—baptism and the Eucharist—but in much modified form, and referred to as ordinances, not sacraments. Catholics baptize babies. Evangelical Baptists (but not some other evangelicals, such as Presbyterians) reject out of hand infant baptism for the straightforward reason that there is no precedent for it in the Bible, which clearly prescribes a "believer's baptism." Baptists also disapprove of a sprinkling baptism, because immersion is the only form described in the Bible. However, and even though the most modest Southern Baptist church has a tank or a tub for baptism, and the very name of their denomination indicates the importance Baptists have always placed on this issue, neither baptism nor any other outward sign is considered mandatory for salvation. This was proved by what happened on Calvary: the thief on the cross was granted salvation by Christ simply because the thief believed.

Southern Baptists downgrade the sacrament of the Eucharist to the mere and occasional celebration of the Lord's Supper, which unites the observant and Christ symbolically, perhaps, but not miraculously and certainly not decisively, as Catholics believe. For Catholics, the celebration of this sacrament relives for the worshiper Christ's words to his disciples at his last supper:

Now as they were eating, Jesus took bread, and blessed and broke it, and gave it to the disciples and said, "Take, eat; this is my body." And he took a cup, and when he had given thanks he gave it to them, saying, "Drink of it, all of you; for this is my blood of the covenant, which is poured out for many for the forgiveness of sins." (Matt. 26:26–28)

Protestants (including evangelicals, for a change) reject the miraculous nature of this biblical event and interpret Jesus' statements as poetical and metaphorical, for the simple reason that since Jesus was standing right in front of the disciples, *obviously* he was speaking metaphorically when he said of the bread, "Take, eat, this is my body." The whole business of the Eucharist is just too arcane, too priestly, too . . . Catholic for Protestant tastes. They want something more workmanlike, and simpler. Church tradition and all that this concept implies? To hell with church tradition, literally, if that's all you've got going for you.

The psychologist William James, that shrewd observer of religious faith who hasn't been much improved upon since he wrote *Varieties of Religious Experience* ninety years ago, probably got it right when he concluded that the problem between the two main branches of Christianity goes beyond doctrine. "Their centers of emotional energy are too different," James wrote. "They will never understand each other."

~~~~~

W. A. Criswell briskly narrated the famous story of Lazarus as told in the eleventh chapter of the Gospel of John. Lazarus was the brother of the Mary who "annointed the Lord and wiped his feet with her hair."

When Lazarus was ill in the town of Bethany, just outside Jerusalem, Jesus was called to perform a miracle and save the man's life. But Jesus took his time; he tarried two days longer in the place where he was. By the time he arrived in Bethany, Lazarus was dead. In fact, he had lain in his tomb four days. (The Oxford Annotated notes that popular belief in ancient times imagined the soul lingering near a dead body for three days before departing. Thus the four days in the tomb for Lazarus would have been a significant span of time—necessary, even, to accentuate the miraculousness of the event.)

Martha, the sister of Mary and Lazarus, went forth to accost Jesus: "Lord, if you had been here, my brother would not have died. And even now I know that whatever you ask from God, God will give you." Jesus replied, "Your brother will rise again. . . .

I am the resurrection and the life; he who believes in me, though he die, yet shall he live, and whoever lives and believes in me shall never die. Do you believe this?" And Martha replied, "Yes, Lord; I believe that you are the Christ, the Son of God, he who is coming into the world."

Then Mary also came to meet Jesus, and she too reminded him that if he had been there, Lazarus would not have died. She wept, and Jesus, "deeply moved in spirit, and troubled," wept also. He asked to be taken to the tomb, which was a cave, and he ordered that the stone blocking the entrance to the cave be removed.

Martha interrupted, "Lord, by this time there will be an odor, for he has been dead four days."

Jesus said to her, "Did I not tell you that if you would believe you would see the glory of God?"

They took away the stone. Jesus lifted his eyes and said, "Father, I thank thee that thou hast heard me. I knew that thou hearest me always, but I have said this on account of the people standing by, that they may believe that thou didst send me." Then he cried with a loud voice, "Lazarus, come out!"

The dead man came out, his hands and feet bound with bandages, and his face wrapped with a cloth. Jesus said to them, "Unbind him, and let him go."

Criswell was silent for a moment. Then he thundered, "Can the modern existentialist raise Lazarus from the dead?

"The sophomoric spiritual sophist?" Criswell's voice dripped with disdain.

"The professional paid religionist?" (I read "Catholic" into his funny if nasty description of gorgeous vestments, incense, and strange incantations.)

"The philosophical religionist?" (That could be me.)

"The pseudo-scientist, with his empty, stupid, unthinkable hypothesis of evolution?" (Also me.)

Furthermore, Criswell wanted to know, can any of these ladies and gentlemen tell us "*who* we are, *where* we came from, *where* we're going, and *why*?" Laughable.

"Then why in the world reject *He who can* tell us these things—He who *already has*?"

Squinting before the bright lights of the television cameras, Criswell, now silent, glared at his congregation. We sat motionless, appreciating the moment. Fine preaching in conservative denominations has about it the flavor of a spectator sport. Southern Baptist preachers are judged and graded; congregations looking for a new preacher hold Sunday-service auditions; two courses in homiletics are required of all male Criswell graduates. The pulpit at First Baptist Dallas is positioned in the middle of the platform, while Catholics and most mainstream Protestant denominations put the pulpit off to the side, reserving for the center the table holding the paraphernalia for the celebration of the Eucharist. Evangelical, fundamentalist, and/or charismatic denominations insist that the pulpit must be front and center because hearing the Word of God preached by a man of God is the surest way to God.

I agreed with W. A. Criswell that sophists, religionists, and scientists cannot raise Lazarus from the dead, and I didn't know who could, but I also wondered whether Jesus in fact did so. It's a fair question, and how you answer it goes a long way toward determining what kind of Christian you are, if any.

Raising a man from the dead? Most modern minds presuppose this does not and cannot happen on this earth, and nothing the Bible says will convince us otherwise. To the outsider or newcomer or Sunday-morning Christian the assertion that divine inspiration of Scripture mandates inerrancy of that Scripture is outlandish, settled long ago when we learned that the world was not created in the six days outlined in Genesis, and that demons are not the cause of illness and derangement, as they are a number of times in the New Testament. From Mark, chapter 5, this story of the Gerasene demoniac:

And when [Jesus] had come out of the boat, there met him out of the tombs a man with an unclean spirit, who lived among the tombs; and no one could bind him anymore, even with a chain. . . . And when he saw

Jesus from afar, he ran and worshiped him; and crying out with a loud voice he said, "What have you to do with me, Jesus Son of the Most High God? I adjure you by God, do not torment me." For he had said to him, "Come out of the man, unclean spirit." And Jesus asked him, "What is your name?" He replied, "My name is Legion; for we are many." And he begged him eagerly not to send them out of the country. Now a great herd of swine was feeding there on the hillside; and they [the demons] begged him, "Send us to the swine. Let us enter them." So he gave them leave. And the unclean spirits came out and entered the swine; and the herd, numbering about two thousand, rushed down the bank into the sea, and were drowned in the sea.

The herdsmen fled, and told it in the city and the country. And people came to see what it was that had happened. And they came to Jesus, and saw the demoniac sitting there, clothed and in his right mind, the man who had had the legion; and they were afraid. (Mark 5:1–15)

The Bible's endorsement of the story of this demoniac tells the doubting mind in the twentieth century just about all it needs to know about the Bible. From this skeptical perspective, the book that is enshrined by believers as Holy Scripture is judged as just another ancient text instead. W. A. Criswell disagrees, of course. He is, after all, the author of the perennial best-seller (in Christian bookstores) *Why I Preach That the Bible Is Literally True.* Rather than allowing any opinion or purported knowledge from the world at large to sit in judgment on Scripture, Criswell insists that the Bible sits in judgment on any such opinion or knowledge, no matter how "scientific" it might claim to be. The doctrine of biblical inerrancy declares that every word of the Scriptures is divinely inspired truth—theologically, philosophically, scientifically, and historically true, as the recitation often goes. The Bible is the first fact, and nothing that contradicts it may ever be a fact. As the bumper sticker around town reads: GOD SAID IT, I BELIEVE IT, AND THAT SETTLES IT!

Jesus Christ was indeed *standing* at the right hand of God. He was seen by believers to rise upward on a cloud at the Ascension and a videocam would have recorded the event. And the corpse of

Lazarus, stinking though it might have been, was definitely cleaned up and raised from the dead. As I quickly came to understand at First Baptist Dallas and Criswell College, there is no appreciation of the faith, ideas, and behavior of conservative Christians without a thorough grounding in this bedrock belief of inerrancy.

There are several relevant passages from Scripture. Second Timothy 3:16 begins, "All Scripture is inspired by God and profitable for teaching. . . ."

In John 10:35 the author refers to the Word of God and adds parenthetically "(and scripture cannot be broken)."

Paul refers to the books of Scripture as "oracles of God" (Rom. 3:2).

Scripture in each case can only be the Old Testament because these authors were in the process of creating the New Testament. Also, inerrantists specify that their doctrine refers to the inerrancy of the "original manuscripts," which, in fact, do not exist. The closest we have to them are Greek papyrus manuscripts of the second and third centuries A.D. Therefore, inerrantists have an out when discrepancies, of which there are quite a few, are discovered in later manuscripts, which number about five thousand in all languages. Most such discrepancies are quite minor. Two are major. Mark 16:9–20, the conclusion to that gospel in which Jesus appears to his disciples after His resurrection, chastizes them for their disbelief, and then charges them to go forth and baptize those who would be saved, is part of the tenth-century Greek text on which the King James translation is based, but it isn't in the earlier manuscripts. John 7:53–8:11, the story of Jesus and the adulterous woman he refuses to condemn, is also missing from the most reliable early manuscripts. Most modern Bibles, including my Oxford and Ryrie editions, include these verses from Mark and John as footnoted apocrypha, stipulating that the stories, even though omitted from the original Gospels, might have been authentic episodes from the life of Jesus.

Quibbles about original manuscripts aside, the logician responds that the methodology of inerrancy—using the testimony of

Scripture to authenticate itself—is circular reasoning. Conservative Christians do not deny this. The professors at Criswell know all about Godel's Theorem demonstrating that any proposition used to prove any other proposition cannot prove itself, but must use unproved axioms for its own validation. The shortest distance between two points is a straight line? This axiom of Euclidian geometry cannot be proved. It is declared to be true and it *works* within the context of the Euclidian system of geometry, but not within some other systems.

Evangelical Christians establish the Word of God as their axiom. One inerrantist writes, "The appeal of Scripture to validate the authority of Scripture is an appeal to an objective content that is God-breathed." Scripture validates itself in the manner that God and Jesus Christ validate themselves, by executive fiat. Jesus said to the Pharisees who were challenging his claims, "Even if I do bear witness to myself, my testimony is true, for I know whence I have come and whither I am going, but you do not know whence I have come or whither I am going. . . . I bear witness to myself, and the father who sent me bears witness to me." (John 8:14–18)

And the Apostle Paul validated his own authority in like manner: "If any one thinks that he is a prophet, or spiritual, he should acknowledge that what I am writing to you is a command of the Lord. If anyone does not recognize this, he is not recognized." (1 Cor. 14:37–38)

The professor for my Old Testament course in college, a shrewd old Jew who was highly renowned in an obscure field within the Semitic languages, did not recognize the authority of Paul *or* Moses. He enjoyed teasing his students, mostly Jews, with all manner of liberal, anti-inerrantist heresy. He wasted no time announcing that Moses did not write the Pentateuch, that each book of the Old Testament is a compilation of many men (and at least one woman, according to Harold Bloom's recent best-seller, *The Book of J*) working in an oral and fabulist tradition during a period of about seven hundred years, from 1000 to 300 B.C., approximately. The Old Testament, he emphasized, is "a historical meta-

phor for a theory of the cosmos." In this metaphor, God is the
literary personification and unification of the three elements of
mankind's experience on earth: individual experience, historical
(tribal) events, and the natural world. All three factors are unified
in the concept of the one God who functions as a single, solitary
cause-and-effect mechanism. When those ancient worthies wrote
that God led their forefathers out of Egypt, it was their way of
saying that history led them out.

Concepts of time and nature, as we understand them, did not
exist, and this point is almost proved by the Hebrews' use of the
metaphor of God, one that we have so much difficulty comprehending today with the same meaning. Do not, our professor warned
us, take the Old Testament at face value: understand it as an idiom
that personifies nature and history and is based, from beginning
to end, on human *experience.* There is not a word of philosophy
in it.

I was much impressed by that professor's explanation that the
word for "truth" in Hebrew is based on the verb "to hold, to
believe." Truth for the ancient Israelites was a matter of character.
There was some sense in which the individual who believes something most passionately knows best. For these people, an ecstatic
vision dearly held was just as true as anything else.

And also know that the Old Testament is *propaganda* preached
by exceptional men to a people who for the most part did not share,
or were not interested in, their way of thinking; thus all the
struggles in the Old Testament between the patriarchs, judges, and
kings of Israel and their stiff-necked tribal constituencies. The
question for the modern student or worshiper is not whether all
this antiquarian folklore is "true" as described—it is not—but
whether the Scriptures can still be a useful metaphor for modern
worship of the monotheistic God.

The footnotes in the Oxford Annotated Bible used in that class,
and which I carried with me to Criswell, assume a liberal interpretation of events. The comment introducing the fabulous episodes
in the story of Elijah in First Kings says, "The element of the

miraculous in the stories must be accepted as an integral part of the writer's method. The ancients did not have the concept of the uniformity of nature."

I was particularly impressed by the Oxford's enumeration of the naturalistic truths behind each of the ten plagues God visited on Pharaoh in Egypt (Ex. 7:8–11:10). The first plague, turning the waters of the Nile into blood, was explained as the annual reddening of the river during the summer due to red particles of earth or perhaps minute organisms. The frogs, gnats, and flies of the second, third, and fourth plagues were annual proliferations, timed with the rise and fall of the waters of the Nile. The locusts of the eighth plague were a familiar pestilence in the ancient Near East (referred to in the book of Joel) and the thick darkness of the ninth plague would have been the *khamsin*, the annual spring dust storm of Egypt.

The inerrantist Ryrie Study Bible acknowledges these natural causes for the plagues but suggests that God multiplied their odious effects in order to make clear His supernatural judgment. The inerrancy of Scripture is vital to evangelicals because, they argue, without this doctrine how would we know if a passage was given by God or manufactured by man? Who would decide? Paul wrote to the Romans: "Let God be true though every man be false" (Rom. 3:4). Dependence on the Bible also protects their Christian faith from the myriad cults that claim to have the proverbial direct line to God. Evangelicals are deeply suspicious of some of the charismatic groups to which they are often and erroneously linked by outsiders. The difference, evangelicals say, is their own strict adherence to the verified Word of God, not to some dubiously claimed communication, such as the golden tablets unearthed by Joseph Smith, the founder of Mormonism.

Liberal Christians, attempting to cope with the problems posed by Genesis and such passages as the raising of Lazarus and the healing of the Gerasene demoniac, reply to inerrantists that the Bible is indeed inspired and, as such, *contains* rather than *is* the Word of God. W. A. Criswell ridicules this accommodating exegesis:

"They believe the Bible is inspired only in spots, and they are inspired to spot the spots!"

Why would God reveal His word in a muddled context that would only give rise to confusion? Evangelicals say He wouldn't. If the Bible is true just here and there but not everywhere, its subject isn't the personal God of revelation and salvation, and it isn't the inspired message of that God, but just the exhortatory and instructional stories of some wise old men. Furthermore, if the Bible isn't complete and sufficient, other sacred books might contain *other* words of God. And then where are you?

Anything less than an inerrant Bible is a slippery slope to liberalism, relativism, secularism, and unbelief. Doubt this passage from Genesis and you end up doubting that miracle in Exodus, then you proceed to wonder what really happened at the tomb of Lazarus, and you conclude your foray into an unfettered biblical exegesis by doubting the resurrection of Christ Himself. You are no longer a real Christian.

A dispute broke out at a recent Southern Baptist convention over the use of the word "quest" as the title for an official journal. "We're not questing for anything!" an opponent of the publication shouted. "We've found the truth!" For evangelicals, it's all or nothing with Scripture. In the language of their theologians, its revelation is either *personal* or *propositional.* If it's merely personal, if we can shop the biblical catalog for those passages, doctrines, and commandments we choose to believe and follow, then we might as well go ahead and empty the churches, lock the doors, and be done with the charade because that faith cannot sustain real Christian belief. The conservatives may be right. Certainly nothing in the history of Christian denominations in the twentieth century can challenge their thesis. The accommodation that more liberal Christians feel is necessary to save the faith has yet to produce any dividends in the pews. Those mainstream Protestant denominations—Methodist, Presbyterian, Episcopalian, and so on—that have made the concessions to the secularist push have been punished with declining and unenthusiastic attendance. One report published in the secular press suggested that they are 50 percent below where they should be, taking into account population growth. In Western Europe, they're just about dead.

In the denominational struggles of the Southern Baptists, inerrantists claim that churches with truly Bible-believing pastors in the pulpits rack up higher baptism rates—more new members—than moderate churches. The moderates, stung by this correct charge, can only assert the *quality* of their own baptisms and slyly point out that the Mormon, Muslim, and Buddhist faiths in America are also growing, so sheer numbers can't be used as the *only* criterion for a healthy church. This battle for the Bible is still raging in the Southern Baptist Convention. Nothing could be more irrelevant for onlookers, most of whom will assume that, for one of many examples, Lazarus was not in fact raised from the dead. What did happen outside Bethany we don't know and I, for one, don't consider myself duty-bound to produce a more plausible explanation. But neither do I call myself a Christian. I hadn't been at Criswell long before I had this one question for those tens of millions who do call themselves Christian, but who also have their doubts about Lazarus or any of the other miracles in the Bible: If you accept the resurrection of Jesus Christ and his ascension into heaven—the most supernatural event in all history—what is your problem with accepting all the others? What is the *logic* of rejecting the other miracles?

Evangelicals propose that if we want Christ's resurrection to attest to His theology we must also allow it to attest to the other events in the New Testament that presents that theology. Let's be consistent. Likewise, they propose that an acceptance of Christ's divinity has logical implications for believing the doubtful events of the Old Testament because Jesus and the New Testament authors accepted those miracles without question. Doesn't their acceptance dictate the modern Christian's acceptance? I should think it does. Their endorsement must either give the benefit of the doubt to those ancient stories or, if one is inclined to discredit the stories, their testimony backfires and instead casts doubt on their credentials for divinity or sainthood, as the case may be.

If you don't accept the other secondary miracles, do you *truly* accept the main one of Christ's resurrection from the dead? Bible-believing Christians have their doubts that you do and, as I was soon to learn in my reading at Criswell, many if not most nonevangelical theologians today do indeed fudge or frankly deny the resurrection of Christ.

Evangelicals believe that the so-called Christian who picks and chooses what he believes is playing games and in most cases doesn't believe anything at all. He has a Sunday-morning religion that might help get him through the week, but not a living faith that will get him into heaven. To my surprise, I found myself, in those first weeks at Criswell College, in agreement with the evangelicals. The cursory dismissal of inerrancy is not so easy, or should not be, *if* one wants to become or remain any kind of relatively thoughtful Christian. Inerrancy is definitely a radical doctrine but so is Christianity itself, claiming as it does that an itinerant Jew born in a crude manger two thousand years ago, crucified on a Roman cross for his heretical message and truculent behavior, is God incarnate, the key to the truth of the cosmos. Mainstream and liberal Christians may politely sidestep the outrageousness of this proposition, while evangelicals bask in the audacity of their faith.

CHAPTER 4

〜〜〜

At the conclusion of the worship service W. A. Criswell came down the steps to the floor of the auditorium to greet congregationists who were responding to the invitation, the tradition of Southern Baptist and many other conservative denominations to challenge the audience, really, to either accept Jesus Christ into their lives if they're lost, or renew previous vows of faith. About a dozen men and women and a few children came down the long aisles or descended the stairs from the balcony. One woman who came forward with her family had a large, red "I Love You" heart on her sweater. Told by the lady that her husband had given it to her, Criswell called out, "I'm glad it wasn't another man!"

The husband replied, "So am I!"

Everyone laughed. Good feeling rolled around the big crowd like a wave at the ballpark, and in fact the atmosphere wasn't all that different from an exciting game. People don't become Southern Baptists or any other kind of conservative Protestant in order to endure lectures about unredeemed transgression, guilt, and the *hope* of salvation based on sufficient penance. They hear a lot about sin, but sin redeemed without a doubt by faith in Christ. Theirs is a world of winners and losers, and they are the winners, washed in the blood of Jesus. We all swept out of the auditorium in good cheer.

Eight hours later Paige Patterson preached the evening sermon titled "Curing Kleptomania," one of a series of messages on the Book of Malachi, the final book of the Old Testament and critical for all Christian denominations because Mal. 3:10 is the biblical justification for tithing: "Bring the full tithes into the storehouse, that there may be food in my house; and thereby put me to the test, says the Lord of hosts, if I will not open the windows of heaven for you and pour down for you an overflowing blessing." Thus Patterson's sermon, too, dealt with inerrancy.

The auditorium of First Baptist Dallas was again almost packed, but with a younger and more informally dressed crowd than in the morning. I saw some blue jeans, but only pressed designer models. This was a collection of clean-cut young middle-Americans I hadn't seen the likes of since watching a rally for Ronald Reagan. A live band with strings, horns, and trap set joined the choir and played snappy hymns as the congregation gathered. Two singers, owners of Honda and Pontiac dealerships, respectively, as Patterson informed us, were excellent. After the invocation came the traditional greeting to one's neighbors in the pews, and because I was wearing the "Our Guest Today" ribbon handed out to all visitors, I was leaning way over to grasp hands offered by a large circle of friendly church members.

Insufficient tithing is stealing from God, pure and simple. Kleptomania. In contrast to his mentor, Criswell, Patterson delivered his message in the more flamboyant stump style of the televangelists. A man in the congregation told me that "the younger people" preferred to come Sunday evening to hear Patterson or some other preacher of fewer years than the eighty-year-old W. A. Criswell.

I could understand why, but they thereby underestimate the shrewd talent of the old man.

Patterson spoke about his own financial agreement with God, drawn up while kneeling on his bedroom floor as a teenager in Beaumont, Texas, as his evangelizing career was already showing signs of precocious promise. Shortly after one of his first sermons, the young Patterson had approached the Lord and promised that if God would keep him supplied with opportunities to preach, then he would give Him 20 percent of everything he ever had.

Patterson said to the congregation, "I don't know whether God decided, 'Okay, that's exactly what I'll do,' but I do know that since that day there probably have not been more than fifteen or twenty Sundays when I wasn't scheduled to preach someplace, and most of those were Sundays when I chose not to. The opportunities have been there and I've tried to be true to what I promised by giving at least 20 percent to the Lord's work."

While Danny Akin hadn't read the entire Bible until he came to Criswell as an undergraduate, by that age Patterson had been preaching for a number of years. Later in the term he told me about those early years:

"By the time I was six years old I understood how to be saved and knew that I needed to be saved but at that time I had no intention of *being* saved. I'd had enough of being in a preacher's family. That's probably why I was as rebellious a little kid as I was. From the age of six to nine were the three most miserable years of my life. I can remember despising the necessity of going to church because my mother insisted I sit with her in the third row, and when the invitation was given she would stand by me with tears rolling down her cheeks. I knew she was praying for me to be saved. But both my folks were careful never to pressure me. They are good old folks from the old time when religious coercion was not acceptable. The kids were given every good influence but never coerced. As I look back, I think I intuitively knew that God was going to call me to preach but I didn't want to do it. Those were three miserable years."

The call finally came when Patterson was nine, on a Friday night during Easter revival when a fairly famous evangelist from Chattanooga, Tennessee, named Fred Brown was preaching at the church in Beaumont. Although Patterson doesn't recall the content of the message, he clearly remembers the "tremendous conviction" that struck him during the service. "I was weeping so I couldn't even talk. Dad just picked me up and hugged me for a minute and then set me down on the front pew and looked me in the eye and asked if I was coming to receive Jesus and I said, 'Yes, sir.' I was baptized on Easter Sunday. By fortuitous accident my wife Dorothy, who was eight at the time, just another little kid to me, was baptized that same night in the church.

"The following Wednesday night during prayer meeting, after my father preached, I came forward again and made public my decision to enter the ministry. This was of course the occasion for all the dear little old ladies in the church to come by and pat my little red head and say how sweet it was and I'd probably get over it. But I knew exactly what the Lord had said do and never had the first doubt. But of course I didn't do anything about it *then!* I was too interested in baseball, basketball, and football.

"There was a man in the church named Charlie Miller, a colorful fellow who ran the rescue mission in Beaumont. Charlie had at one time been a prizefighter and lost his career in the ring due to the bottle, and then he had reformed and become chauffeur for the famous opera singer Amelita Galli-Curci for a short while—before he lost that job to the bottle again. Then one night he was saved at the Pacific Garden Mission, a famous mission on State Street in Chicago where, by the way, Billy Sunday was also saved, along with a number of other famous baseball players. Charlie had come to Beaumont to run a mission for homeless men. He was seventy-five when I was a kid, and I can remember how impressed by him I was. He would be up preaching to the men and sometimes one of 'em would be high on alcohol and try to challenge him. Oddly enough, Charlie was very formal with the men, preaching in a coat. So he'd take the coat off and walk down the aisle and with one blow knock the guy out cold and leave him lying there while he put his coat back on and finished the sermon. I was fourteen then, and he struck me as my kind of preacher.

"Charlie walked up to me one day in church and asked if I had committed my life to preaching.

" 'Yes, sir.'

" 'Do you plan to start when you're sixty-five?'

" 'Well, no sir, but I'm only fourteen.'

" 'You start Tuesday night. Be at the mission.'

"I almost worked myself to death trying to get something of a sermon ready to preach at the rescue mission. And I did. Dad seized that opportunity and said that since I was about to turn fifteen, and my birthday fell on a Sunday, he wanted me to preach the following Sunday night. At that time First Baptist in Beaumont was the sixth largest church in the Southern Baptist Convention. I was scared absolutely to death, but the Lord blessed me and I got through it, preaching from the book of Joshua, the famous text 'Choose you this day whom you will serve, whether it be the gods of the Canaanites in whose lands you dwell, but if it be in my house, we shall serve the Lord' " (Josh. 24:15).

Patterson discovered he enjoyed the work. He was relieved to know that not only was he committed to preaching, but also he could actually *do* it (not everyone can). He became a child prodigy of sorts, receiving invitations to preach from all over southeast Texas. By the time he was sixteen he was seldom home on Sunday. He preached revivals at night and also worked in a bookstore and played all the sports in junior high school, football only in high school. Then in his senior year he had the opportunity to preach around the world.

He tells the story: "Dad had just been elected as executive secretary of the Baptist General Convention of Texas and was invited to the dedication of the First Baptist Church in Tokyo, an English-speaking church there. They had a big-dog preacher—big dog, big name—scheduled for every night but one, and they got to talking about it and decided they ought to have a youth night. Is there a youth evangelist we could have? 'Well,' someone must have said, 'T. A. Patterson has a son who does youth revivals. Why don't we ask him to bring his son? That won't cost us any extra money.' So my Dad borrowed the money for me to go and on a Thursday night in 1957, sandwiched between all the big dogs, I preached in Tokyo, Japan. I was seventeen. Then for two months I preached all over Japan and in many other countries—Korea, Taiwan, Thailand, India, Jordan, Lebanon, Israel, Italy, Spain. In Spain, Franco was persecuting Protestants and all of our churches there had been officially closed. So we met in secrecy under the possibility of police interruption. You can imagine the effect that had on a seventeen-year-old kid. And many of those were difficult sermons because that was the first time I had preached with an interpreter. When you're a fast-moving speaker like I am, an interpreter cramps your style badly. You have to learn what you can use and what you can't. But it was a great experience and I still look back on that as a very pivotal time in my life because while I had always been serious about doing God's work, it was on that trip that the immensity of the world's problems and the tragedy of people living as they live all around the globe got my attention for the first time. Because I do believe in heaven and I do believe in hell and I do believe that Jesus is the only way, the stark terror of all those millions of people without the Lord got hold of my heart. There were many times on the trip when I couldn't sleep at night. My ministry took a turn toward the serious at that time, which has never left me. Until this day when I look at the masses of people out there and see them as Isaiah described them—sheep without a shepherd, milling around with no idea what life is all about, or eternity either—I cannot help but be deeply and profoundly moved by that."

The members of First Baptist Dallas claim to be in total agreement with Patterson's faith. His problem is in getting them to act on it. Concluding his sermon on Malachi and the spiritual importance of tithing, he issued an invitation for those who wanted to tithe to the church to come forward along with those who were accepting Christ into their hearts for the first time. The band played and Patterson and Criswell stepped down to the floor of the sanctuary, eyes shifting from side to side and up at the balcony. Four people came forward—with vows, not tithes. Patterson returned to the pulpit to give us one more chance, and the band played on and the choir sang. Three more people came down, then four boys from a local detention center were led forward, but all with vows, not tithes. No surprise, really. Only 10 to 15 percent of most congregations do tithe the full amount; First Baptist Dallas achieves 15 to 18 percent.

On this evening, Patterson came up empty-handed. After the service I greeted him. He smiled ruefully and expressed regret that I happened to have showed up "on the first evening in years" that he had delivered the tithing sermon. Today, any blatant appeal for money from worshipers brings forth images of Jim and Tammy Bakker and reinforces every outsider's "worst impression" (Patterson's phrase) of fundamentalist bookkeeping. Nevertheless, Mal. 3:10 is in the Bible and the Bible is inerrant at First Baptist Dallas. As another evangelical bumper sticker reads: ANYBODY CAN HONK. TITHE IF YOU LOVE JESUS.

CHAPTER 5

W hen the atheist Bertrand Russell was asked what he
would say if ushered into the presence of God after his
death, he replied, "Not enough evidence, God! Not enough evidence!"

In a way, the assorted neoorthodox and liberal Christian theologians of this century, led by the estimable Europeans Karl Barth
and Rudolph Bultmann, see it that way, too, but unlike many of
their intellectual brethren they haven't felt compelled to leave the
faith entirely. Instead, they've changed its focus radically, and the
first doctrine to go was any notion of biblical inerrancy. Evangelicals see themselves in a struggle to the death with these revisionist
thinkers and practitioners of Christianity.

Credit for developing the first of the liberal theologies is often
given to Friedrich Schleiermacher and his *Religion: Speeches to Its
Cultured Despisers*, written in 1799, impenetrably verbose in the
German academic manner but nevertheless earthshaking within

the trade. *Speeches* was a work of existentialism, to use the term in the loose manner to which we're accustomed. Religious observance is the individual's own business. Christianity is the highest expression of the religious urge—intuition should tell us this, Schleiermacher believed—but it is not dependent on any particular dogma; the Resurrection is not even essential.

A century later, Bultmann suggested famously (in these circles) that we must "demythologize" the Bible because too much of Scripture is simply unbelievable in the age of the electric light bulb. If there's truth in that, and there is, how much more truth in *this* age of genetically engineered calves, atomic clocks that measure time in nanoseconds, and a cosmology that declares the universe to be ten billion years old and a similarly incomprehensible number of light years in diameter. Not only is our world no longer a Gothic cathedral, as the standard line goes, it is no longer any kind of cathedral at all. It's a highly computerized laboratory. The airplane pilot has more confidence in his instruments than in his God, who is no longer the copilot. God seems to be dispensable; radar isn't.

Science, not Scripture, is now inerrant in the modern world. The precipitous decline of dogmatic Christian belief began with the era of modern science, of course, but the conflict between the two was not initially apparent. Christians have always asserted that a necessary first premise for the scientific enterprise is the God Who created a good universe operating under a uniform set of rules discoverable by the human mind. There was nothing to fear from science because it could only reveal more and more of the intricate design that is, for most believers, the best, intuitively felt proof of God's existence. This teleological proof found poetic expression in the proverbs of the Old Testament and Paul's letters in the New Testament: "Ever since the creation of the world [God's] invisible nature, namely, his eternal power and deity, has been clearly perceived in the things that have been made" (Rom. 1:20).

Thomas Aquinas, adapting for Christian purposes the ideas of Aristotle rediscovered for the Western world through translations from the Arabic, proposed that reason and faith were *separate and equal* paths to God, with reason directing us mainly to the "general" revelation of God's creation and to our own moral natures, and faith revealing the "special" revelation brought by the person of Jesus Christ. This duality was opposed to the received wisdom of the church of the thirteenth century, which insisted on the primacy of faith, but it caused no trouble as long as the created world discovered by scientific reasoning matched the world required by orthodox Christian faith—the world of the Bible. The difficulties arose when reason began to cast doubt on those truths, specifically, the cosmology and anthropology of the book of Genesis, and miracles in general.

The advances in scientific knowledge of the past four centuries have undercut the textual integrity of the Scriptures as a whole, but perhaps even more damaging is the nature of the scientific enterprise itself, which postulates *anti* supernaturalism as a necessary first principle for its endeavors. Thus the initially peaceful coexistence of reason and faith has become, in the secular mind, an irreconcilable contradiction. Faith is now opposed to reason—opinion, to put the best light on it, or ignorance, to put the worst. The Reformation thinkers had said all along that splitting reason from revelation would be fatal because it would give man an independent role and thus separate him from an *objective,* inerrant source for knowledge—Holy Scripture. They were correct.

Writing a few years after Bultmann's most dramatic announcements, Dietrich Bonhoeffer suggested in his letters from the prison camp that the time might have come for Christians to join with avowed unbelievers in accepting that this world no longer requires the concept of God to be the deus ex machina that provides an explanation for whatever is beyond the purview of our science. Rather than restricting religious belief to the "god of the gaps," in Bonhoeffer's phrase, and standing by helplessly as those gaps in our knowledge get smaller and more insignificant by the year, some Christian scholars have proposed a reassessment of the whole situation. Harvey Cox, author of *The Secular City* and a believer in a transcendent God, nevertheless understands rampant disbelief in the age that has seen the passing of the "closed metaphysical world view." Cox flips Voltaire on his head. A mere two centuries after the French thinker's remark that, if God didn't exist, we would have to invent Him, Cox has suggested we drop the whole subject for a while.

In *Honest to God,* a brief and influential book of thirty years ago, Bishop John A. T. Robinson of the Anglican church expresses sympathy with those would-be Christians who believe that they have rejected the one and only gospel, while in fact they have merely rejected "a particular way of thinking about the world which quite legitimately they find incredible." He urges that we forge ahead, and if this means creating *new* religions, so be it:

If our defense of the Faith is limited to [that faith delivered to the saints two thousand years ago], we shall find in all likelihood that we have lost out to all but a tiny religious remnant. A much more radical recasting is demanded, in the process of which the most fundamental categories of our theology—of God, of the supernatural, and of religion itself— must go into the melting.

These theologians and their followers are unconcerned with any proofs of God. The historicity of the bodily resurrection? Totally irrelevant. It may well have happened (Barth, for one, believed it did), but it still doesn't matter. Bultmann suggested that a truly relevant New Testament would conclude with Christ on the cross. The Jesus of history and the Christ of faith are two different subjects entirely. We can never know or even approach the Jesus of history, but this Jesus has nothing to do with contemporary Christian faith anyway, which is or should be totally concerned instead with the *kerygma,* the proclamation of the existentially risen Christ. A follower of Bultmann writes, "I see the growth of a community of self-giving love as the basic thrust of the will of God in human history, and I see that community as exemplified primarily in the church founded by Jesus. . . . The crucial evidence upon which such faith rests is the impact upon the Christian of Jesus and the saints."

Such veneration on the basis of faith is superior to any longing for or attestation to the historical Jesus and his resurrection. The proclamation of Christ is in fact the *new* resurrection. Any attempt to link faith with the historical Christ is doomed for two reasons. First, the truth about the man Jesus and his alleged resurrection is lost to us forever. Second, too many modern minds simply cannot accept the Bible as evidence anyway, and this situation will only get worse, not better. Any linking of belief and verifiability will inevitably diminish belief. The neoorthodox assert, if only implicitly, that basing Christian belief today on the inerrancy of the Bible and the historicity of the Resurrection is not so much faith as formula. Faith alone is safer for modern times; it is also, in some way, more meaningful. From this point of view, the beauty of faith encompasses doubt, too.

Barth proposed that the Bible is a tool of God for his encounter with *me*. Faith and faith alone are all we need for this encounter. Existentialist Christians have broadened that idea by saying that Christ doesn't help me because He is the Son of God; He is the Son of God because He helps me. He came to serve mankind, not to be served. Jesus is the human face of God. He is the Man for Others.

One group of theologians went so far as to suggest, as part of Nietzsche's legacy, that we just kill God off. This death of God school was in vogue twenty-five years ago, featured even on the cover of *Time* in 1966, with large red letters against a black background asking "Is God Dead?" The question carried the authority of a proclamation. One of the leaders of this group, William Hamilton, suggested in another context that it's time to call the bluff of all revised Christianities. Hamilton said it was time to "put up or shut up, to be an 'in' or an 'out.'" He opted for the latter, accepting instead "the world of rapid change, new technologies, and the mass media." He said we must grow out of our "anguished quest for salvation from sin [and] into a confident, optimistic, secular stance."

Others in the death of God school proposed a more existentialist death, so to speak, and although Bonhoeffer was not an official member of this school, his eloquent statement speaks for this vision of our dilemma:

So our coming of age leads us to a true recognition of our situation before God. God would have us know that we must live as men who manage our lives without Him. The God who is with us is the God who forsakes us [a reference to Mark 15:34, Christ's calling out to God from the cross]. The God who lets us live in the world without the working hypothesis of God is the God before whom we stand continually. Before God and with God we live without God. God lets himself be pushed out of the world [and] onto the cross.

Some of the death of God theologians are hard to distinguish from outright atheists, which figures, but one difference sometimes drawn is that the radical theologians generally grant that historical Christianity has been a necessary stage for human development, or some such, while many atheists dismiss it as pernicious from inception. Atheists are materialists and positivists, while the theologians reserve some role for what they call "the vertical dimension"—the soul, or whatever. Jesus might play a profound role in that vertical dimension but no more so than, say, the Buddha. Is the religious attitude merely a stage in the development of mankind? We have heard recently about the end of history and the end of nature, but we may see the end of religion first. Monotheism may not be, after all, the logical conclusion for our religious instinct. Perhaps a secular, atheistic humanism is, or will be.

The new wave of Christian theologians has entertained such provocatively named concepts as the *invisible* church, *implicit* faith, *anonymous* Christians, *religionless* Christianity, *liberation* theology, and my favorite, *Christocentric* atheism. In most of these new doctrines, and especially the last one, Jesus is a martyr, a model, an exhortation for the ages—but not God incarnate. He chose God, God didn't choose Him, and His alleged resurrection is, to cite one example, merely a "hope for the world in which we live, a hope for the meaning of life."

There is literally no end to the revisionist doctrines constructed in the cause of preserving something that can be called Christian faith and that can be authentically lived as such, while setting aside the old forms of belief and observance that simply don't square up with our new knowledge of God's world. The proponents of these formulations deny that they in any way denigrate *authentic* Christianity; they claim to preserve it, and often they find evidence for their models within the New Testament. The real Christ, they say, is not a revived corpse.

Read enough of this twentieth-century theology and you will be awed by the irrelevance of much of it to anything the man in the street might believe. If widely read, which it's not, it would speak more clearly to agnostics than to Christians. In any context it might as well be labeled "For Professional Use Only." But I'm a sucker for words so I find some of these neo-Christian formulations quite elegant. My favorite comes from Bishop James Pike, the Episcopalian who was profiled in *Look* in 1966 and then three years later explained his resignation from his denomination in that same magazine. Pike said, "There are several phrases in the Creeds that I cannot affirm as literal prose sentences, but I can certainly *sing* them."

The layman may be puzzled by such pronouncements because many philosophers are, too. The logical-positivist school, for one, takes a dim view of religious and metaphysical language, wondering whether such propositions—evangelical, neoorthodox, liberal, or any other sort—really mean anything, certainly anything verifiable in the real world. If they do not, we should acknowledge this and conclude the debate. "Is Theology Poetry?" was the title of one of C. S. Lewis's most famous sermons. He answered no, these philosophers say yes.

The most famous illustration of their point is Cambridge philosopher John Wisdom's parable of the gardener. Two visitors to a garden find some vigorous plants in an otherwise neglected and dying environment. No one in the neighborhood has seen a gardener at work. One of the visitors insists that a gardener (read God) has been coming, perhaps at night. The other says no, and besides, any gardener would be looking after the whole place better, not just the few plants. As they continue their study of the garden, the two observers find more signs that might indicate the attention of a gardener, but others cast doubt on this, and there are even some signs that a person of malicious intent might have been at work. The one observer still insists that a benevolent gardener is coming to look after the hardy plants; the other observer still says no.

Wisdom's idea is clear: the different beliefs about the gardener-God "reflect no difference as to what they have found in the garden, no difference as to what they would find in the garden if they look further, and no difference about how untended gardens tend to fall into disorder." The two different beliefs, in short, have no meaning beyond that invested in them by their proponents. In the real world, they're moot, neither verifiable nor deniable. This last point is the idea behind a corollary to Wisdom's parable, a challenge to theists proposed by Oxford professor Antony Flew: "What would have to occur to constitute for you disproof of the love of, or the existence of, God?" He argues that since *nothing* could dissuade the theist—not even a series of Holocausts (my example)—there is really nothing to talk about.

In some of these analyses of theological propositions, the concept of God is deemed of a kind with our concepts of truth, justice, beauty, even love: *values,* which, if not apprehended and honored, do not exist. If the tree falls with no one around to hear the crash, the correct answer to the old question is that there is still a crash. But is there any truth, justice, beauty, love, or God on the planet Mars? Not until we arrive.

These questions about language and meaning are complicated, but a good deal of the murky Christian theology of the past fifty years gives credence, or at least sympathy, to the argument of the positivists. I was told at Criswell that Antony Flew prefers to debate with evangelical scholars, who at least are advancing assertions about the real world. Paul Tillich's *The Courage to Be* is a marvelous dissection of religious faith, but what do the words "the Ground of our Being," Tillich's famous formulation for God, really mean or convey? In the neat aphorism of the Greek writer E. M. Cioran, "We cannot pray to a God who is *probably* true. . . . We do not beseech a *nuance.*"

Conservative Christians, including most definitely the Protestant evangelicals at Criswell College, absolutely agree. They rebuke all revisionist ideas about God and their manifestations in the churches as meaningless God talk, church chat, religious existentialism, paganism masquerading as piety. C. S. Lewis's assessment of these developments is caustic and classic. No teetotaling Baptist, conversant with doubtful spirits of all sorts, he denounced this theology as "Christianity-and-water."

With friends like these, evangelicals say, God doesn't need enemies. "God is love"? That's not good enough. What's a tautology but a tautology? God *does* love, but He is also holiness and righteousness. The genuine Christian faith calls men to change; men do not call that faith to change. If religious faith is just another commodity in a consumer culture—Christianity à la carte—then it's finished. As the apostle Paul warned the Colossians, "See to it that no one makes a prey of you by philosophy and vain deceit, according to human tradition, according to the elemental spirits of the universe, and not according to Christ" (Col. 2:8). Evangelicals argue that the liberal appeasements might play with intellectuals and the sophisticated classes but wreak havoc with the basic Christian believer *and* the moral structure of society in general.

Writing in the *The Suicide of Christian Theology*, John Warwick Montgomery draws a nice metaphor: the gun was loaded in the eighteenth century with the loss of biblical revelation and a clear vision of God, aimed in the nineteenth century with the death of God, and fired in the twentieth with the dehumanization of man, the inevitable result of humanism and relativism.

The right, represented most popularly in recent years by Allan Bloom's *The Closing of the American Mind*, surveys the manifest ills of our culture and concludes that the major cause of the dissolution is the erosion of values. Alexander Solzhenitsyn's commencement address at Harvard in 1978 was an earlier and much briefer expression of this tenet: "The humanistic way of thinking that has proclaimed itself as our guide did not admit the existence of intrinsic evil in man, nor did it seek any task higher than the attainment of happiness on earth. It started modern Western civilization on the dangerous trend of worshiping man and his material needs as if human life did not have any higher meaning."

At the heart of all conservative apologetics today, Christian, Jewish, or unspecified, is a pragmatic appeal: believe because it's good for you, because the alternative is nihilism, because society requires the binding power of religious faith or, at the least, mere observance. That utilitarian tradition goes back several centuries. The rational Christians of the Enlightenment did not necessarily accept all the tenets of the faith—John Locke wrote *The Reasonableness of Christianity*, but he thought the only essential Christian belief was that Jesus was indeed the Son of God—but even the doubters acknowledged the sagacity of portraying the truth of these propositions for purposes of social control. The concept of a fiery hell had been in deep trouble with the knowledge class for centuries, but Locke, who apparently didn't believe in the literal hell, thought it played well with the masses and should be retained but not required. The free-thinking Voltaire acknowledged Christianity's utility. It was wise social policy. Tocqueville saw the religious spirit of America as a main source of its strength, and he's quoted over and over by Christians in this regard—but Tocqueville was ambivalent about his own faith.

However, conservative Christians don't stop with advocating the mere utility of their faith. They are convinced of its truth, and convinced that without it we are literally lost souls. The only alternative to faith is despair. Either-or. Only the orthodox Judeo-Christian worldview makes sense of the universe. One writer said, "Existentialism is a philosophy born of Christian despair, a way of thinking that has retained the Christian meta*psychology* while abandoning Christian meta*physics*. The feeling of anxiety and loss that mark this philosophy is rooted in the fear of the secularized Christian's never being released from his subjectivity."

We are mired in our subjectivity, striving desperately for objectivity. But we *have* this objectivity, Christians assert. Only the Christian God gives us a taste of that triumph. Only Christianity and its Bible give our experience an objective, *externally* derived value. Without it the universe of our experience is a vast sea without a shore, in author Francis Schaeffer's phrase, a prayer delivered in a room without windows or doors. The metaphors pile up and some are quite beautiful.

Only Christianity gives us hope; it best answers our *need* for hope. Regarding Eastern and pseudo-Eastern doctrines, the Christian apologist and novelist G. K. Chesterton said, "They call it peace; we call it despair." Only Christianity raises mankind into something great. Christians don't sacrifice to their God. He has sacrificed for them. The image of God incarnate in the little baby in the manger, born for us, *resonates;* the image of the dead Jew on the cross, dying for us, *resonates.*

In the second decade of this century a group of conservative Christians published a series of twelve small paperbacks titled *The Fundamentals,* their rebuttal to all the liberalisms current then and still to come. These books argued that true Christian faith, like it or not, is necessarily dependent on an acceptance of supernatural occurences (quite a few of them, in fact: the Ryrie Study Bible lists thirty-five specific miracles in the New Testament). Anything else is *something* else; a new religion perhaps, but not Christianity.

These authors proposed five fundamental tenets of the Christian faith: the virgin birth, bodily resurrection of Jesus Christ, His

blood atonement for our sins, His second coming and premillennialism, and the inerrancy of the Bible. The term "fundamentalist"
was soon coined as the label for the Christian who accepts these
beliefs. Those who waffled on one or more of them were moderates
or liberals or, in the deep suspicion of many fundamentalists,
pagans afraid to come out of the closet. William James's remark
about Protestants and Catholics—"Their centers of emotional energy are too different; they will never understand each other"—
goes double for conservative and more liberal Christians. Soon
enough the split within the Christian community was complete,
and it will probably remain so until the end of time: liberals see
accommodation as necessary for the sake of both the truth and
survival, while conservatives see it as heresy in both respects, a
Trojan horse for unbelief, a prescription for denominational decline.

~~~~~~

Every theistic faith requires repudiation of all other theistic faiths
(the polytheism of Hinduism and the de facto atheism of Buddhism
are more congenial) and that's the way it should be; arrogance is
the honest way because a tolerant religious faith is a compromised
faith. But we cannot be totally honest today. In the Western world,
at least, we have, with a few exceptions, the ecumenism requisite
in an era of instant communication and devastating weapons.
There will be no more Crusades and no more pogroms, presumably. It's necessary to go through the motions so that everyone may
live together—as C. S. Lewis joked, in the manner in which you
tell the other man that his wife is attractive and his children smart
and cute.

   Occasionally, however, we do glimpse the contradiction inherent
within ecumenism. The orthodox are sometimes too honest; they
slip up. In Central America, where evangelical Protestantism is
booming at the expense of traditional Catholicism, the church
sometimes refers to the new Protestants with the pejoratively
loaded term "sects." On a papal journey to Mexico, John Paul II

urged Catholics to seek "a more solid training in the truths of our Catholic faith so as to form a front against the solicitations of the sects and groups that try to pull you away from the true fold of the Good Pastor." While evangelical eschatology requires the survival of Israel if only so the Jewish state can participate in the apocalyptic prophecies, Bailey Smith, former president of the Southern Baptist Convention, declared that God doesn't hear the prayer of a Jew. Smith is not anti-Semitic; he was merely expressing the Christian belief that Judaism is an incomplete and insufficient faith. He subsequently explained this and cited the tears he had shed in the Holocaust Museum in Jerusalem. Likewise, the Vatican's Cardinal Ratzinger had to squirm to get out from under his remark that Jews can find ultimate fulfillment only in Jesus. Then John Paul II stated similarly that the visitation of the Holy Spirit at Pentecost marked "the new and everlasting covenant," and he got into trouble with Israel. Why? Only because he said it aloud. He has to believe this, as the Jews well know. He's the pope.

Meanwhile, regarding the easily ecumenical liberal Christians, the naysayer E. M. Cioran had the final word. Their faith, Cioran said with deadly accuracy, no longer has the energy to be intolerant.

CHAPTER 6

〜〜〜

My parents left the Methodist church in Houston when their favorite pastor Don Pevey was transferred to Corpus Christi. My father has attended assorted Sunday services since then, but only when the weather is too bad for golf. His churches of choice are Unitarian and Congregational—Christian ethics without much, if any, Christian dogma. I once asked him what he believes about God. "Don't know," he said with a contradictory finality and that defensive edge you often hear from the backslid when the subject of religious faith is broached. (When I more recently reminded him of his answer he barked, "And I don't trust those who do.") I turned to my mother. "It's today, not tomorrow" was her cryptic reply, and I took this to mean that whatever she believes, it doesn't include eternal life, heaven, hell, or the like. She acknowledged this. My friends, if absolutely pinned down on the matter, and after they get over their anger or embarrassment or frustration at even having to address this subject, will label themselves agnostics or deists or, better yet, secular humanists, which has a positive ring to it. The Jews are Jews, of course, sui generis and accepted as such by everyone. I am also acquainted with some Westernized Buddhists and a few New-Agers for whom Jesus is mainly a Capricorn.

Liberal Christians are correct when they argue that traditional faith is lost for most of us in the twentieth century; conservative Christians are correct when they respond that nothing has been found to replace it. Ninety percent of my friends claim to believe in *something*, but these beliefs are so inchoate and unarticulated they have no positive function in our lives. It's all negative. Check the marketplace and read *Newsweek* cover stories on Shirley Mac-Laine and it's difficult to avoid Dostoevsky's conclusion that when we cease to believe in a real God, the result is not a belief in nothing, but rather in everything. Samuel Beckett stated that he had nothing to express, nothing with which to express, no power and no desire to express, together with the obligation to do so. So it is on the religious left, as I call our quadrant of the statistical pie, and without any attempt to give it hard-and-fast boundaries. We know who we are.

I can cite one of the more famous atheists of this century, Sartre. In a conversation with his companion Simone de Beauvoir, published in 1974, the aging great man said this: "As for me, I don't see myself as so much dust that has appeared in the world but as a being that was expected, prefigured, called forth. In short, as a being that could, it seems, come only from a creator; and this idea of a creating hand that created me refers me back to God. Naturally this is not a clear, exact idea that I set in motion every time I think of myself. It contradicts many of my other ideas; but it is there, floating vaguely. And when I think of myself I often think rather in this way, for want of being able to think otherwise."

A rather surprising statement. In another context Sartre drew an analogy between a keenly felt atheism and the man who enters the cafe to meet a friend. But the friend isn't there. The man waits. The friend doesn't arrive. The man's presence in that cafe is now *defined* by the absence of the friend. This is the main fact of the situation. Whatever he now does—exhibit patience or get angry, stay and wait or get up and leave—is a response to what isn't there.

I know people who would say the aging philosopher was just worn out by this point, and slipping badly. But consider Bertrand Russell, another prominent naysayer. The man who wrote *Why I Am Not a Christian* also wrote to a friend, "The centre of me is always and eternally a terrible pain, a searching for something beyond what the world contains, something transfigured and infinite—the beatific vision—God. I do not find it. I do not think it is to be found, but the love of it is my life. It's like the passionate love . . . of a ghost. . . . I have loved a ghost, and in loving a ghost my inmost self has itself become spectral."

Deduct some points for hyperbole but it does sound as if the hound of heaven was gaining ground on Russell. Alas, the beast came up short. For my own part, a couple of years after that epiphanal morning in Sunday school, my attendance at church was finally deemed optional by my parents, and I never went back. That was about as easy a decision as I ever had, but shortly thereafter, in high school, my crowd was reading Bishop Robinson's *Honest to God* and Paul Tillich's *The Courage to Be*, paperback best-sellers espousing an unshackled, existentialist Christianity—something that could be believed, even if it were only words on a page.

I wouldn't pretend that my friends and I got too deeply into the implications of all this. I wouldn't claim that we do so now. It was a game we played. *Existentialism.* I loved the lilt of those syllables. We were also reading Camus and Sartre and Nietzsche and *Hamlet*. It never occurred to any of us to read the Bible. We didn't get our heretical books from our parents or teachers, most of whom, like my parents, tried to keep up the old observances, if only for their children's sake. We public school students in Texas in the sixties stood in silent prayer every morning in homeroom and pledged our allegiance, too, but it didn't do any good. I doubt that many if any of those kids had the kind of explicit denial of Christian faith that spoke to me that Sunday morning. We did not think of ourselves and our extracurricular reading list as in any way revolutionary. Unbelief was simply in the air. It wasn't even unbelief, really, in the sense of being a negative reaction to the real thing. Nor was it a positive assertion of some alternative, a carefully honed positivism, perhaps. It was just neutral. (It was also keenly influenced by all the Jews in the school. The place was sometimes called Hebrew High and for some reason I became a Jew-lover, to parody a phrase that had some currency at the time. I responded to the Jews' literate, cosmopolitan culture, and to one Jewish girl's big breasts.)

In college in New York City I took those religion classes but I didn't see this as a sign. Nothing was stirring within me, that I could feel. This was theology, an interesting subject for study, a conundrum like quantum physics. I never atten d a worship service. At some point I toyed with the notion of going to Union Theological Seminary, a bastion of liberal Christian thought then and now, right across 120th Street from Columbia. I didn't do it. I went to work instead.

For the following twenty years, many of them in New York, some in Texas, that easy decision of the boy in Sunday school, meaningless at the time because it was without repercussions, was finally subjected to the more rigorous examination posed by the working life of a married man at large in the wide world. Saint Francis of Assisi and many others have declared that until you have suffered you cannot know God. Today, operating under the presupposition of psychological motivations, we would be more likely to say that until that time you would not *need* God. The idea is implicit that the psychological priority of the needing undercuts the objective truth of the knowing. In any event, I wasn't doing much suffering that I was aware of, but I would nevertheless spend whole weekends with Nietzsche or one of the others. Now, there's only one reason to do this after you're out of college. It's reasonable to assume that Lewis's hound had indeed finally caught my scent and, aware of this myself, I was hoping to drive him away with the heavy artillery. At stake was a lifetime's carefully constructed skepticism. I told myself I wanted to know what was true, but, like everyone, I really just wanted to be more comfortable and secure in what I already believed, even if that was nothing at all. I came up with another slogan about life as a "meaningless miracle."

In 1979 I twice went out of my way to see John Paul II during his visit to New York City. The first time was on Madison Avenue outside St. Patrick's, where he was scheduled to appear briefly on a balcony above the street before going inside for a ticketed affair. I thought this was a good man, albeit with some reactionary Catholic politics, and I wanted to see him. I'm not sure why. He was majesterial in his gorgeous white vestment that looked in the pale light of the city's canyons as if it had been painted by Vermeer. He waved to the thousands of us massed below him. That benediction gave me the chills. The next day I detoured into Central Park to watch him speed past on his way to mass at Yankee Stadium, and from the curb I got a look at his rough peasant's features, and they were good. Back in my apartment in Brooklyn I fell to my knees to pray. I *tried* to. Perhaps that was the silliest thing I've ever done.

Paige Patterson was precociously chosen and never looked back; I was precociously hostile but have been looking back ever since, in some way. Atheists have doubts, too, I suppose—about atheism. One day several years ago I was seated in a psychiatrist's office. The woman was a friend, yes, but this was business. More or less out of the blue, triggered by some context now forgotten, the question came to mind. I asked her whether my whole life, climaxed by those episodes that had finally brought me to her surprisingly uncomfortable chair, had been one long religious crisis played out in ignorance of the main thrust of the plot. She replied without hesitation, "I think so." I have to take into account that she is a follower of the Indian seer Krishnamurti, of whom more in a moment. She might also have been merely seconding Jung's observation that a spiritual crisis was the essence of the problem of almost everyone he treated, or Saint Augustine's famous formulation that there is in each of us a God-shaped vacuum that can only be filled by . . . God. Until we understand this, Augustine lectured, and then acquiesce to the truth of it, we shall be hopelessly lost.

~~~~~~

There's a mildly disdainful word for twentieth-century types who are having trouble squaring the circle of traditional belief: searchers, people keenly aware of the God-shaped vacuum but unable to derive or sustain a believable concept of God with which to fill it. I separate these people, and they are legion, into two camps that might be labeled, and not all that facetiously, Type-A and Type-B. The Type-A's ask the question and demand an answer; they *will* find something to believe in and if they find something new the following year, shifting from Christianity to Buddhism to transcendental meditation and back to another Christianity, so be it. I would meet such searchers at Criswell College. One of my roommates at Columbia was a classic case, and twenty years later he's still at it. You would think that these serial searchers would decide after a while that their quest for the truth is all *too* productive, but they aren't cursed with relativist doubts, they aren't deterred as they tack this way and that. They want an answer and will have one. John Calvin said we are all factories for the manufacture of idols. A more contemporary evangelical, Lesslie Newbigin, writes in *Foolishness to the Greeks,* "The shrine will not remain empty. If it isn't filled with Christ, it will be filled with some other idol."

Type-B's, if you will, are people like me and Bertrand Russell, and perhaps Sartre, with the sense, intellectually or emotionally or both, of our culture's loss of faith and perhaps also feeling the need for that faith, but with an equally keen sense of the insufficiency for ourselves of answers that simply do not hold up to our scrutiny. We wonder whether, just because we need a faith, one is necessarily available (believable), and whether we might not have to learn as a culture to live without one. While not deaf to the right's judgment that the modern world is empty in its heart, we reject the idea that we can return to some premodern epistemology and theology, however much we might want to, and, while sympathetic to the tortured efforts of liberal Christians to reshape that faith, we can't go along with the results so far.

We consider the cornucopia of revealed truths, including the Eastern doctrines, as almost prima facie evidence that there is no one revealed theological truth, and therefore we see no reasonable option other than a retreat into notions of "psychological" and "existential" truth—the relativism that drives everyone on the right crazy. We are either still searching for some private truth (seeming to believe in the search for its own sake, in the manner of science), or have given up looking for truth by redefining it as something only science can determine, knowing full well that scientists will play along: "*Before* the Big Bang? That's not our purview."

For us, if Sartre's famous battle cry of existentialism, "existence precedes essence," makes sense at all, it seems to follow that existence also *precludes* essence. I don't know what logicians would say to that, but it's true in all hearts that were suckled on this stuff. We can't make any particular leap of faith. Ours is the dogmatism of skepticism, in effect, and some of us get along well enough with it, once we concede the inherent contradiction in the premise. Pyrrho of Ellis, a third-century B.C. Greek, is the model for this orthodoxy. His truest peace came from accepting the fact of the moment and embracing it. The Hindu-bred Krishnamurti follows in that tradition. How do we conquer suffering? By suffering. Our usual reflexes of putting the mind to work, analyzing the feeling, substituting language for life, are all mistaken. We cannot achieve an equilibrium for the mind by seeking causes and cures. We thrive only by living the feeling, allowing the word "suffering" to be *only* the word. The best way to handle this world is to embrace it with a radical openness, clearly the path of least resistance. A book with this message for its title, *Be Here Now,* was one of the first of the new generation of New Age texts, selling millions of copies in the sixties. I tried it then, without much luck. Now in the nineties I can't locate my copy at all.

A good place to meditate on all these matters is sitting on one of the black cushions, surrounded by the blackish, nearly nihilistic canvases of Mark Rothko at the Rothko Chapel in Houston, a shrine of the religious left on the campus of St. Thomas University, a genuinely Catholic school about six blocks from my former home. On the table in the Rothko lobby is a selection of sacred texts: the Qur'an, Tao Te Ching, Bhagavad Gita, Upanishads, Tibetan Book of the Dead, Torah, and Bible. The brochure presented to every visitor likens the chapel to a big tree: "It has a mysterious beauty and offers hospitable shade to everyone."

Perhaps so for some, but I found the place depressing. I walked over to the Rothko every once in a while, squatted down on one of the meditation pillows, and observed the visitors as they came around the corner and saw for the first time those famous religious paintings. I never saw one face register anything approaching joy. I saw surprise, puzzlement, disappointment, anger, even, but, more than anything else, blank stares. People walked around for a minute or two, then left, and I assume the crowd attracted to the chapel in the first place would be those most likely to respond to its meaning and message. Where is the hospitable shade? Where was it for Rothko? The painter committed suicide before his pictures were hung.

The Rothko is a perfect twentieth-century chapel: a room for prayer but without windows or doors. It is the perfect embodiment of a godless world, the array of God-seeking texts on display notwithstanding, or actually proving the point: belief in everything, belief in nothing. The conflict between orthodox believers and the religious left is not, as it is implicitly portrayed in the secular press, entirely the work of reactionaries who refuse to get with the program of the new and godless world. Orthodox religious belief is a rearguard action and destined to lose, perhaps, and certainly the more obscurantist element of the faith (the Bakkers, say) adds to the sum total of falsehood, but the world of the winners—the skeptics—is no bargain, either, or not yet.

How is it that the painting, sculpture, music, and literature of the creative class are simply incomprehensible to the vast majority of the populace? Something is amiss. John Adams, a summa graduate of Harvard, composer of the worthy opera *Nixon in China*, acknowledged in *The New York Times* that "something is wrong" when even he has no idea what the composer Elliott Carter is getting at with his sounds. I felt the same way while trying to read *The Flanders Road*, Nobel-winner Claude Simon's alleged best book. There must be some connection between the disbelief on the part of most artists today in any kind of organizing principle for the universe (God), and their refusal to employ readily grasped organizing principles in their work. There must also be a connection between artists' disdain for those "classes" that still believe in God and their delight in confronting those rubes with offensive images, such as the photograph of a cross dipped in the jar of urine.

W. A. Criswell was correct. Not only can we on the religious left not raise Lazarus from the dead, we have no beliefs at all, no authority to tell us who we are, where we came from, where we're going, or why. Our shrines are either stuffed full of patently false idols, shuffled at random, or they are kept empty on purpose.

The suspicion might be rising at this point that I'm some sort of neoconservative. I'm not. I couldn't care less about someone else's traditional values; I yield to no one in my nostalgia for the sixties. Nevertheless, we would all agree that this culture is nearly overwhelmed by all the bullshit and bad faith, by the literally spellbinding vacuity, top to bottom, left to right. We do worship the worthless, as Solzhenitsyn asserted, and this idolatry is the engine of the whole system. Everyone knows it. Those Eastern Europeans who aren't already rushing west to ransack the shelves are determined to avoid this fate—but how? In the journal pieces

I have read they find only one option: some form of adherence to the received religious tradition. The religiously orthodox are correct when they argue that the irreligious world is not sustaining the rest of us and we even joke about this with a bumper sticker of our own: LIFE'S A BITCH—THEN YOU DIE.

CHAPTER 7

Jim Parker grew up on a farm outside Abilene, Texas, about thirty miles from Stamford, my birthplace in the north central part of the state. Parker and I are about the same age. Our paths have diverged widely in the nearly forty years since my parents moved out of that region, and Parker's is the road much less traveled. He's now a professor at Criswell College in the Department of New Testament Studies, although the semester I was in residence he was teaching the class on ethics. Paige Patterson had urged me to sit in on this one.

"Parker's just an ol' pig farmer," Patterson said with some exaggeration. "You'll enjoy him."

So there I was, waiting for our teacher early in the morning on my second day of classes at the college. I asked the student next to me whether Parker had any objections to our bringing cups of coffee to the table. Parker? Of course not. He finally shuffled in a little late, looking sleepy yet startled. He has a friendly, open face and longish, grayish hair. His jacket that morning was cut from some funky leatherlike material; by faculty standards, as I discerned them, Parker was hip, but cleaned up from the first time he had met Paige Patterson, years ago, when he had a shaggy beard.

He turned to the class and said with a grin, "I'm the first to admit that it's unethical to have a class at seven-thirty in the morning, but it's all part of the Fall."

A hearty guffaw issued from the student ranks—twenty strong for this upper-level offering. Parker intoned a brief prayer (every class begins with a prayer, delivered by the professor or sometimes a student of his designation) and then proceeded with all the normal first-day things.

A student walked in late and surveyed the occupied chairs.

"Here," Parker motioned. "You may sit at my feet."

We laughed again and I knew why Patterson had wanted me in this class. Here was someone at Criswell whom I would instantly "relate to," and Patterson had known that would be the case. Parker may have been raised a pig farmer—to wit, he was a 4-H student in Abilene—but his demeanor betrays the irony inherent in a secular education today, and that is the education Parker has had, for the most part. Criswell was only the third out of the eleven schools at which Parker had studied or taught where his evangelical views were the norm rather than the exception.

Finishing up his general instructions, Parker advised everyone to bring a Bible to class, concluding with another quip: "It's incredible the light the Bible will shed on commentaries." This sally, he admitted, was not his own. It originated with a professor at Princeton, from where Parker has a couple of master's degrees. He dismissed us and I stood by as he answered the crush of questions.

"Oh, yes!" he exclaimed after I had introduced myself. Patterson had indeed informed the faculty that I would be around for the term. Then he paused. "Patterson told you to sit in *here*?"

"He made me promise."

We discussed the awful hour with, I thought, an unspoken hint of elitism burrowing beneath the conversation: Ivy League schools don't have seven-thirty classes, with the possible exception of first-year language labs. More than anyone else at Criswell, to my knowledge, Parker was educated in the secular world, including Princeton and the University of Basel, Nietzsche's home base, and beginning at Baylor University, the nominally Baptist institution in Waco, Texas. There's no alcohol in Waco (the county is dry, as they say in Texas) and no dancing on the Baylor campus (the subject of a recent dispute), but that doesn't mean the education at Baylor is orthodox Christianity. Parker's battles with the Baylor professors were a rude awakening for his own traditional belief. Indirectly, that undergraduate experience set him on the circuitous course that earned him four advanced degrees and finally brought him to Criswell College.

"I grew up as one of six kids on a farm right outside Abilene, Texas," he told me. "I raised pigs for 4-H. That's where Patterson gets the 'pig farmer.' My dad was a commissioned-order buyer for livestock, and then he started a radio broadcast of farm and ranch news, which he still does. We didn't really grow anything on the farm—just ran a few head of cattle, and there was always a horse or two around. My mother worked in special education in the public school system. She is Southern Baptist, my father Episcopalian. My mother is much more active than my dad is, but he at least goes every Sunday that he ushers—and they have it rigged so you usher once a month!

"I was always responsive to church. I had some really good Sunday school teachers over the years. And, on rare occasion, going to my father's church gave me an early realization that there are other Christians than Baptists, and that there are other ways of expressing the same faith."

Parker was in the tenth grade when he had that pivotal experience that all Christians encounter at some point. It changed his life. He had made the standard profession of faith and was baptized when he was ten years old—"about the time a lot of Southern

Baptists do it. Mature reflection leads me to believe that nothing really happened then. It's hard to say, but I don't think so. There were certain evidences in my life that nothing happened. I was pretty indistinguishable from the secular kids—a cultural Christian, if you will. I wouldn't have stood out.

"Then in the tenth grade we had a winter youth retreat at Lake Brownwood—it was freezing cold—and I think that's really where I became a Christian. It became clear in my mind that I needed to make a clear, full commitment to Christ—everything I was, am, and will be. No particular sermon triggered this emotion, I had just reached an existential crisis, a fork in the road. I knew this was a choice with lifelong consequences. It was rather overwhelming. My life-style was profoundly affected. People noticed. For one thing, before that I had cussed like a sailor—or like the people at cattle auctions! Overnight that kind of little thing just stopped. My cousin noticed. He told my sister, 'Jim doesn't cuss anymore. What's wrong with him?'

"But that wasn't the substance of what happened, of course. I just really began to develop spiritually at that point. I was very interested in reading the Bible, praying, attending church activities, witnessing. I got some flak. You know, all of a sudden I was a 'religious fanatic.' This didn't bother me at all. I was secure in myself, with who I was. I'm still that way. The opinion of others doesn't bother me. I ran for president of the student council and lost because I was too weird, blazing my own trail, not caring what people thought I should do. But they did make me chaplain!

"I knew after the retreat that I wanted to go into some kind of religious work. Pastoring would have been the most likely option, I suppose, and I thought I might want to be an evangelist. The expression that's used is 'God called me to some kind of special service,' and I did have that sense, and it was a wonderful sense to provide direction and purpose. I remember thinking in college about all the poor students with no idea where they were headed. It was nice that I knew."

I recalled Paige Patterson's testimony about his own sleepless nights in Europe on his tour of the world as a teenage preacher, despairing for all the lost souls, the sheep without their shepherd, "milling around with no idea what life is all about, or eternity either."

Parker continued: "I had to decide about college, and knew that Billy Graham had gone to Wheaton, outside Chicago, so I wrote them. It's a top-quality academic evangelical college—today, probably the most ideal Christian college. Most Christian schools have no idea what Christian education is all about. At Baylor, say, the idea is that you have a religion department and chapel, and they require every student to take a couple of courses in religion and attend chapel for one or two semesters—and that makes it a Christian university, different from Texas A&M. It doesn't dawn on them that the Christian worldview should affect the content of all disciplines, some more than others, of course. Math, hardly at all, except in that the reality of the external universe would be affirmed, the legitimacy of mind and reason. Stuff like that. But the social sciences—well, one's view of the nature of man is profoundly affected by the Christian perspective. Or should be. Wheaton understands that this Christian worldview actually affects the content of the discipline itself, whereas most Christian schools teach these disciplines with the secular presuppositions and methodologies. They separate piety from intellectual discipline, which makes for schizoid students, and that's why there's such a high attrition rate by students who leave the faith at 'Christian' colleges.

"I didn't go to Wheaton. It was just so far away. I went to Baylor instead, down in Waco. A lot of my friends were going there, and it was *the* Baptist school in Texas to go to. But first, the summer after high school, I sold Bibles for the Southwestern Company in Kentucky. Worked like a dog. Learned how to handle rejection! But it confirmed my desire to go into religious work. At Baylor I majored in religion and am still a Christian in spite of it. Baylor had this schizophrenic atmosphere I mentioned. They wanted to be a big, prestigious university, and the only way they saw to do that was teach all the courses the same as you would get them anywhere.

"The Religion Department employed the cafeteria approach. A few professors were pretty conservative, with traditional views, including Kyle Yates, who really helped me a lot, but most were liberal. From my experience at home I had been aware that there are different expressions of Christianity, but Baylor was the first time I was personally exposed to people who called themselves Christians but who would not affirm what the church historically affirmed. The basic truths had been reinterpreted right out of existence. Teachers tried to convince me that Scripture is not reliable. The Ten Commandments were not special revelation from God but rather the guidelines of human beings, developed so that these wandering groups of Semitic tribes could live in reasonable peace with each other. Attributing this code to God gave it the ring of authority, like a child will tell a sibling, 'Well, Mother said to do it!' In other words, the fundamentally secular interpretation of the Old Testament. That's what I was taught at Baylor."

And what I was taught at Columbia. Parker continued: "I asked why the ideas of some fourth-rate, sun-crazed, wandering tribesmen should be authoritative for me today at all! Why not pick any other screwball group and take their ideas as authoritative? I don't remember the answer. It would have been double-talk then just like it's double-talk today. These folks don't really believe in the miraculous but they hide behind all this gobbledygook. That's something I learned about liberal theologians: they just can't talk straight. Oh, *sometimes* they can be explicit. I remember one teacher saying about something attributed to God in the Bible, 'My God would never do that.'

"They thought 'conservative' and 'intellectual' was a contradiction in terms. If a conservative position was presented at all, it was in caricature, ad hominem, which can have powerful appeal. I was taught that missions and evangelism were religious imperialism. I had no idea about the implicit admissions behind a statement like that. First of all, you have to be assuming that the Christian faith is not true because if it *is* true, evangelism is no more religious imperialism than distributing penicillin is medical imperialism.

"Some professors were syncretists with the idea that all religions are saying the same thing, with no one religion being a valid truth claim. This was perplexing because my Sunday school teachers had been saying for years that Christianity is reliable. I knew that what I had been taught at home was wrong *or* what I was hearing at Baylor was wrong. The teachers I was *entrusted* to were undermining everything. Most of the students came to Baylor as conservatives. Then they fell like flies. And this has perplexed me to this very day: Baylor can teach the most egregious apostasy and heresy and anti-Christian ideology, but scales fall over the eyes and ears of Texas Baptists. Their Baylor is the child that can do no wrong.

"I had heard about this stuff existing way up North—the source of all evil and heresy!—but I just couldn't believe it at Baylor. So I went in to see Abner McCall, the president at the time, and shared my concerns. And he said something like, 'Well, son, you just have to understand, we all believe the Bible, we just interpret it differently.'

"I wasn't too bright, maybe, but I knew something more than that was going on. In fact, as I told him, isn't Marxism just another political philosophy and interpretation of economics? Now, remember, McCall was real conservative politically, one of the leaders of Democrats for Nixon, so I knew he could relate to that provocation. Why don't we have any Marxists teaching economics?

" 'Now, now, that's different,' he said. Well, the reason it's different is that in the one case—political economy—he believes one system is right and the other wrong, but in religion, it just doesn't matter. McCall is a wonderful man, incredibly brilliant in law and political theory, but his theological sophistication is paint-by-numbers.

"I certainly do *not* oppose secular teaching in other colleges. I just think it should show its colors. The atheist professors at Baylor were straightforward. A geology professor said—on the last day of class, naturally—'Either God created man or man created God. I'll leave that up to you. But as far as I'm concerned, if it's not in the rocks, it doesn't exist.'

"That was no real threat because I knew there are a lot of things he doesn't find in the rocks that he believes in, such as love. The real threat came from the Religion Department because they're not straightforward and honest. Of course the reason they're not is that if they said publicly, 'No, we don't believe in miracles,' then the Southern Baptist Convention would come down on them and clean house. So we push them into the dishonesty." (As it turned out, the struggle for control at Baylor between denomination conservatives and the moderate leadership at the school erupted in full-scale civil war late in 1990.) Parker continued:

"I had a friend who had been at Moody Bible Institute for two years before transferring to Baylor, and he introduced me to literature that developed these issues in a scholarly way. So basically I was self-educated. And Kyle Yates gave me direction, too. I'd go into his office when I was worked up about something and he'd say, 'Well, yes, there are people who believe such things, but I'm not one of them. And here are my reasons.'

"Early on at Baylor I still wanted to be an evangelist. That kind of backwoods, redneck stuff was not encouraged. They wanted to get that anti-intellectual stuff out of me as quickly as possible. But the philosophical and historical questions were also interesting to me, and I could see that I wasn't going to get them all answered to my satisfaction at Baylor. Up to that point I hadn't been a particularly outstanding student. At the end of my freshman year I went to one ol' professor and asked him what I'd need for the Ph.D., and he said I'd need seven more years after Baylor and I'd have to learn French and German and Greek and Hebrew. And it struck me that I was talking about the next decade of my life. A major commitment. So I started Hebrew the next semester, and then German; I took a minor in Greek. I figured I had to have all these tools. I quit most of my outside activities, took heavy loads because I wanted to cut off as much time as I could, went to summer school, and finished in three years. I paid for it with a combination of jobs, grants, and loans.

"I wanted to know whether Christianity is *true,* and I began to be convinced it is. There are really good reasons for believing it to be so; it's not a matter of shutting your eyes and piously believing in the face of the facts. Now, it wasn't because of this apologetics, as it's called, that I became a Christian, but being convinced of the truth of Christianity allowed me to *remain* a Christian. I could never have held on to that double-talking liberal nonsense at Baylor. If I had determined that was my only option, I would probably have done what so many others do, and jettisoned it altogether. I hope that's still true today: I couldn't live with what I know to be delusion."

~~~~~~~~

Few people could, presumably, but the key word is "know." One man's fact is another's delusion. It all depends on one's presuppositions. This was perhaps the key point impressed upon me, time and again, by Jim Parker and everyone else at Criswell College: presuppositions have priority. If you approach the subject of Christian belief with an ironclad antisupernatural presupposition, of course you can't find God in the universe. That presupposition, evangelicals argue, is wrong. Even worse, it usually is not even identified for what it is and thereby escapes critical analysis. You can find evangelicals—Paige Patterson is one of them, as he told me—who respect Sartre as an atheist because at least Sartre stared the beast in the eye and wrote "No Exit" by way of conceding defeat.

Parker and I discussed these matters over quite a few lunches during the term, the first time some kind of Hawaiian food, the second Vietnamese, then elsewhere. He acquired this eclectic taste in cuisine while studying in Basel, Switzerland, for three years, and he indulges it to the extent possible in Dallas, Texas. He was the first person at Criswell with whom I spent a good deal of time off campus, and as he began to ply me with a number of books and articles—the stack soon became unwieldy—I suspected he had been tacitly put in charge of my case. After all, he was a bachelor with more free time than other faculty members, he had vast experience in dealing with skeptics, and he clearly enjoyed the give and take of belief and doubt (although so did Paige Patterson and Danny Akin and just about everyone else—especially the professors—whom I would meet at the school).

"Not at all!" Parker exclaimed when I asked him. He just wanted to make sure that I understood what the issues are, and the main issue, he insists, is truth, of which he finds very little in religious observance today. Parker thinks about as highly as I do of America's ballyhooed "return to religion"—that is to say, not highly at all. Yes, 90 percent of Americans say they believe in God, about that same percentage believe in the divinity of Jesus Christ, 75 percent accept heaven and hell as actualities, and so on. But less than 50 percent attend any church at all, fewer yet attend regularly, and, according to one telltale poll of Methodists, one in twelve who claim allegiance to that denomination acknowledge God as the "most important" factor in their lives. That ratio would not be much different for the other mainstream denominations, Catholicism included. And which figure means more, the 90 percent or the one in twelve? The latter. Parker and I agree on that. So does C. S. Lewis, who wryly observed that Christianity is either a matter of utmost importance, if it's true, or of no importance whatsoever, if it's false. One thing it is not is moderately important.

What do most Christians truly believe? "They're deists," Parker said, and then delivered a brief lecture on the history of deism, beginning with one Lord Herbert of Cherbury, the first modern deist. Deism, also referred to as "natural religion," acknowledges the proverbial Divine Presence but denies any kind of supernatural revelation or intervention attributed to the personal God of the theistic faiths. Deism takes care of why we're here at all, then leaves us pretty much free to do as we will on earth.

Thomas Jefferson was a deist. He put together a Bible without all the miraculous material, and it's a much shorter volume than the original. A remark I heard several times at Criswell is that deists invite God in for the Creation, then show Him the door.

"Belief in the supernatural is gone," Parker added. "People have bought into philosophical naturalism but they also want the warm fuzzy. So they're deists. Also, a lot of people are just mad at the theistic God."

I agree with this assessment. People are hurt, angry, suffering, and they understand from Sunday school and church that the God of theistic Christianity is responsible for everything that happens on earth. They're not interested in the fine points of Christian theodicy—the problem of God's relations with mankind, the problem of evil. They understand that Jesus Christ was appointed to redeem their sins and suffering, but they're not sure about this because they're vaguely influenced by the prevailing antisupernaturalism, and why all the problems in the first place? Adam and Eve and the serpent? Unlikely. And yet, we *are* here and our conscious selves and the midnight sky do seem, in moments of self-satisfaction, rather miraculous. So, sure, there must be some kind of God around who started it all.

Deism is a nonanswer, an emotion more than anything else, not really a belief. Nor does it hold up well under scrutiny because an uninvolved God is really a malevolent God, given the way matters have turned out. But deists don't have a malevolent God in mind. Most of them have little at all in mind.

Parker closed one of our sessions of soft evangelizing with an observation about those millions of us who walk away from the church at an early age. In other areas of experience, he said, people may continue to grow—our politics may evolve, for example—but we almost never return to reconsider our initial rejection of religious faith. "The void in your lives is obvious," he said, "but the rejection is never reexamined. In this one area, people quit growing."

Evangelicals and other Christians argue that the only alternative to unquestioned belief in *something* is unquestioned doubt about *everything*, a philosophical naturalism leading to a skepticism that has two problems: no one actually lives that way, and it is a contradiction, because the programmatic doubt is not itself doubted.

Parker left me, the token philosophical naturalist at the table, with three questions he wanted answered before I left the table or, failing that, before I left town or, failing that, before I finished this book.

- How does scientific, philosophical skepticism explain man's moral nature?
- How does it hold together logically?
- How does it avoid nihilism?

The first question was one of the subjects of Parker's Ethics class, and he summed up the Christian answer in his first lecture: "A transcendent source for human values is the only one that guarantees a valid, normative ethical system." Otherwise, morals are relative, and this is not good enough either practically, because we must live in an ethically ordered society, or epistemologically, because we do have a moral sense and we do know right from wrong. "If Christians have the problem of evil to explain," Parker said as a challenge to me, "atheists have the problem of good."

In his lectures for the Ethics class Parker devoted many hours to explaining how the nontheistic ethical systems—emotivism, empiricism, intuitionism, ethical egoism, utilitarianism, instrumentalism, and more—can neither sufficiently explain our moral nature nor guarantee an ethical norm. But ethics is also another of those matters on which liberal and conservative Christians can agree in principle but disagree on how it's worked out in practice. John A. T. Robinson writes, "The only intrinsic evil is the lack of love," but evangelicals respond that while it's possible, even easy, to love mankind in the abstract, we cannot love all, or even many, men and women in particular. Therefore the Bible defines love for us with the Ten Commandments, and God enforces it.

Richard Robinson responds in *An Atheist's Values,* "Which is more profitable, to do [something] because God commands so, and punishment awaits . . . or [because] society as a whole will benefit, with a diminution of misery?" Robinson suggests that obeying rules is *prudence,* not morality. Then he adds, "The false assumption that nothing but religious belief will ever make people obey the moral laws is widespread in the Occidental world, and it has harmful effects. It leads people into all kinds of intellectual dishonesties in their frantic effort to save religious belief for the sake of saving morality. . . . The capture of morality by religion . . . has turned out harmful for the world now that religion is declining."

Arthur Schlesinger, Jr., wrote in *The New York Times,* "As a historian, I confess to a certain amusement when I hear the Judeo-Christian tradition praised as the source of our concern for human rights. In fact, the great religious ages were notable for their indifference to human rights in the contemporary sense. . . . Religion enshrined and vindicated hierarchy, authority, and inequality and had no compunction about murdering heretics and blasphemers. . . . Human rights is not a religious idea. It is a secular idea, the product of the last four centuries of Western history."

Answering this slander, Parker referred me in one of our luncheon conversations to the passage in Romans proving God through the argument from design: "For what can be known about God is plain to them, because God has shown it to them. Ever since the creation of the world his invisible nature, namely, his eternal power and deity, has been clearly perceived in the things that have been made" (Rom. 1:19–20).

Among those things is man's moral nature, inscribed in our hearts. To the extent that ancient societies that had never heard of the Bible nevertheless had highly ethical structures, they were perceiving and abiding by this general revelation. If we have the ethics from general revelation, why do we need the special revelation of Christianity? We are fallen. Divergent behavior merely proves the incompleteness of common revelation in a fallen world.

Parker told me a story from his two years at Princeton, where he picked up the Master of Divinity, the basic professional degree for ministers, and the Master of Theology, a specialization. Some of the liberal students in a missiology class were propounding the view that whatever the individual believed to be good and true was in fact so. The evangelical students disagreed, and a friend of Parker's asked one of the other students whether the guard in the concentration camp who believed he was doing the right thing was therefore justified in his actions. The cultural relativist said yes. Parker's friend jumped up, grabbed his hair, and shrieked, "Madness!"

Theistic ethicism may be in vogue. The cover story in the December 1989 *Atlantic* asked "Can We Be Good Without God?" and answered in the negative. Not even a good Constitution is enough. We need a Holy Writ as well. If only man is the judge, there is no judge. In class Parker cited a statement by Ludwig Wittgenstein to the effect that any book written on ethics that was really about ethics and not about language would "explode" every other book.

Then he smiled and said, "That book has been written."

~~~~~~

I knew that Parker's second and third questions about the internal logic and alleged nihilism of philosophical skepticism were the ones that finally drove C. S. Lewis to Christianity. Lewis failed to see how the purposeless workings of the natural world produced human beings who then looked back on that natural world with the keenest sense of purpose. If the materialist system is closed, there is no purpose. But there is purpose, so the system is not closed. It's open. We obtain our sense of purpose, our need for love, our desire for the healing presence of God, as well as our moral sense, from the personal God who resides *outside* the natural world. It was the only answer that made sense to Lewis. His corpus may not be great technical apologetics (he was soundly beaten in a debate with an Oxford atheist, a defeat that apparently chastened his doctrinaire zeal), but his best books and sermons are great *belief*.

He concluded his sermon "Is Theology Poetry?" this way:

The waking world is judged more real because it can thus contain the dreaming world: the dreaming world is judged less real because it cannot contain the waking one. For the same reason I am certain that in passing from the scientific point of view to the theological, I have passed from dream to waking. Christian theology can fit in science, art, morality, and the sub-Christian religions. The scientific point of view cannot fit in any of these things, not even science itself. I believe in Christianity as I believe that the sun has risen, not only because I see it but because by it I see everything else.

The evangelical author Francis Schaeffer buttresses Lewis's argument with the image of the two floors of our human experience, which I interpret, rather loosely, in the following way. Our physical, scientific, historical selves reside on the lower floor. In the upper room are our qualities of love, hope, purpose, meaning, soul. We cannot live on just the lower story. Animals presumably are not beset with concerns about meaning; we are. If the upper-floor qualities that define our personalities arose from the lower floor of impersonality, we are trapped with aspirations beyond fulfillment. We cannot get to the upper floor. But this is illogical as well as intolerable. We *do* have these feelings. We *do* get from the lower story to the upper one, whether by some irrational leap of faith (or despair) that makes no sense and cannot sustain the connection, or by the work and message of Jesus Christ and the will of the Christian God.

I was intrigued when I first read these arguments because I had followed the same reasoning years before, but I substituted premises and therefore drew the opposite conclusion. While Lewis and Schaeffer presupposed our sense of meaning and purpose, I presupposed the workings of evolution and the natural world, and I decided that I must therefore be a machine because nothing but a machine could evolve from a machinelike, purposeless process. I have a clear memory of my conclusion, and the logic still seems unavoidable: I am the machine that doesn't feel like one.

Theists scoff. One professor at Criswell who did so was Kirk Spencer, the young science teacher who was in the process of earning his doctorate in geology from Southern Methodist University, several miles north of the Criswell campus and, despite its name, a secular institution. "If they create life in a test tube, would this prove that life 'just happened'?" Spencer asked his upper-level Natural Science class at Criswell. "No, it would prove that intelligence is necessary to create life."

I'm of two contradictory minds on this issue. Despite my preceding conclusion about being the machine that doesn't feel like one, I also come dangerously close to agreeing with Spencer. I've always thought that the chemists can manipulate their organic chemicals and macromolecules for a million years and never produce a single virus. When I mentioned this at Criswell, some people probably figured they had a closet creationist on hand, a guy ready to cross over. If I had added that I also suspect, somewhat unfashionably in my circle, that we are alone in the universe, they might have been almost certain.

My hunch about the inherent hopelessness of efforts to create living organisms from inert chemicals in the laboratory—abiogenesis—comes dangerously close to being a brand of vitalism, the naïve intuition that something beyond the processes of what we consider the natural world must be responsible for life on earth. This heresy is common enough among common minds but is held in deep disdain by the massed forces of the scientific community, with notable exceptions, among them Nobel Prize winner Sir John Eccles, who has declared the Darwinian model "defective." The reviewer of a recent Eccles book wrote in *The New York Times* by way of a punning retort, "Sir John's current struggles to defend the metaphysical [recall] Ophelia's lament for Hamlet, 'O! what a noble mind is here o'erthrown.'"

Another renegade, the British astronomer Sir Frederick Hoyle, devised the most popular debunking of abiogenesis when he claimed that the spontaneous generation of a bacterium is about as likely as believing that a tornado smashing through a junkyard of airliner parts would create an airworthy 747. Hoyle is often quoted by creationists, but they don't cite this subsequent statement: "The intelligence responsible for the creation of carbon-based life in the cosmic theory is firmly within the Universe and subservient to it." Francis Crick, codiscoverer of the structure of DNA, also expresses doubts about abiogenesis on the primitive earth. Maybe the first microbes came from outer space. But Crick acknowledged that this "directed panspermia" theory doesn't answer the ultimate question about where those microbes came from.

One final exhibit: *The Mystery of Life's Origin: Reassessing Current Theories*, a book published in 1984, received a rave review from the *Yale Journal of Biology and Medicine*, which concluded, "the volume as a whole is *devastating* [my emphasis] to a relaxed acceptance of current theories of abiogenesis."

A typical example of this relaxed acceptance may be found in Timothy Ferris's superb book on cosmology, *Coming of Age in the Milky Way*. Ferris writes, "Darwin's theory of evolution, though it does not explain away the ancient conundrum of why there is such a thing as life, does make it clear that life may arise from ordinary matter. . . ."

Darwin doesn't even make this claim for his theory. He left open the question of genesis. A couple of paragraphs later Ferris suggests that no "thinking person" can any longer accept the Christian verdict that "there is no life, truth, substance, or intelligence in matter." All this statement proves is the power of presuppositions. Ferris accepts the presupposition of scientific naturalism that matter is in fact the source of its own vitality. Certainly this is the consensus of scientists, but plenty of thinking people, even scientists, don't agree. One of them is the English chemist and sociologist Michael Polanyi, author of *Personal Knowledge*. Polanyi is sympathetic to liberal Christianity and also a vitalist. "The rise of man can be accounted for only by other principles than those known today to physics and chemistry," he writes. "If this be vitalism, then vitalism is mere common sense, which can be ignored only by a *truculently bigoted mechanistic outlook* [my emphasis]. And so long as we can form no idea of the way a material system may become a conscious, responsible person, it is an empty pretense to suggest that we have an explanation for the descent of man."

Polanyi and many other vitalists accept evolution. Some evangelicals also accept evolution, usually in one form or another of "progressive creationism," God acting over a long period of time, six *metaphorical* days. (This is Kirk Spencer's position regarding the geology of the earth; he considers some fundamentalists' insistence on six actual days of creation simply untenable.) All such attempts to reconcile Scripture and science come under the rubric of "concordism" and Einstein is widely quoted in this regard: "Religion without science is blind and science without religion is lame." But again, as with Hoyle, any religion Einstein envisioned was a far cry from orthodox theism.

Paige Patterson told me one day, "I'm not sure that final proof for macroevolution would be per se the death of theism, but it is hopelessly antithetical to the message of Scripture. Acceptance of evolution as compatible with biblical Christianity is an unthoughtful acceptance. The evolution of a body is perhaps explicable, given some uniformity among the various species. How would we explain the evolution of a soul? None of us would argue that there's anything eternal about a catfish. It is an explicit declaration of Scripture that there is an eternal aspect to man—a soul."

If we don't have a soul, what is this feeling that we do? And if we do have a soul, where did it come from? The catfish? That's the brief argument for vitalism. To believe that the human soul popped up out of nowhere, Patterson suggested, "takes more faith than believing what the Bible says."

CHAPTER 8

Church services, required chapel services, classes, lunches with students and teachers, and reading, stacks of reading: I was feeling my way at Criswell College, studying, in effect, a very foreign language spoken on some unknown planet orbiting a different sun. The people there looked on me with pity, partly for not knowing what is so sweet in their hearts, so productive in their lives as they judge them and therefore, by definition, so manifestly true. But they had to give me credit, and they did: I was working as hard as I could to find out, arriving home at my apartment every evening absolutely exhausted, often confused, once or twice ready to call it quits on the grounds that I would never understand them, no matter how reasonable they were in their dealings with me, and they would never understand me, no matter how reasonable I was. So we should just agree to disagree and leave it at that—which is what we do, after all, in the real world, with most people secure enough, if not happy, in their chosen beliefs and appropriately smug about the poor bastards still out in the cold.

One such frustrating moment came in Cultural Milieu of Modern Man, a required upper-level class taught by Professor Luis Pantoja, who's from the Philippines and the director of admissions at Criswell. On the first day of classes Pantoja walked in, named the course and quipped, "Some of you may have to check the dictionary on that word." I thought he was perhaps correct, based on the myriad pronunciations I had already heard around my table. Paige Patterson had suggested I take this class for the obvious reason that I probably knew more about the cultural milieu of modern *secular* man than anyone in that building. Patterson imagined the class and I could mix it up pretty well, but a couple of weeks into the term when I spoke to the students at Pantoja's request about my own journey into unfaith and my agenda at Criswell College, they greeted my presentation with what I took to be a flabbergasted silence. Then one student asked me by way of a challenge, "Don't you know that Jesus said, 'I am the way, the truth, and the life; no one comes to the Father but through me' " (John 14:6).

I replied that I knew that the author of the gospel *claimed* that Jesus said that, but that's not the same as my knowing that Jesus actually said it, or that Jesus meant what evangelicals say he meant, or that Jesus wasn't deluded while making this claim. We were stymied by that issue of presuppositions, but I didn't quit that class or any of the others. Most of the time I was a happy kibitzer. I became intrigued, in fact. The theology was fascinating, the classes fun, the teachers full of wit, the students real people (a few nerds, an equivalent number of flaming troublemakers, skiing nuts, baseball fans, and golfers), and I didn't have to write the papers or take the tests. And where was the lockstep indoctrination I had feared from a Bible college? I sought for it in vain. Everyone was a conservative Christian, but much of what I heard from Danny Akin, Jim Parker, and other teachers in the Criswell classrooms was assorted challenges to the students, to the point of riling them up. Speaking to captive audiences that agreed with their own beliefs, the professors constantly challenged those beliefs by calling attention to opposing views and requiring students to know them and understand them. "Liberal" was one of the first words that came to mind as a description of the atmosphere in Criswell College classes.

On the first day of Cultural Milieu—"An examination of the various facets of Western culture (music, art, literature, theater, etc.) and an evaluation of the cultural contributions and deficiencies of each from the perspective of the Judeo-Christian worldview"—Luis Pantoja discussed the assigned texts, one of which was *The Cosmic Center: The Supremacy of Christ in a Secular World,* by D. Bruce Lockerbie.

"Lockerbie is a Christian humanist," Pantoja said, and paused with the mischievous smile. "There *is* such a thing, you know." A few of us laughed.

"The Bible is humanist," Pantoja continued, "because it has a *high* view of man. Man is fallen but God redeemed man because we were created in His image."

The basic idea of the course, I realized, is to confront the students with the secular world beyond the walls. Pantoja is an excellent choice for the assignment. His playful smile can be almost taunting and revealing more of that irony that I had not, I'll admit, previously associated with conservative Christians.

He assigned two movies for viewing: *Return of the Jedi* and either *Kramer vs. Kramer* or *On Golden Pond.* Then he added, "Some of you may be too fundamentalist to go to the movie theater, but these are on video, too." (Here I thought I picked up a little sarcasm about rigid fundamentalism.) Surely enough, the question of nudity in movies was raised. Someone knew that *Kramer vs. Kramer* was R-rated. Pantoja reminded the students there's a distinction between exposure and endorsement: "All things are lawful for me," Paul wrote, "but not all things are helpful" (1 Cor. 6:12).

"We have you read Rudolf Bultmann, but that doesn't mean we endorse him," Pantoja said. "You can send your kid to religious school but that doesn't mean he won't still see *Playboy*. Some of you probably have those magazines in the closet somewhere. You struggle with this." One student acknowledged that he has struggled with the temptation of pornography all his life. A broad discussion finally came down in favor of seeing the movies, for the sake of knowing the world in which the students live. However, Pantoja did allow for "conscientious objection." After viewing the movies, the students were to make twenty-five "significant observations" on the present condition of Western culture as portrayed in the movie. What does the movie convey as "real, true, right, and good?"

Under these criteria, Pantoja added, "Dustin Hoffman is a superb actor" does not count as a significant observation.

The students would also be required to view the Ramses exhibit about to open in Dallas and one other cultural show or event of their choice (opera, ballet, symphony, or art exhibit). Regarding the ballet Pantoja said, "Herschel Walker did it, so can you." Walker is the former Dallas Cowboy running back who performed in a ballet, and apparently did quite well with the lifting parts. This would not be the last reference to the Dallas Cowboys I would hear in Cultural Milieu. Later in the term, when Cowboys coach Tom Landry (an evangelical himself) was summarily fired by the new owner, the ethics of the move and the effects on the team would be widely discussed. I wasn't around when Walker was traded from the Cowboys to the Vikings, but I assume this move was also carefully analyzed.

Pantoja quoted an evangelical source in defining culture as the "knowledge, beliefs, art, law, customs, and any other capabilities acquired by man as a member of society."

"What is the biblical foundation of culture," he asked?

We were silent. The answer is Gen. 1: 26–28.

Then God said, "Let us make man in our image, after our likeness; and let them have dominion over the fish of the sea, and over the birds of the air, and over the cattle, and over all the earth, and over every creeping thing that creeps upon the earth." So God created man in his own image, in the image of God he created him; male and female he created them. And God blessed them, and God said to them, "Be fruitful and multiply, and fill the earth and subdue it; and have dominion over the fish of the sea and over the birds of the air and over every living thing that moves upon the earth."

"God has a specific cultural design," Pantoja expanded. "God made provisions for man." He added a point I had not known (there would be thousands of these over the semester), that early biblical men and women were apparently vegetarians. Meat eating did not begin until Noah's era. (Gen. 9:3: "Every moving thing that lives shall be food for you; and as I gave you the green plants, I give you everything.")

Pantoja asked the class, "Is it proper to say that Paul was a product of his own culture when he wrote about women? Yes! The gospel *is* culture-bound! Do you agree?"

From the silence in the room I wasn't sure all the students did. Pantoja continued with another rhetorical question: "Is monogamy a stipulation of ancient Near Eastern culture?"

No.

Pantoja invited us to consider the phrase "the Lamb of God," used in reference to Jesus. "This phrase is culture-bound, isn't it? Other cultures don't have any lambs. But would the gospel have said 'Behold the pig of God'? No. That wouldn't be kosher!"

He acknowledged that God's covenant with Moses was similar to the tribal king's covenant with his people, but that parallelism does not prove the Mosaic material is *hopelessly* culture-bound. In some areas, God accepted His people's cultural traits, and worked with them. In others, God corrected them (wholesale, it would seem, in the message and work of Christ in the New Testament). The question, Pantoja said in conclusion, is *how much* cultural accretion can you remove from the Bible and still maintain the true gospel? How are we to communicate this culture-bound gospel to our twentieth-century society?

A black student asked, "What segment of the culture *defines* 'culture'?" An excellent question and Pantoja shrewdly dodged it. Time was up.

Pantoja might also have raised the issue of slavery, which is a given throughout the Old and New Testaments. Jesus never directed individuals to free their slaves. Paul acknowledged slavery but also urged owners to free their slaves as soon as possible. While the Bible's message can be legitimately read as mitigating the harshness of the institution of slavery (and Gandhi credited Christianity with awakening his own revulsion against the Hindu caste system), it was not until the eighteenth century that Christians began to condemn slavery as absolutely sinful, and they reconciled this change of heart as a "progressive revelation."

The culture-bound nature of Holy Scripture is acknowledged by even the most benighted of Baptists today, if only implicitly, but it is still a tender point. Some of the students in the Cultural Milieu class seemed uncomfortable with Pantoja's questions, because the answers require careful alignment with the doctrine of inerrancy. In its acceptance of slavery, for example, the Bible is not inerrant, judged by today's ethics. Jim Parker responded in Ethics class by pointing out that Scripture deals with slavery as it deals with divorce. In saying this, Parker emphasized, he was by no means equating those two practices, but God hates both, and both are manifestations of our fallen nature. His instructions in each instance are designed to limit the scope of the evil. In the Old Testament, slavery is actually an indentured servitude, and owners are instructed to free their charges after seven years. In the New Testament, holders are urged to free their slaves. And today, many Christians of all persuasions, including evangelicals, are in the forefront in the battle against apartheid, a system-wide slavery. Thus, Parker said, Christians have continued to grow ethically as they have implemented the implicit ethics of Christ's message.

"But let's face it," I said to him one day, "if I *were* to become some kind of Christian it's highly unlikely I would be a Southern Baptist. Too many cultural differences between them and me."

He replied that people do certainly make the decision about denomination, if not the more fundamental conviction decision, based on cultural and political factors. "Some may think that if they are more sophisticated culturally, their religion therefore has to be more convoluted and arcane—sophisticated. The evangelical wing of the Anglican church is a good compromise for evangelicals for whom the conservative cultural milieu of American denominations is forbidding."

And yet Parker, who is certainly culturally sophisticated, has chosen to remain in the conservative milieu of a Southern Baptist church in Texas. I pointed this out. He shrugged. "I'm much less conservative than Southern Baptists have been traditionally," he said, "but they're moving, so I'm not sure how big the gap is now. A lot are still vocally on the right, but a lot also share my views. I'm real concerned about ecology issues, real concerned about race issues—and Southern Baptists have come a long way on race."

They have had to. Their Convention was established in 1845 in part to protect the institution of slavery, behavior reconciled with Scripture on the basis of the apparent acceptance of the institution in both Testaments. At the conclusion of my first worship service at First Baptist Dallas, after W. A. Criswell had preached on the lessons of Lazarus, one of the people who had come forward during the invitation was a black woman, a secretary, as the pastor informed us after speaking quietly with her. There were a few other blacks in the congregation that morning, and one black woman in the large choir. Criswell joked about how difficult it is to get a man to come stand beside a pretty single woman who is accepting Christ into her life, and I wondered whether it wouldn't be even more difficult to get someone to stand beside a black woman. But these days, it's not tough, at least in the cities. Any urban Southern Baptist church today will bend over backward to welcome blacks in its services, if only in the spirit of tokenism that marks the fundamentalists' television programs, almost all of which have a black man, and sometimes a black woman, in some role (often as one of the singers), and where the cameras always find the black people in the audience. (Most black Baptists in America attend churches that belong to one of two mostly black conventions, separate organizations from the Southern Baptist Convention that claim about eight million worshipers.)

Given the history of racism in Southern Baptist churches, most of which were white-only until recent years, and given the diametrically opposed political agendas of many white and black Baptists, it would be easy to lodge a charge of hypocrisy and tokenism against the congregation at First Baptist Dallas. I was in no position to judge that morning. A woman—white—finally joined the secretary and took her by the arm.

Some weeks later, prior to one of my first classes at Criswell, I overheard at the table a racist joke about Jesse Jackson's campaign for the presidency. No one laughed, but no one admonished the student, either. I mentioned the episode to Paige Patterson, and he frankly acknowledged that while Southern Baptists had made great strides on race, while Criswell College enrolled dozens of black students every term, while one of its most renowned graduates, Darrell Gilyard, is a spellbinding black preacher with a national reputation, there was and is work still to be done.

That point was made most emphatically at Criswell several months after my departure, in a speech by former Criswell Vice President for Academic Affairs Richard Land, now chairman of the Christian Life Commission, the watchdog unit of the Southern Baptist Convention in charge of ethical issues. The venue was First Baptist Dallas and Criswell College's annual School of the Prophets, a preachers conference and revival. The subject was racial prejudice. Jim Parker mailed me a cassette tape of the speech in which Land labeled "a shame and a disgrace" the failure of Christian churches to resolve their own problems with racism. He derided conservatives for excusing racism as a "liberal issue" and challenged them to reconcile their stock excuse for inactivity on racism—"you can't legislate morality"—with their efforts to do just that on another front, abortion.

Racism is a sin problem, a spiritual problem, but also a political problem, Land stated, and he lauded the freedom riders of the sixties. He urged the preachers to become the freedom riders of the nineties—"even if your deacons don't like it." Regarding apartheid he said, "It is wrong and will always be wrong." Then he quoted Patrick Henry: "Give me liberty or give me death." I would like to have seen his audience's reaction to that provocation. He challenged the preachers to establish interracial *social* friendships. "How many in the audience have African-American friends?" he asked rhetorically, implying that the correct answer was few.

"That must change," he answered softly. Almost sarcastically he dismissed a question about interracial marriages as a false issue. He reminded the preachers of the disgraceful fact that black children are still not welcome at certain vacation Bible schools—a blatant racism few would openly defend—while not letting them off the hook for the much more common and subtle practice of red-lining certain neighborhoods "in which we just don't go door-to-door because somebody might say . . . yes."

The speech was a harsh attack on the racist traditions and residual practices, in some quarters, of the Southern Baptist denomination. But by that time I was not surprised, because other than that one episode with the Jesse Jackson joke, I picked up no signs, no sense, of Southern-issue racism at Criswell College, and I heard time and again—if not so harshly as in Land's speech—every determination to attack it at its roots. At Criswell College, at least, I believe they are working hard to overcome old attitudes. Bigotry exists, of course, because it exists everywhere—Land told his audience that they cannot possibly understand how "totally" blacks live in a world of racial slights—but I was willing and happy to acknowledge that Jim Parker was correct: some and maybe many Southern Baptists have come a long way on race.

Darrell Gilyard, the twenty-eight-year-old Criswell graduate who is rapidly becoming one of the most popular guest pastors on the Southern Baptist circuit, isn't so sure. "I don't think race relations will ever get much better," he told me in his office at Victory

Baptist Church in Dallas. "Racism is sin. The outward display and manifestation may decrease, but racism increases along with sin. The only way to deal with it is through the love of Christ. When a white man loves God and a black man loves God and you bring those two together, they'll love each other."

Gilyard's church is an attempt to do just that. Victory Baptist is the only conservative Christian congregation in the Dallas area with a racially mixed congregation: about five hundred members, 55 percent white, 45 percent black, a few Hispanics and Asians. Gilyard began the church in 1989 with just six members and he said to anyone who would listen, "This is what we're gonna do, folks. Not a black church, not a white church, a mixed church. If we can go to school together, if we can play football together, we can go to church together."

And it's easy for Darrell Gilyard to get people to listen. He got *A*'s in homiletics—*A*-pluses. He's a small, trim man prone to convulsions of laughter that literally double him over, and behind the pulpit he focuses that energy on the Word of God with a tenor voice that could bore a hole in the back wall of the auditorium. It must be impossible to wool-gather during a Darrell Gilyard sermon. But, he told me, he has one major advantage as a speaker: "The black preacher has a God-given delivery, a God-given imagination." When I asked whether this wasn't a rather broad statement, the sort of stereotyping that can work good or ill, he admitted as much, but then added, "Most white preachers would tell you the same thing. Ask any of them. Ask Paige. There's a delivery that a black preacher has that few white preachers have. Your typical run-of-the-mill white preacher is monotone, while *delivery* is what has gotten the black preacher by. You take that natural, God-given ability and add some *content* and you've got an unbeatable combination. The doors are wide open for a black preacher with content."

This combination is what Gilyard delivers at Victory Baptist, and he knows exactly the kind of folks he's after: "With the blacks, I call them buppies. Your typical black church is all emotion, a bunch of rah-rah." (Gilyard sometimes refers to this style as rousology, a terrific coinage.) "Well, the educated blacks aren't going to the typical black church, because they want more than emotion; they want substance, too. They want exciting substance. These are the blacks we try to reach. Their doctor is prepared, their dentist is prepared, they want a preacher who's prepared, too.

"The typical white church is so dead it's not funny. The whites we reach are tired of that. They're looking for some *life*, something more than programmed religion. Everything is a balance here, right in the middle. And a lot of mixed couples come here because they feel comfortable."

Mixed couples in Dallas? "More than you think," Gilyard said, "but they're in the closet. This isn't California."

Gilyard himself grew up in Florida in circumstances that have made his Christian testimony just about as well known as his preaching. He has never met his mother; he met his father (his parents were not married; each had a spouse) only in 1989 after a viewer saw Gilyard on Jerry Falwell's *Old-Time Gospel Hour* and recognized his features as those of a man she knew who had told her he had left a baby boy in Florida. Then Gilyard said on the program he had never met his father. The woman made the connection.

In Florida Gilyard lived under a bridge part of the time in his teenage years. "There were times when I had a home; I didn't live under the bridge the entire time, but for the most part. Every day I'd pray. At nine years old I had accepted Jesus Christ." Until Gilyard was about seven he had been raised by the kindly and godly woman on whose doorstep he had been left by his parents. When she died the wandering began.

"I'd ask God how he could allow a boy to grow up like that. One afternoon I could sense God speaking to me. He said, 'Trust me. I have everything under control.' I decided I would take my eyes off my circumstances and put my eyes on the Lord. I told myself, 'Darrell, you're not a loser. You may not have what the other kids have, but you're not a loser. God doesn't make losers.' And this gave me peace. You would have thought I was living in a castle somewhere. I was about sixteen."

When he finally met his father and learned of the "drug-infested community" that had destroyed the rest of his family he decided that God had actually taken him *out* of that environment for the purpose of putting him into one in which he could trust Jesus Christ—in which he *had* to trust Christ. Eventually in Florida Gilyard joined the First Baptist Church in Jacksonville, whose pastor Jerry Vines, soon to be president of the Southern Baptist Convention, encouraged him to attend Criswell College in Dallas. He received a full scholarship.

Gilyard had no idea of the segregationist background of the Southern Baptists until he studied church history at Criswell. "And it angered me when I found out. I was so naïve, with my background. It shocked me. But I don't blame the present generation for the sins of the fathers." Gilyard of course knew about W. A. Criswell's "birds of a feather flock together" blunder: "Dr. Criswell is a product of his day. He's a sweet man, I love him, he's had me down to the church to preach. Believe it or not, I've never personally been victimized by racism. I guess the reason I feel this way is that I never looked for it. I don't see color. I just see people."

When I suggested that this trait made him a rare human being, Gilyard said simply, "I wish I weren't."

One morning in Cultural Milieu, Luis Pantoja jolted the class with the observation that atheists are perfectly capable of contributing to the general well-being, and have done so. "You don't have to be a Southern Baptist to be a good president," he added with sarcasm, leaving unstated the observation that conservative Christians feel betrayed by the former Baptist president from Georgia. A president many evangelicals liked very much, Ronald Reagan, was nobody's angel in the pews. He was seldom even in the pews.

"Sometimes we Christians think of culture as all degenerate, degenerate, degenerate, but that's not true," Pantoja said. "Don't give up on the world!" He referred to the definition of culture cited in one of the textbooks as "human achievement and divine gift; human dexterity and divine grace." The human and the divine are inextricably linked. However, Pantoja added, Christian humanists never allow cultural achievement to be its own end. It is preservation and not redemption. It is also tainted, of course, by mankind's fallen stature. Pantoja said, "Culture is a tribute to our sagacity but also a monument to our pride."

This particular morning I thought the class was sitting on its hands. They knew what their teacher was saying to be true, but they were simply not very sympathetic to it. Many come from fundamentalist families and churches, where the message is that culture as it manifests itself today is mostly bad, right down to the R-rated beer ads on television. The assault by conservative Christians on the National Endowment for the Arts began after my term at Criswell, but reports I received later verify that most of the people at Criswell believe there should be some kind of oversight on the funding of controversial projects. I'm sure some of them would like to jettison the NEA altogether, while realizing that isn't going to happen.

Pantoja's students were more comfortable with his emphasis of the importance of 1 John 2:15–17:

Do not love the world or the things in the world. If anyone loves the world, love for the Father is not in him. For all that is in the world, the lust of the flesh and the lust of the eyes and the pride of life, is not of the Father but is of this world. And the world passes away, and the lust of it; but he who does the will of God abides forever.

Some Christians go to extraordinary lengths to bridge this gap between Christianity and culture. In class one day Pantoja handed out a Xerox of an article in *The Dallas Morning News* about Andrew

Greeley, the Catholic priest, sociologist, novelist, and defender of the sacred import of popular culture. His most recent book was *God in Popular Culture*.

"I suppose the elitists will ridicule the idea of finding God in science fiction, mystery stories, pop singers, and comic strips," Greeley says. "That's their problem, not mine. But God lurks everywhere." Greeley salutes Bill Cosby as the "most influential teacher in America because of the 'paradigms of love' on his TV show;" Woody Allen as "God-haunted" and the "most explicitly theological filmmaker in America today"; Madonna's song "Like a Virgin" as "the timeless cry of the human heart for renewal"; and Bruce Springsteen, whose latest album *Tunnel of Love* is "deeply religious" and its release perhaps more important than a papal visit.

I don't ridicule such rampant ecumenism. I just don't find it edifying. In rebuttal I recommend this passage from Acts, one of my favorites in the New Testament:

Now while Paul was waiting for them at Athens, his spirit was provoked within him as he saw that the city was full of idols. So he argued in the synagogue with the Jews and the devout persons, and in the market place every day with those that chanced to be there. Some also of the Epicurean and Stoic philosophers met him. And some said, "What would this babbler say?" Others said, "He seems to be a preacher of foreign divinities"—because he preached Jesus and the resurrection. And they took hold of him and brought him to Areopagus, saying, "May we know what this new teaching is which you present? For you bring some strange things to our ears; we wish to know therefore what these things mean." Now all the Athenians and the foreigners who lived there spent their time in nothing except telling or hearing something new.

So Paul, standing in the middle of the Areopagus, said: "Men of Athens, I perceive that in every way you are very religious. For as I passed along, and observed the objects of your worship, I found also an altar with this inscription, 'To an unknown god.' What therefore you worship as unknown, this I proclaim to you. The God who made the world and everything in it, being Lord of heaven and earth, does not live in shrines made by man, nor is he served by human hands, as though he needed anything, since he himself gives to all men life and breath and everything. . . .

"Being then God's offspring, we ought not to think that the Deity is like gold, or silver, or stone, a representation by the art and imagination of man. The times of ignorance God overlooked, but now he commands all men everywhere to repent, because he has fixed a day on which he will judge the world in righteousness by a man whom he has appointed, and of this he has given asurance to all men by raising him from the dead."

Now when they heard of the resurrection of the dead, some mocked; but others said, "We will hear you again about this." So Paul went out from among them. (Acts 17:16–33)

For anyone who hasn't approached the New Testament in decades, whose impression of the book is encrusted with a thousand discarded pieties, the clarity and honesty of that reporting might come as a surprise. It did with me. Duly noted is the colorful mocking of Paul by some skeptics; beautifully phrased is his gentle denunciation of the altar to the unknown god: "What therefore you worship as unknown, this I proclaim to you."

Greeley's piece, by comparison, is a desperate accommodation. Contemporary culture isn't just un-Christian, it's anti-Christian, pagan, devoted twenty-four hours a day to each and every vanity condemned by Jesus. Any other pretense is unseemly. T. S. Eliot said that Christianity is always modifying itself into something that can be believed—a necessary challenge, but doomed when it becomes eviscerated in the process.

"May the Force be with you." Greeley would no doubt propose that this is an essentially sacred passage from the scriptures of George Lucas. It is, but this sacredness has nothing to do with the personal God of the Bible. "My stars!" Pantoja exclaimed in class. "I've heard Christians say 'May the Force be with you!' The ideas we appropriate! That idea is pantheistic. The Holy Spirit is not a force, but a person! God is not a force, but a person."

In one of his last lectures in Cultural Milieu, Pantoja drew what seemed to me a valid distinction between a truly Christian belief, in which the central value is God, and the competing liberal Christian, secular humanist, and frankly pagan worldviews, which may use the language of faith but without the slightest sign that it is central. Is God even a peripheral value in the pop culture perpetrated by Madonna? Of course not. The satisfaction of the vanities is the chief integrating value in the secular, capitalist world embodied in pop culture. To assert that this culture needs the Christian God and the values He demands is one thing, and perhaps true. But to go through contortions in order to *align* this culture with the Christian God is another, and nonsense. Common grace— God's providential care—is an excellent Christian doctrine, but when this grace becomes too common it is no longer grace. God is a value today in the wide world only when ceremoniously invoked, just as parents are a factor in a child's play only when they walk into the room. The difference is that God has not walked into our little playpen in a long time—if He ever did, which an increasing number of people are doubting.

CHAPTER 9

The students at Criswell surprised me daily. In rapid succession I talked with three who could not have had more different takes on their faith. Jace Stover would observe Passover as easily as not; he would like for his future children to celebrate the Jewish holidays in their household. "Judaism," Jace emphasized, "is not a false, merely an incomplete religion." That's the mandatory Christian attitude, of course, but it's not usually followed up by observance of the Jewish holidays. A few nights later over pizza, Manny Mateus, an Ecuadorian who now lives in the States, expressed a surprisingly laissez faire attitude toward other beliefs—prompted, perhaps, by a far-flung family that, for the most part, doesn't agree with and isn't intimidated by his own conversion to Christianity. Then the shy, mild-mannered Shawn Ostoj told me about his mother, who was deeply into occult matters—spells, Ouija boards, and the like. "It works," Shawn concluded. "There's something to it."

However, these three students do share one trait. They are searchers of what I have dubbed the Type-A variety—people who *will* find something to believe in. Before grasping Christianity as the one true explanation of everything, Jace and Manny and Shawn had each tried a wide variety of worldviews, including Hinduism, Eckankar, Mormonism, transcendental meditation, and Sri Maharishi. All three also have one or both parents who are not Bible-believing Christians.

Jace's mother, who was raised a Southern Baptist, tells him, "It's too simple." He describes his father as "moral but not religious," which, as he well knows, is not good enough for Christianity. After Jace became an evangelical, his parents asked him if they were going to hell, and he reluctantly replied yes. The same holds for Jews. Their religion is not just "incomplete"; it is fatally so. Jews will go to hell if they don't accept Christ before the coming tribulation. But as a general rule Jace tries "not to judge people"— meaning that he doesn't tell them to their faces that they're going to hell. Mainly he "feels sorry for them."

Appropriately for the man who might observe Passover, Jace suggested we have dinner at what he assured me was the best Jewish deli in Dallas, on the north side. Indeed, the Reuben sandwich was first-rate, with excellent rye bread. Our conversation over dinner was so intense we were both surprised to learn from the cashier that right down the row of tables from us a major altercation had broken out, with a great deal of shouting and threats. Jace and I hadn't heard a word of it.

He's a former military man and has retained the bearing and predilection for weaponry and warfare. At Hardin-Simmons University, which he attended for two years, he had two pictures on his wall: one a battle scene, and the other a view of Christ on the cross, depicted from behind. I rose to the bait and asked why.

Because, he said, he could understand the battle scene, but not the Crucifixion. Regarding his collection of rifles and pistols, Jace said he has no problem with the "turn the other cheek" admonition of Christ because "it doesn't apply when someone puts a bayonet in your face." In this opinion he's joined by many conservative Christians, but not all, by any means, as I would learn later.

What irritates Jace Stover is why people don't accept Christ in the first place. Why can't they see the transparent truth of Christianity? "The answer is not quitting drinking, whoring, etc. The answer is Jesus Christ," he said. Then he asked rhetorically, "What's the great sacrifice here?"

Jace gets "constantly angered" at people who talk about the sacrifices required by Christians. He doesn't see it. What's the problem with giving up what you can't keep anyway?

Jace can also get angered at "the church crap," the inter- and intradenominational quarrels that have marred Christianity from the beginning. Once Jace walked away from the church, on just that account. That "church crap" drives a lot of people away from Christianity or, at the very least, away from the standard denominations and toward what are referred to as Bible churches—nondenominational congregations that just teach the Word of God, and the believer takes it from there. Dallas is full of these churches. The Baptist and all other Protestant denominations were founded on such libertarian principles, summed up in the Baptist description of its own denomination as a "priesthood of the believer," but now denominational politics have wracked the Southern Baptists, too.

As Jace described his momentary disenchantment with denominations, I passed on the remark I had heard to the effect that should Christ come back today incognito, he would shun the denominations and might not be a "Christian" at all. He would walk the earth a second time as a solitary holy man. Jace nodded his head and said he understood this rejection of the denominations.

Manny Mateus invited me to dinner one night in a pizza joint he said was the best in town, but wasn't. Manny arrived in his bank clerk's attire of coat, tie, and wire-rim glasses. He lived with his mother and a couple of siblings. He spent his teenage years and early twenties "looking for someone to love me." I asked him whether he got love and support from his father. "No. Just advice about sex and money."

In Ecuador, Manny fooled around with the teaching of Sri Maharishi and Hinduism. After the family moved to Texas, he began to drink heavily. A Christian he was dating warned him about it. She took Manny to a singles party at a church and he was impressed by the sober good fun of the kids, just as Danny Akin had been back in Atlanta. Then one evening Manny went to two different functions: a church fellowship party and a family party with a lot of drinking. He was struck by the contrast. Another friend interested him in reading the Bible, and when Manny encountered various Matthean injunctions to "Trust ye in me" and "Trust in the Lord in all matters," he began to cry. "This," he realized, "is the truth for me!"

I asked him whether that attitude, which skates dangerously close to a generous and unbiblical relativism, is his real attitude or just a witnessing strategy when dealing with the likes of me. In reply he told me the story about when he witnessed to his uncle, who listened politely and said, "Fine, Manny. That's the truth for you. That's not the way I see it." Manny claims to have learned from that encounter to avoid overt expressions of self-righteousness.

These Criswell students—a sizable minority, I believe—who have adopted a series of faiths don't understand why their families and friends might judge their conversion to Christianity as merely one more episode. They say that the emotional strength they derive from Christian faith is of a different order entirely, completely unlike the partial and transitory satisfactions derived from those others. I believe that. Only now do they truly *know*. They wish everyone did. Manny said to me, "I want you to see my life as the truth, more than I want you to hear what I say."

The main reason those Criswell students who converted to the Christian faith believe it to be the truth is this abiding sense that Jesus Christ has changed their lives for the better. He answered their questions and their needs, as He did for their Christian friends, and they don't see any competing belief having the same success in healing people's lives. At some point in Dallas I dismayed another student with my observation that my few friends who had returned to Christianity lately had chosen Catholicism. Frankly, I said, they're more comfortable with the culture of Catholic worship and its sophisticated intellectual background. They're uncomfortable with the enthusiasm and the commitment required of conservative Christians. I was interrupted: If this is so, why are so many evangelicals former Catholics who didn't find anything to sustain them in the dry observances of that denomination?

People are different, I said. They have different needs.

Yes they do, but some are also wrong.

Over pizza I asked Manny what he knows about what I labeled an existential Christianity—an acknowledgment that belief in Jesus Christ can be a formidable force for positive change within lives, but without any concern that this change is the sign of supernatural intervention. Not much, he said, so I explained briefly the idea. Then I concluded, with some exaggeration, I suppose, "I would have no quarrel with being labeled an existentialist Christian of some sort."

Most Criswell students would have challenged me on the spot. Why believe something that isn't true, that doesn't even claim to be true, that amounts to worshiping ghosts? But Manny listened quietly and with interest and no immediate judgment. He's a scholarly type, intending at that time to study apologetics on the graduate level and then perhaps to teach in a seminary in South America, where there's only one Southern Baptist seminary—in Argentina. He surprised the students in our Cultural Milieu class when he acknowledged one morning that he had no hard-and-fast prohibition against alcohol. When I asked him whether he was worried about the salvation of his family he replied, "I'm worried about you." Indeed, his prayer delivered over pizza had asked the Lord to lead me to wisdom, and then as we parted company in the parking lot outside he asked me if I minded another prayer. I said no. This was my policy at Criswell. Prayers for my salvation could be offered at any time, and I would bow my head and sincerely participate. Manny prayed that I might know Jesus Christ and serve Him with this book.

~~~~~~~

It suits, or at least it doesn't contradict, some people's personality to assure you that you're going to hell. Shawn Ostoj isn't one of these dogmatists. A shy gentleness is the most obvious characteristic of his personality, and a literalness unencumbered by the fine points of doctrine the main attribute of his faith. He understands how the Old Testament God of retribution and jealousy could be a stumbling block for many would-be Christians; an old lady in a nursing home had recently told him just that. Certainly God could squash Satan if He chose to but He hasn't and Shawn doesn't know why. The powers of Satan in the universe are manifest; Shawn's mother's success with the casting of spells is sufficient proof of that. When Christ returns for the Second Coming, He will be "up in the clouds—visible to everyone." And it will happen very fast and soon.

Shawn came to Christ after flirtations with a number of New Age–oriented beliefs during his tenure with the Marines in Hawaii. He was convinced about Christianity on the strength of the biblical prophecies. "I could argue with religion on many grounds," he told me one day in the student lounge, "but I couldn't argue with the truth of those prophecies." His conversion required only a couple of days.

The Old Testament prophecies of Daniel, Ezekiel, Jeremiah, Isaiah, and others, and Jesus' fulfillment of some of these prophecies in his ministry in Palestine, are major exhibits used by evangelicals when defending the historical truth of their faith, but Shawn was the only Criswell student I talked with who converted mainly on the basis of these prophecies. Not many people will. For one thing, the spirit of the prophecies is unremittingly *Old* Testament, layer upon layer of excoriation, apocalyptic vision, obscure allegory, the Lord did this and the Lord did that. In no part of the

Bible does my Columbia professor's depiction of God as a metaphor for history ring more true than in the prophecies.

I compare Shawn's Christianity with, say, Jim Parker's. As best as I can judge from the outside, Shawn's faith seems to be almost pictorial in its simplicity; Parker's isn't. In fact, he spent almost a decade going to school to make certain that it is not. Is his and Shawn's Christianity even the same faith? It's not my call, but the notions of Shawn, Jace, and Manny put to rest any idea of a blind homogeneity I might have had about conservative Christianity. These three young evangelical students, chosen practically at random, will certainly proclaim the same tenets of belief, but are these tenets actually prescriptive, much less restrictive, on the faith that they feel and live? It didn't seem like it.

<p style="text-align:center">~~~~~~~</p>

One day in his office on the tenth floor my New Testament mentor Danny Akin said to me, "I have no allegiance to the Baptist church. I'm grateful for it, but it could drop dead tomorrow and I wouldn't shed any tears.

"God put me together in such a way that I just couldn't accept Christianity because my momma does, or whatever. I can't be happy with that. I want to know what *I* can believe to be true. I urge everyone to read the great philosophers, the other religions, Shirley MacLaine. Read everything from every perspective you possibly can. When the Bible says 'Beware of vain philosophies,' a lot of people take that to mean they should have nothing to do with them. I have heard preachers state that Paul made a mistake in debating the Athenians. But as Norman Geisler points out, in order to *be*ware, you must first be *a*ware.

"I am more humble than I was in my approach to truth, to epistemology, although I'm still a Bible-believing Christian. Truth doesn't come as easily as I once thought it did. There is a way in which it can be simple, but another in which it is most complex. I'm not going to be arrogant or condescending with someone who differs with me—agnostic or atheist or whatever. Now, I've run into the opposite attitude on their part, people who are amazed that we Neanderthals are still around, talking with me as though I were some backward country bumpkin. That disappoints me. They boast of their pluralism but they're not being honest. Their pluralism is really fundamentalism."

That was a point I heard many times at Criswell, where they preach and teach what they believe to be the truth, where they have nonnegotiable presuppositions, and where no one is on the faculty or enrolled as a student if he or she doesn't believe just about what Paige Patterson believes. But, they argue, this state of affairs also holds at what they sometimes refer to as the secular seminaries. One of the books provided me by Jim Parker was *Escape from Skepticism—Liberal Education as if Truth Mattered*, by Christopher Derrick, a Catholic author, teacher, and former student of C. S. Lewis. Derrick urges that we at least acknowledge that a secular education is in fact a religious education—the religion of secular humanism and atheism. His book is a more calmly argued version of some of Allan Bloom's theses in *The Closing of the American Mind*.

"An education is answers, not merely questions," Derrick writes. He argues that "academic freedom" in the natural sciences is a contradiction in terms, an absurdity. There's no freedom involved in studying chemistry, because the point of such study is truth. Laws have to be followed. Likewise, Derrick and Parker (and Bloom) propose, if the point of study in philosophy and sociology is also truth (and if it's not, why are we studying it?), then there can be no freedom involved here, either. The whole issue is bogus, they insist. There is no such thing as "value-free education." Laws have to be followed. Which laws? The issue is one of presuppositions, of course. From the evangelical perspective, we will follow either the Word of God (Jesus said, "Know me, and the truth shall make you free") or what amounts to the no-word of man (philosophical skepticism).

The professors at Criswell would of course like to see the Christian presupposition underlie all formal education, as it does at their school, but they know this isn't going to happen and they would settle for truth in advertising by the secular schools—exactly what Jim Parker does not feel they practice at Baylor, as just one example, nor does he see the situation getting any better. Christian education will continue to fade, he believes, and its secular replacement will continue to wrap itself in the flag of academic freedom.

To fight back, Parker has recently founded the Trinity Institute, a nonprofit organization that he would like to see grow into an American equivalent to the well-known L'Abri study center in the Swiss Alps, founded by the evangelical Christian author and speaker Francis Schaeffer. Right now there's no place to study at Trinity, but Parker hopes to raise the money to buy a facility he has located in the countryside southeast of Dallas. For this purpose he's trying to set up an importing company that will specialize in cosmetics manufactured in Mexico and for sale in the Soviet Union. The prospectus for the Trinity Institute reads, in part: "The purpose of the Institute is the support and advancement of trinitarian theism and biblical revelation. The objective is to propagate the Christian worldview to the thinking community with intellectual integrity and personal sensitivity. The Institute will perform the negative task of analyzing and critiquing the various anti- and nontheistic worldviews vying for the allegiance of people's minds today. . . ."

Danny Akin said to me, "Liberals don't take us seriously. I believe in reading them. I wish they believed in reading us. Liberals are smart and we're stupid: that's what people learn in many seminaries. Paige Patterson was at Samford University in Alabama—a Baptist school, but liberal as all get-out—and he talked with a small group that came to his room late one night, evangelicals who were under constant bombardment from the rest of the school. And they asked Paige whether there were 'others like him'! They had never heard of Carl F. H. Henry or Norman Geisler. One guy had heard of Francis Schaeffer. Their professors had never acknowledged to them that evangelical scholars even existed."

When I showed up at Criswell I didn't know this, either. I did know of Francis Schaeffer because Paige Patterson, in our first conversation, had recommended a couple of his books. But I had no idea of the furious pace of evangelical publishing; I supposed that the liberals were still writing, but I hadn't read any of their newer stuff, either. John Burns, professor of New Testament and Greek and also the school's librarian and foremost bibliophile, directed me hither and yon in the library stacks on the tenth floor, one floor up from the classrooms. Every professor I met gave me suggestions for reading; so did some of the students, but, all in all, as Paige Patterson had advised me would be the case, the students were more doctrinaire than the teachers in their presentation of the faith, and certainly so in the classroom. Some of them weren't comfortable with the dicey issues, such as the culture-bound Bible discussed by Luis Pantoja, or challenges to inerrancy of Scripture that came up in almost every class. Some students have been jolted when they learned that those two major passages from the King James version (Mark 16:9–20 and John 7:53–8:11) aren't part of *the* inerrant Bible, after all; one young man even left school over the issue. Toward the end of one of Jim Parker's lectures in ethics a student raised his hand and said, "I don't want to be an academic hillbilly, Professor Parker, but you're leaving me in the dust."

I could believe it. Although an upper-level course attended by seniors, mostly, Parker's material was out of the blue for most of them—as it would be for most college students anywhere, at least in this country. Ethics is difficult. Also bothersome for some of the Criswell students, I thought, was Parker's calm and reasoned presentation of attitudes and thoughts inimical to Christian theism. And he answered all those challenges to the faith with ideas, not polemics. And as I had observed in some other classes, some students seemed uncomfortable with an unthreatened consideration of falsehoods and heresy. Ethics for many Criswell students, even the seniors, is still a matter of the Ten Commandments, the Sermon on the Mount, and Paul's exhortations. It's disturbing for some of them even to think about alternatives.

One reason Parker feels his own faith is solid enough to think about alternatives is that he studied at liberal Christian or secular colleges, with the sole exception of Trinity Evangelical Divinity School in Deerfield, Illinois, where he picked up a master's in New Testament studies. He was in the minority at Baylor, Princeton, and the University of Basel, in Switzerland, where Karl Barth's son Marcus was on the faculty, where Nietzsche and Karl Jaspers had taught.

"I've had to fight for my faith on my own," Parker told me. "Attending a conservative school is a double-edged sword. On the one hand, faith isn't torn down, but on the other, it isn't tested, either. That's the reason I try here to expose the students to the real conceptual challenges to Christianity, not to straw men."

<hr>

I have no doubt that the general tone of Criswell College comes from Paige Patterson. A lot of the moderates in the Southern Baptist Convention revile the president of Criswell College for his leadership of the conservative wing in the denominational battles centered on inerrancy, and I don't doubt Patterson is a tough, perhaps even ruthless, political infighter when necessary, but the man's freewheeling personality has left its mark on the school. Everyone at the school assured me that, say, Bob Jones University in Greenville, South Carolina, would not feel quite the same. (Then again, attire at Criswell got so lax during the term of my residency that regulations were tightened for the following year.) Students at Criswell often made remarks indicating pride in their leader's irreverent reverence. Like Akin, Patterson doesn't stand on propriety (although I never heard him referred to as Paige), and I eventually learned that this devil-may-care insouciance got an early start during a local-option election on alcohol back in Beaumont. One afternoon he told me all about it.

"It had really gotten rough. Dad was constantly receiving threats. I heard they were putting a parade together and a bunch of us kids thought up this float. We scraped up the money to buy an old wrecked car, put it on the back of a flatbed truck, and about five of us got in it with catsup poured all over us—I was out on the hood, thrown through the windshield—and on top of the car was our sign: FINISHED PRODUCT OF THE BREWER'S ART. We narrowly lost the election.

"Dad was a whole lot less combative than I, but nevertheless he had strong convictions and stood for them at whatever cost. That was drilled into me. The event that really set it off was at Hardin-Simmons, which had entered into an agreement with the government and had borrowed money from it, something no Baptist school is ever supposed to do, of course. They had built some dormitories with the money, and as a result the government imposed some stipulations, notably that every male student had to take ROTC. I had a 4D classification militarily—an exemption for clergymen. I really resented being forced to take ROTC just because Hardin-Simmons had done something that wasn't Baptistic, but I acquiesced. I went over to get my uniform and the sergeant was pure military, stationed there with no convictions one way or the other, cursing a blue streak as he handed out the uniforms. I was very idealistic at that point, and I just told him, 'Sir, beg pardon, but you have no business being on the faculty of a Baptist school and talking that way.' He asked if I thought I was big enough to do something about it, and my Christian commitments at that point didn't include passivism, so we stepped out behind. But a campus patrol came by and saw the crowd gathering and broke it up. So my first day on campus I ended up in the president's office. That was my first denominational battle, so to speak."

From Hardin-Simmons, where he wasn't a good student although he did well in his major, Greek and biblical studies, Patterson proceeded to New Orleans Theological Seminary. He and his long-standing girlfriend Dorothy had married by this time, and they both took master's degrees in theology at New Orleans. She had the better grades—about the second highest grades in the history of the school at that time, as Patterson now recalls.

"I was increasingly interested in the intellectual side of things, though without any intention of teaching, and certainly not of being the president of anything. No intention at all. But I went on to get my doctorate."

Dorothy Patterson got hers later, from Luther Rice Seminary.

"I was pastor at the time of Bethany Baptist Church in New Orleans, and on the side, with a man named Leo Humphrey, ran a coffeehouse ministry on Bourbon Street. We'd visit in homes till about ten and then go down to Bourbon Street till three in the morning. That was the late sixties and early seventies, the height of the runaways and hippiedom. I stayed in New Orleans until I was almost through with my doctorate and then moved to First Baptist Church in Fayetteville, the first large church I was pastor of. We had 2,300 members, located just off the campus of the University of Arkansas. We were there five years. A wonderful ministry there. Every Thursday night about nine-thirty we had the Lion's Den, advertised on campus as the place to be when you're worn out and tired of studying. Mrs. Patterson had refreshments and we talked about the things of God. Kids came in from everywhere. We were there till one or two in the morning sometimes. One time a visiting biker gang rolled up on their choppers. Somebody had invited them. We had another coffeehouse ministry, this one called The Ear—a big ear was the entryway.

"We would go into the bars and the nightclubs. That was unheard of for a pastor in a place like Fayetteville, but it appealed to the kids. They liked the fact that we—my wife and I, then some others—would talk about Jesus anywhere, without getting obnoxious. But the adults were typical aristocratic Southerners, dignified and cultured. I was a shock. To begin with I was young—twenty-seven, by far the youngest pastor that church had ever had.

"One night I got thrown out of a club—nothing ugly, the guy just said, 'Preacher, you're running off my business. I know where to get in touch with you if I need you but I'd like for you to leave.' So I stepped out on the front steps and the bouncer was sitting there. Big guy with a can of beer in his hand. I said, 'Looks like it's been a rough night.' He said it had been.

"Then I said, 'I don't want to offend you, but if you died where you're sitting right now would you be in heaven or hell?'

"He just took that beer can and crushed it and beer shot everywhere. Then he turned and looked at me and said, 'I can't believe you asked that question. I was just sitting here contemplating how I was going to take my life tonight when I got home.'

"I said, 'There's no reason to do that, you know. Nothing's that bad, especially not when the Lord loves you as much as He does.' We talked for about thirty minutes and he committed his life to Christ. The next Sunday he came forward during the invitation and I just stuck the microphone in his hand and told him to tell 'em what had happened. That was the event that began to turn the congregation's vision. The Lord probably used that as much as anything else to help us with our young people. We had a tremendous college ministry there. The Lord was gracious to us, but wherever Christians act boldly, but not foolishly or obnoxiously, and people see the *adventure* of Christianity, they tend to look into it. From the five years there, we now have, I think, fifty-two kids who are in the Lord's work, scattered around the world.

"I have to be the most unconventional educator you ever saw, in many ways. I'm just as liable to go down to a bar and get everybody's attention and preach as I am to come teach my class. Nowadays I'm always sure that I've got somebody with me to testify to what I'm doing, because I don't trust the false conclusions some people might want to come to. I still love working on the street, with people who are down and out, because by all means if you help them, they're the most grateful people in the world. I tend to be, believe it or not, uncomfortable around the aristocrats and sophisticates of society. I've learned how to adjust and do okay but, natively, that's not who I'm comfortable with. I'm comfortable with ranchers and farmers and butchers and bakers and candlestick makers.

"One day the phone rang and it was W. A. Criswell and he asked why didn't I come to Dallas to be president of his school. That didn't appeal to me at all. As a matter of fact I had four or five invitations right about then, including one to go back on the faculty in New Orleans as professor of evangelism, another to go to Canada and start the new seminary up there, one to go to another church, and of course I was happy where I was. This was the least appealing of all my options, but because of who he was I agreed to come talk to him. And while I was here it just seemed like the Lord in every way was saying, 'That's what I want you to do.' When I arrived we had twelve full-time students. I made the fourth professor. The rest has happened since then, in fifteen years."

CHAPTER 10

<hr>

My Old Testament class at Criswell was taught by the quiet and courtly Ray Clendenen, who also teaches Hebrew and, like Danny Akin, was completing work toward his doctorate from the graduate humanities program at the University of Texas at Arlington, with a major in linguistics, a minor in history. His dissertation was on the book of Malachi. Old Testament was another class in which some of the students were uncomfortable with challenges to their faith, as Clendenen lost no time explaining to them some of the details of the critical approach to Old Testament hermeneutics (principles of exegesis) that I had learned in my course at Columbia.

In 1678 Richard Simon, a French priest, wrote *A Critical History of the Old Testament*, attacking the traditional Mosaic authorship of the Pentateuch, the first five books of the Old Testament: Genesis, Exodus, Leviticus, Numbers, and Deuteronomy. In 1879 Julius Wellhausen identified four different sources for the Pentateuch and labeled them J (Yahwistic), E (Elohistic), D (Deuteronomistic), and P (Priestly). Among the criteria used by Wellhausen for his distinctions among sources were the different words, "Yahweh" and "Elohim," used for God in certain sections and under certain circumstances. Different names for individuals and places are also used in different sections, and the changes are generally consistent with the change from Yahweh to Elohim.

And then there are the alleged dual accounts of the Creation and the Flood. Genesis 1:1–31 presents the first six days of creation. On the seventh day God rested. Then Gen. 2:4 reads: "These are the generations of the heavens and the earth when they were created. In the day that the Lord God made the earth and the heavens, when no plant of the field was yet in the earth and no herb of the field had yet sprung up. . . ." And the creation story is told again, succinctly, in the next five verses, and there is a change of order from the first version: in Genesis 2, man is created before vegetation.

Likewise, liberal exegesis alleges another redundancy in the sixth chapter of Genesis: two different introductions to the story of Noah and the Flood. Genesis 6:5–8 reads:

The Lord saw that the wickedness of man was great in the earth, and that every imagination of the thoughts of his heart was only evil continually. And the Lord was sorry that he had made man on the earth, and it grieved him to his heart. So the Lord said, "I will blot out man whom I have created from the face of the ground, man and beast and creeping things and birds of the air, for I am sorry that I have made them." But Noah found favor in the eyes of the Lord.

Two verses later, this prologue is repeated in different language. In Exodus, God's call to Moses to lead his people out of Egypt and His appointment of Moses' brother Aaron as aide-de-camp and mouthpiece (Moses was not eloquent, as he admitted) are described in the third, fourth, and fifth chapters, then recapitulated in brief format in the sixth chapter and the first part of the seventh, with the change that the rod that the Lord turns into a serpent is Moses' rod in the first version (Ex. 4:2–5), but belongs to Aaron in the second (Ex. 7:8–12). (My Oxford Annotated footnotes the cultural background of the serpent trick. Serpent magic was practiced in Egypt from ancient times. God's sign of turning the rod into a serpent was the reverse of the usual trick, whereby the snake is made rigid by hypnotism and then picked up by the tail.)

At Columbia, I had no notion of the evangelicals' argument that Jesus accepted the truth of the Old Testament, that His acceptance dictates our acceptance, otherwise what is the logic of accepting His divinity? Ray Clendenen made exactly this point in answering a student's question about why this young man, as a prospective pastor, should worry about liberal-conservative debates rather than simply accept Christ as Lord and Savior and being done with it. Clendenen told the student he could not preach the divinity of Jesus without attesting to the inspiration of Scripture and without being prepared to answer questions about the world of the Old Testament. He proposed that a fair distinction between liberal and conservative Christians could be derived from the rigor of their approach to the Scriptures, and he suggested *The Pelican Guide to the Old Testament* as a good introduction to liberal exegesis and hermeneutics, available in the library. He also cited the best of the evangelical responses.

Another student interrupted Clendenen and asked, "What's the possibility of a person's being saved who takes the Bible and twists it around?"

"The Bible," Clendenen replied calmly, "is *literature* written by God. The evangelical approaches the Bible with the understanding that it is true; the liberal does not assume this as a matter of faith, but this does not mean that the liberal necessarily denies that it is inspired. I would never venture to say a person was saved because of a particular view of Scripture. We are complicated creatures."

He cited the example of Karl Barth, the neoorthodox German theologian who, in Clendenen's opinion, accepted the personal

God of salvation and other tenets of evangelicalism but denied inerrancy. (Paige Patterson said to me about Barth, "His education was one way but his leaning was another. Why else would a guy leave his home every Sunday afternoon with a big family Bible under his arm and go to the jail and preach to the prisoners? Barth did that. I'll be shocked if Barth's not in heaven. I think he came to know the living Christ. I think he did a lot of harm with his theology, but personally I believe he was saved.")

In a subsequent class Clendenen admonished the students further about drawing drastic distinctions between well-meaning Christians who interpret this or that part of Scripture differently. Good evangelicals do not, or should not, interpret the inerrancy doctrine to mean "mechanical dictation." The student who had asked whether liberals were saved spoke again about the New Age movement and about liberals "twisting things around."

"Evangelicals too!" Clendenen interjected. He credited liberals with at least reading the text carefully—"more carefully than we do. Evangelicals can skip verses and impose their theology on the text. Don't let the liberals excel us in taking Scripture seriously"—a remark that surprised me.

Another student spoke up. "My concern as a minister isn't trying to prove someone right or wrong. If they disagree, that's them. My job as a minister is to preach the Word of God. I don't care about this theology."

Most of the class seemed to agree, nor was Clendenen surprised in the least by this discussion. Criswell has its Green Berets. They want to preach; the niceties of theology are of no interest to them. They *are* fundamentalists. Clendenen repeated the evangelical admonition that in this day it's not enough to preach; it's also necessary to know.

Paige Patterson sometimes draws the analogy between privates and generals. The students at Criswell are training to be generals, he reminds them. All the private needs to know is how to point the gun and pull the trigger, but the general needs to be aware not only of his own plans but also those of the enemy. Therefore it behooves the future leaders of the evangelical faith to know not only what they believe but also what the enemy believes. Somehow the subject of Old Testament criticism also came up in one of Danny Akin's classes, and Akin said he found validity in the critical approaches if they didn't operate with an ironclad antisupernatural bias. But at any rate, he added, "You can't just say any longer 'I believe the Bible.' You have to go further." And, of course, all truth is God's truth. The Bible is true but God's truth is not restricted to the Bible. This doesn't mean that the Koran or the Upanishads are Holy Scriptures of *special* revelation but they can indeed contain general revelation. So can the writings of Sartre.

~~~~~~

Clendenen briefly outlined the evangelical response to the literary-historical criticism of the Old Testament. Regarding the two Creation accounts, one of which has the order of sequence as vegetables-animals-man, while the other has it man-vegetables-animals, he answered that the second sequence can be explained if the verb in the passage is translated as the past perfect tense, as it can be legitimately, so that God formed man from dust and placed him in the garden He *had planted* in the east. Another explanation is that the vegetation of chapter one could be general vegetation, the garden of chapter two a specific garden (Eden).

Clendenen suggested that perhaps Moses was indeed working with a collection of sources, which he put together under divine inspiration. Clendenen has no problem with that explanation for alleged inconsistencies, but he reiterated why evangelicals consider it vital to defend the historicity and divine inspiration of the entire Bible: "If the Bible isn't true historically, what basis do we have for accepting its theological truthfulness? None."

There are, however, exceptions to the rule, dictated by outright mistakes and contradictions. For example, 1 Kings 6:1 begins, "In the four hundredth and eightieth year after the people of Israel came out of the land of Egypt, in the fourth year of Solomon's reign over Israel . . ."

This number 480 is important because it pins down the time of the Exodus by backdating from that fourth year of Solomon's reign, which is known from independent Assyrian sources to be about 960 B.C. However, the date for the Exodus thus calculated, 1440 B.C., is believed by some evangelicals (although not by Clendenen) to be too early for the Exodus. Their lines of evidence point to a date somewhere in the thirteenth century before Christ. The 480 years of First Kings were probably calculated by multiplying 12, the number of generations since the Exodus, by 40, often used as the length of a generation in the ancient world, whereas the more accurate 25 years for the span of a generation yields a better date for the Exodus. First Kings 6:1 is thus used as ammunition against inerrancy. Inerrantists reply that the number is simply "figurative," an interjection by the scribes that is within their editorial jurisdiction, and therefore subject to human error.

"And by the way," Clendenen concluded his quick account of this problem, "I don't believe you can date creation by this means of genealogies. It's impossible." He explained that most scholars acknowledge that the Old Testament genealogies, which run on for column after column and certainly give an appearance of completeness, nevertheless leave out some names. They are open-ended. "Don't play dating games with the genealogies," he advised.

Clendenen doesn't worry about any of the dozens, maybe hundreds, of other inerrancy problems raised by the Old Testament. Neither do any of his students, I was certain. And I wasn't worrying, either. So who *does* care about these questions, which seem to the outsider to be of a kind with the proverbial "How many angels can fit on the head of a pin?" used to denigrate the Scholastics of the Middle Ages. From my reading I gathered that combative liberal Christians and anti-Christian zealots dwell on them most incessantly, the former trying to shore up their arguments against an inerrancy doctrine they see as fatal to the faith in the long run, and the latter just having more fun with the foolish. And evangelicals are obliged to respond to each quibble because they have painted themselves into a corner on the inerrancy issue.

I really enjoyed Clendenen's handling of these discussions, which extended over a series of classes. He obliged the students to know the criticisms and how to handle them. An observer walking into the classroom in the middle of some of the discussions might have been confused by Clendenen's evenhanded approach. Is the man even an inerrantist? Yes, he is, but he didn't shy away from the toughest passages, one of which is Gen. 6:1-2: "When men began to multiply on the face of the ground, and daughters were born to them, the sons of God saw that the daughters of men were fair; and they took to wife such of them as they chose."

There are several theories regarding who these "sons of God" were. Angels, probably. It is widely believed that this story explained to its contemporaries the presence on earth of the Nephilim, who are referred to two verses later as "the mighty men that were of old, the men of renown." The Nephilim were gigantic people of superhuman powers—the offspring of divine-human couplings. In an aside during the Nephilim discussion Clendenen referred to the angel that Joseph Smith, the founder of Mormonism, claims led him to the golden tablets of the Book of Mormon in Palmyra, New York. Evangelical Protestants look on Mormonism just as I do: absolutely beyond belief. To help them understand how liberal Christians and nonbelievers view their own orthodoxy I should have drawn an analogy with how they themselves look on the Mormons.

Clendenen said that he had always assumed Smith was either crazy or simply a liar, but the angel could have been a demon in disguise. This possibility was batted around by the class, with enthusiasm. This would be the norm for all discussions at Criswell: angels and demons, demons especially, were a big favorite for discussion. The students are drawn to these colorful exemplars of the supernatural world that the secular mind dismisses out of hand. If you accept Christ and accept the Bible, you should accept angels and demons. Likewise, it will help you to find Christ if you hold powerful feelings about the spirit world, which is everywhere in the Old and the New Testaments. But in class after class at Criswell, the teachers warned against any preoccupation with Satan and his dominion. Danny Akin was typical when he said, "A lot of dealing with the demonic is a sham. If someone is in serious trouble with demons, leave it to God."

How do evangelicals read passages about angels fornicating with humans without construing them as fragments of ancient mythology? By two expedients: the standard one, presupposition of the inerrancy of Scripture, and also the argument from personal experience. Although my question one day to Paige Patterson was not about the Nephilim, his answer addresses this passage, too, in language I would hear closely paraphrased by others at Criswell College: "To this point in my life everything I've ever trusted the Bible in has proved to be true. Everything it has told me not to do has indeed proved beneficial to avoid. Everything it has told me I would experience in the Lord if I trusted Him, I've found to be true. So when I come to things in the Word of God that I do not completely comprehend, I go as far as I can in the direction of logical explanation, but when I reach a point when such explanation is not altogether satisfactory I choose to believe that it is in fact so because I haven't found anyplace where I definitely know it *not* to be so. I can find a lot of places in the Bible where my experience neither confirms nor denies the passage, but I've never found one not to be true. So at this point in time I must trust it."

Nevertheless, I came to one early conclusion about the Old Testament: anyone entertaining Christianity as a plausible faith for his life should *not* begin here, at the beginning. The modern mind that starts its study of Christianity with the Creation account, Adam, Eve, the Fall, the Flood, and the miracles, and then continues with the stories of the proverbially jealous, vengeful God—this searcher will probably never make it to the Gospel of Matthew. Blame this on an antisupernatural presupposition if you wish, but Christian embarrassment with the Old Testament is not unique to these times. Marcion and other Christian authorities writing as early as the third century A.D. wanted to jettison the Old Testament from the Holy Scriptures. However, they were considered heretics because of this idea.

The evangelicals at Criswell know that the God of the Old Testament is often perceived from our vantage as a personification of a tribal deity, and is therefore a stumbling block for many. Paige Patterson said: "The Bible never conditions salvation on the amount of things you believe. It's perfectly possible to come to Christ and be saved and not have resolved the problems of the Old Testament. It frequently happens that people don't even *know* about the Old Testament. We have to insist on the cross and the Resurrection as the starting point for people coming to the Lord, and then urge them to spend their lives working out the details in the Song of Solomon, Ecclesiastes, and Genesis.

"We are dealing with Semitic literature and while we can demand of it that it be true or false, as we can with everything, we cannot fairly demand of it precisely the same identical kinds of standards that we demand of Biology 101. I know there are Christians whose faith does read Semitic literature with the same standard, but I'm saying that of course Job was written in poetic language. I believe every word of it happened just as it was recorded, but I also believe there is much that was said that was not transcribed. And much is related in classic, Near Eastern formula, so, yes, it *could* be infinitely more palatable to us in our scientific era.

"When we argue inerrancy, we don't mean Scripture tells us everything it could, or even that one author was cognizant of what all other authors were cognizant of. By inerrancy we mean that our experience of it has proved true in every case, and we therefore affirm that it is true in all events, unless proved wrong."

With that acknowledgment of the problems and qualifications

associated with the Bible and inerrancy, Patterson sounds rather like a Barthian, neoorthodox, professing that faith and faith alone define and justify Christianity. But he's not neoorthodox because he believes the Bible is inerrant and he believes this, in the final analysis, because of the Resurrection.

CHAPTER 11

~~~~~~~~

I heard a great deal about presuppositions while at Criswell, but always with the clincher that the theistic Christian presupposition is more than that. Their Christian axiom is grounded in the proof of the Resurrection. Faith alone is not enough because all other religions have faith, too. A neoorthodoxy grounded in faith is just the initial loss of footing at the top of the slope. It is closet existentialism, religion as personal experience—relativism, in a word, and a skunk by any other name still stinks. Evangelicals aren't interested. They want "true truth." In this regard they're in bed with the logical positivists: let's talk about something real, or not talk at all.

The main theistic faiths of Judaism, Christianity, and Islam are the only world religions that claim that the cosmic order has been definitively, divinely revealed in the affairs of men on earth. Jews disagree with Christians regarding the Resurrection, of course, but they set the precedent for both Christianity and Islam with their own ordering of historical events as evidence of God's direct intervention on behalf of his chosen people. Christianity just carried this theme to its logical conclusion with its claim that the prophesied Messiah had come to earth, that God *Himself* had finally stepped into human history and become incarnate.

Did the Buddha die for his people? Did Mohammed? Did the Buddha rise from the grave? Did Mohammed? No, so if Jesus was in fact resurrected from the dead, what evangelicals term the "truth claim" of Christianity has a validity unlike that of any other faith: theirs *is* the one true religion, Christ on the cross is the only atonement for our sins, Christians are justified in their worldwide evangelizing, heaven and hell are realities, and the problems with the miracles of the Old and New Testament are resolved in favor of faith—better yet, factuality—because, as John Montgomery writes in *The Suicide of Christian Theology*, "If God did in fact intervene objectively in history in the person of Christ, there is no logical reason (only an emotional one—dislike of the miraculous) for trying to explain away his miraculous interventions in Old Testament times."

There's nothing wrong with any of this logic. If Jesus rose from the dead, everything follows. The Christians are right, everyone else is dead wrong. However, *believing* that he rose from the dead is not enough. Evangelicals will not accept mere belief because people believe a lot of things. Followers of other religious faiths have powerful episodes in their lives that they consider as attestation to their faith. If this is the only criterion, voodoo is a "true" religion. So belief is not enough. Belief is neoorthodoxy. *Knowing* is orthodoxy.

Maybe this distinction isn't of much interest to the average Christian, but it's vital to those who insist on the intellectual soundness of their faith. It has been important to many Christians, and before them, Jews, from the earliest days. Moses' people needed signs of his relationship with God. Jesus' disciples did, too, and Jesus got irritated with their constant pestering for signs. Nevertheless, their evangelical successors today are adamant that

Christianity must have a truth claim superior to all other such claims. Paul wrote these classic lines to the Corinthians, who were having difficulty with the new doctrine of a bodily resurrection of the dead: "But if there is no resurrection of the dead, then Christ has not been raised; if Christ has not been raised, then our preaching is in vain and your faith is in vain. We are even found to be misrepresenting God. . . . If for this life *only* we have hoped in Christ, we are of all men most to be pitied" (1 Cor. 15:16–19; my emphasis).

To me, that statement is a body blow for much contemporary, liberal Christian apologetics. Paul was an evangelical. He explicitly denies the value of some mere *proclamation* of the risen Christ, the *kerygma*. The note in the Ryrie Study Bible succinctly summarizes this First Corinthians passage: "If the bodily resurrection of Christ is untrue, then preaching the gospel is a lie, Christian faith is without meaningful content, and Christians are hopeless concerning their prospects for the future."

Of course Rudolph Bultmann, the chief twentieth-century advocate of the *kerygma* as what Christianity must be all about today, had studied Paul's admonitions to the Corinthians, and he could only argue that this was the apostle's way of framing the essential, existential question. What else can a revisionist Christian claim? The evangelicals, on the other hand, agree with Paul: if Jesus Christ was not resurrected from the dead, everything collapses. It's all or nothing with inerrancy, and likewise with the Resurrection.

~~~~~~

It was my good luck that the speaker in two consecutive chapel services at Criswell during my term of residency was Gary Habermas, a professor at Jerry Falwell's Liberty University in Lynchburg, Virginia, and one of the evangelical world's leading experts on the Resurrection. He and Oxford atheist Anthony Flew debated the Resurrection, and the transcript and commentary of the encounter has been published in the book *Did Jesus Rise From the Dead: The Resurrection Debate.*

Habermas began his presentation at Criswell with the eight facts surrounding the crucifixion event that almost all Christian scholars, even the most liberal, acknowledge as historically true:

1. The crucifixion of Jesus.
2. His burial.
3. The subsequent despair of the disciples.
4. The empty tomb (although there is some disagreement here).
5. "Something happened": the perception by the disciples of literal, bodily appearances after that crucifixion.
6. The transformation and renewed passion of the disciples, who were thereby ready to die for their faith.
7. The conversion of two skeptics, James the brother of Jesus, and Paul.
8. The establishment of a new Sabbath.

Habermas then listed five models of Christian faith that have been derived from these facts, beginning with the least doctrinaire, an acknowledgment that something happened but we'll never know what, to the insistence of the evangelicals that Jesus rose bodily from the dead. Most Christian scholars today, according to Habermas, believe that Christ rose as a "spiritual body," not a physical body, and that the disciples "saw by the eye of faith," so that a videocam would not have recorded the post-Resurrection appearances or the Ascension.

This consensus is not good enough for Habermas and other evangelicals for three reasons. First, if the resurrection was not bodily, the conquest of death was not total, and that total conquest is of mighty significance to them (as it was to the Iranian prophet Zoroaster, who lived about 1400 B.C. and is usually credited with first teaching the doctrine of an afterlife). Second, the biblical, historical evidence supports a bodily resurrection. Those were Habermas's two points. I add a third one: for nonbelievers, a noncorporeal resurrection, some event that was visible to believers only, cannot be distinguished from hallucination, "vision," derangement, you name it, and will never establish itself as solid grounds for real belief. Thus I agree with the evangelicals: the noncorporeal resurrection is an accommodation doomed to failure.

Those scholars who refute the bodily resurrection suggest, among many other things, that the descriptions in the Gospels are hopelessly tainted by their authors' agenda to emphasize corporeality in order to counter all the confusion about a noncorporeal resurrection, which, they argue, was Paul's initial conception of the event, as described in his first letter to the Corinthians.

That city, as Danny Akin quipped in his introductory remarks on the two letters, was the "New Orleans, San Francisco, and New York City" of the ancient world—a dissolute metropolis of 250,000 free men and women, 400,000 slaves, and 12,000 officially sanctioned prostitutes (1,000 at each of the twelve temples of Aphrodite, copulation with any of whom was a sacred rite)—and one Jewish synagogue. It's clear from Paul's letters that the congregation in Corinth was having a difficult time assimilating into its pagan rites the Christian doctrine of the bodily resurrection. There must have been libertines, ascetics, ecstatics, and antiresurrectionists vying for authority within the same congregation. Immortality of the soul they knew about, but immortality of the body? What could this mean? Paul explains it to them in this fashion:

For not all flesh is alike, but there is one kind for men, another for animals, another for birds, and another for fish. There are celestial bodies and there are terrestrial bodies; but the glory of the celestial is one, and the glory of the terrestrial is another. There is one glory of the sun, and another glory of the moon, and another glory of the stars; for star differs from star in glory. So it is with the resurrection of the dead. What is sown is perishable; what is raised is imperishable. It is sown in dishonor, it is raised in glory. It is sown in weakness, it is raised in power. It is sown a physical body, it is raised a spiritual body. If there is a physical body, there is also a spiritual body. (1 Cor. 15:39–44)

The contemporary reader makes what he can of this explanation. The ancients also had trouble deciphering it, according to

many Christian scholars today, who assert that the initial understanding by all concerned, including Paul, was that the resurrection was *strictly* spiritual and in the eyes of the beholder, and not
bodily at all. But this doctrine proved virtually indistinguishable
from the pagans' "immortality of the soul," so the resurrection
accounts in the four Gospels emphasize the physical nature of
Christ's resurrected body, as in Luke 24:39: "See my hands and
my feet, that it is I myself; handle me, and see; for a spirit has not
flesh and bones as you see that I have."

Today's antiresurrectionists claim that these passages are late
additions to the story, obvious signs of a covert theological agenda
as well as evidence of the inevitable elaboration that accompanies
the oral storytelling tradition. One liberal school of thought con-
tends that it was not until the first part of the third century A.D.,
two hundred years after the events of the Resurrection, that corporeality became widely accepted Christian dogma, an achievement of the convert and scholar Tertullian.

～～～～～

Christ was either liar, lunatic, or Lord—bad, mad, or God. That's
the choice that conservative Christians would like to restrict us to
(even C. S. Lewis went along with this framing of the question),
under the assumption, I suppose, that people raised in any sort of
Christian tradition will be unlikely to label Jesus Christ a liar or
a lunatic. Mainstream and liberal Christians refuse to accept this
gerrymandering and introduce the obvious fourth choice: legend.
This hypothesis doesn't argue that the whole story of Jesus and his
resurrection is legendary, but rather that legendary material crept
into the gospel accounts. We are reminded that the ancient peoples
would not have understood our contemporary criteria for "truth."
Belief in resurrection and incarnation was more acceptable in the
ancient world. When Paul and his associate Barnabas were in
Lystra, in Asia Minor, Paul healed a man who had been crippled
for life and the native people then hailed him and Barnabas as
gods, Hermes and Zeus, respectively (Acts 14:8–13). Elijah raised

two people from the dead, one in First Kings, chapter 17 and another in Second Kings, chapter 4. The first story reads like this, in part: "Then [Elijah] stretched himself upon the child three times, and cried to the Lord, 'O Lord my God, let this child's soul come into him again.' And the Lord hearkened to the voice of Elijah; and the soul of the child came into him again, and he revived" (4:32–37).

And Lazarus was raised from the dead, of course.

One passage from Matthew's Resurrection account is cited as classic mid-Eastern mythology: "The tombs also were opened, and many bodies of the saints who had fallen asleep were raised, and coming out of the tombs after his resurrection they went into the holy city and appeared to many" (Matt. 27:52–53).

Doubt is cast upon miracles in general. Why were the disciples confused after the feeding of the 5,000? Because it hadn't happened. Why in the Gospel of Mark does Jesus several times warn the beneficiaries of miracle healings not to inform anyone? Because the miracles didn't happen, and the author was inserting this statement by Jesus as a way of explaining why nobody knew about them. This was a point I had wondered about: with so many miracles being performed by Jesus in public, such as the feeding of the 5,000, how could anyone have still doubted him? Yet most people did. One of Jim Parker's master's theses was on this subject of the "Messianic secret" in Mark, and Parker defended the proposition that Jesus wanted secrecy in order to conform with the Palestinian expectation that the work of the Messiah would precede his claim to titles and prerogatives.

Scholars who debunk the bodily resurrection draw the analogy between Jesus and the Buddha, in whose extant teachings there is no hint that he was divine. Yet, as the traditions of Mahayana Buddhism were codified, about the time of Jesus, in fact, the man Gautama was transformed into an earthly incarnation of the divine spirit. (On the other hand, this transformation required centuries to evolve, whereas the Christian tradition for the Resurrection was practically instantaneous.) The story of the seventeenth-century messianic pretender Sabbatai Sevi is often used to show how quickly legends of divinity spring up, or used to. Miracle stories about Sabbatai Sevi were circulated almost immediately after his public appearances. Perhaps these were real miracles? Perhaps, but if so the Messiah was a turncoat: he soon converted to Islam.

Liberal and secular criticisms of the Resurrection accounts dismiss them as being written down too many years after the fact—twenty, at least—to guarantee authenticity, as proved by the famous inconsistencies between them. For example, two of the Gospels, Matthew and Mark, state that there were two angels present at the tomb, but Luke and John report one angel. In Matthew's account of the discovery of the empty tomb, Mary Magdalene "and the other Mary" were present; Mark includes Salome in the group; Luke omits Salome but includes Joanna; John mentions only Mary Magdalene. There are numerous other problems with the accounts, all of which are used to refute the doctrine of inerrancy. All these attacks draw the same rebuttal, the only one available, really: the accounts do not claim to be exhaustive. However, this defense is tested severely by this description in the Gospel of Matthew: "And behold, there was a great earthquake; for an angel of the Lord descended from heaven and came and rolled back the stone, and sat upon it. His appearance was like lightning, and his raiment white as snow. And for fear of him the guards trembled and became like dead men" (Matt. 28:2–4).

Critically minded scholars wonder how the "detail" of a dramatic earthquake could possibly have been omitted by all the other accounts, if it were true. In short, according to the liberals' argument, the ancients lived in a world in which the most radical supernatural events were believable to most people, our modern ideas about historicity were unknown, and truth was something very different from our own science-based concept. The Christian doctrine of the resurrection of a corpse arose from that untenable worldview.

In great detail, evangelicals counter this thesis and the arguments that flow from it. They offer elaborate discussions of the differences between the Sabbatai Sevi story and the resurrection of Christ. They advance highly technical arguments involving the "creedal" primitiveness of some of the bodily resurrection passages, indicating that they date from the earliest and therefore most reliable oral tradition. They cite the verisimilitude of the Resurrection passages, that storytelling detail that convinced C. S. Lewis and many others of the authenticity of Scripture in general. John 20:3–8 is often a chief exhibit in this regard:

Peter then came out with the other disciple, and they went toward the tomb. They both ran, but the other disciple outran Peter and reached the tomb first; and stooping to look in, he saw the linen cloths lying there, but he did not go in. Then Simon Peter came, following him, and went into the tomb; he saw the linen cloths lying, and the napkin, which had been placed on his head, not lying with the linen cloths but rolled up in a place by itself. Then the other disciple, who reached the tomb first, also went in, and he saw and believed.

This passage is too detailed to have been made up, these conservative scholars assert; after all, the author of the gospel wasn't a skilled novelist. In C. S. Lewis's view, the New Testament authors were either profoundly shrewd scribes—but he found no reason to believe this—or they were transmitting a profound truth in the simple and blunt manner of which they were capable. But the author of a monograph on the Resurrection, part of a package of material given to me by Jim Parker, directs anyone entertaining this argument to several other first-century works that contain equivalent naturalistic passages in undoubtedly fictional contexts.

But most important of all, evangelicals argue, is the key role of eyewitnesses to the Resurrection. The main passage here is from 1 Corinthians, in which Paul writes: "For I delivered to you as of first importance what I also received . . . that [Christ] appeared to Cephas, then to the twelve. Then he appeared to more than five hundred brethren at one time, most of whom are still alive.

. . . Then he appeared to James, then to all the apostles. Last of all, as to one untimely born, he appeared also to me" (1 Cor. 15:3–7).

"Most of whom are still alive": creditable eyewitness testimony, in the opinion of evangelicals. In addition, as Habermas noted, "*This* resurrection followed the most unique claim in the history of religion"—Jesus' own prediction that after three days in the tomb he would rise again.

I was amazed to learn at Criswell how much scholarship, old and new, is devoted to the Resurrection. The average Christian knows what he believes and doesn't worry about it, but the teachers and scholars on both sides of the question are still trying to prove what they believe. I happened to be heavily into my Resurrection reading—very absorbing material, by the way, well argued on both sides—when I took a break from school one weekend and drove home to Houston, where I had lunch with the old friend who had told my wife I'd either quit the job at Criswell or convert. He's a pagan and part of that crowd that was reading *Honest to God* in high school. His name is Steve Hanks.

I said over the enchilladas, "You know, Steve, what happened at the Resurrection is a more interesting question than I had thought." I was teasing him, but I was also serious. What exactly did or didn't happen on Calvary, and then on those fateful days that followed—I employ the melodramatic word because it's hard to deny that *something* happened, with unparalleled repercussions—is an intriguing question. All the arguments pro and con about the empty tomb, the worldview of the ancients, and the dating of various passages will never convince most skeptics, but the argument that something must have happened in order for the disciples to have become so instantly radicalized is cogent, if not sufficient.

Steve was alarmed. I *was* on the brink. Evangelicals submit that if we can't come up with a better, solid explanation, we are in some way bound to accept the attestation of the ages: Jesus Christ rose from the dead. Steve's opinion of that logic was expressed in his exclamation to me—"Wait a minute, Mike! *Any* explanation is more plausible than that Jesus rose from the dead!"

My own layman's study of the Resurrection debate convinced me that here, too, we are dealing with presuppositions. Steve's exclamation is a definition of philosophical naturalism: miracles don't happen. The evangelicals' truth claim is grounded on the historicity of the Resurrection, but that claim to historicity is itself rooted in the presupposition of the inerrancy of Scripture, or at least the inerrancy of the Resurrection accounts. Inconsistencies in these accounts are explained as incompleteness. Eyewitness credibility is accepted without question, but these are the same eyewitnesses who accepted all the miracles of the Old Testament.

I asked Paige Patterson these questions: Since the New Testament witnesses to the Resurrection believed in the Old Testament, isn't that belief in some way logically prior to belief in the Resurrection? Don't we have to accept Adam and Eve *before* we accept the Resurrection?

Patterson replied, "I may choose to believe a witness to a car wreck even though I know that person believes in Martians."

"But in a court of law that belief in Martians would be used to impugn that witness's credibility," I said.

"It might be, but he could still be telling the truth," Patterson said.

Evangelicals assert that the historicity of the Resurrection does not rest on a doctrine of inerrancy. Many noninerrantist scholars, some of them not even conservative Christians, argue that the historicity of the Resurrection is as sound as the proof for many other events in the ancient world—the assassination of Julius Caesar is a commonly cited example—*if* one does not hold the antisupernatural presupposition. But of course we do hold it: while evangelicals want to say that the Resurrection proves the miracles, liberals assert, in effect, that belief in all the miracles undercuts the eyewitness testimony about the Resurrection. And Hume argued famously that testimony can never be proof for a miracle, and no miracle has ever had any other kind of proof. Ergo . . .

In short, and as usual in this world, the two (or more) sides in the Resurrection debate know what they want to believe, know what they *do* believe on some level deeper than language and logic, and accuse the other side of holding the untenable presupposition. They are preaching to their respective choirs.

~~~~~~

The Resurrection debate is inextricably tied to the subject of Christology—the theological interpretation of the person and work of Jesus Christ—and Christology was one of the three subjects covered by Danny Akin in his Systematics class I was attending. Criswell College requires three different systematics classes. This one covered Christology, pneumatology (doctrine of the Holy Spirit), and soteriology (doctrine of salvation). The other two cover prolegomena, bibliology, theology proper, Creation, angelology, anthropology, hamartiology, ecclesiology, and eschatology. Hamartiology I had never heard of, nor was it in my dictionary. It turns out to be the doctrine of sin.

Akin's Systematics course rounded out my basic schedule for the term at Criswell: Old Testament, New Testament, Cultural Milieu, Religious Belief Systems, Ethics, and Systematics (I dropped Natural Science until the end of the term when the discussions turned to the specifics of the creation-evolution debate). Paige Patterson accepted my schedule as reasonably representative if in no way comprehensive. Sixty-seven courses, taught by twenty-five professors and adjuncts, were offered to the 350-plus students at Criswell that spring, running from Basic English Grammar and Marriage and Family Counseling to New Testament Exegesis (Colossians) and Intermediate Hebrew, both of which required solid skills in the ancient languages.

The bookshelf that holds the Resurrection debate is a long one indeed, but a whole library would be required to house everything that has been written about Christology. The subject would seem to come down to one simple question—was Jesus of Nazareth divine?—but matters turn out to be much more complex. Most church-goers today probably don't realize that hundreds of years were required for the establishment church to codify its doctrine of Christology. They probably assume that the inherited tradition was clearly transmitted from the first verses of the New Testament, but in fact Matt. 1:1, which begins, "The book of the genealogy of Jesus Christ, the son of David, the son of Abraham . . ." is a painstaking effort to place Jesus firmly within the line of *human* ancestry leading back to Abraham. Mary was with child by the Holy Spirit, certainly, but that fact seems no more important to the author of the gospel than Joseph's family tree—forty-two generations—as recited in the first seventeen verses.

Christological doctrine is not self-evident in the Scriptures. In fact, there's not a great deal of pure theology anywhere in the first three Gospels. The story of Jesus and of the early church is *not* the Christian religion. A good many people have argued in the last two centuries that without the genius, passion, and energy of the expositor Paul the story of Jesus would have remained just that and nothing more. This was the theory I had somehow absorbed. According to this school of thought, Paul's justly famous doctrinal letters elevated Jesus' sermons and parables *about* the kingdom of God into the religion of Jesus *as* the kingdom of God—Christianity as we know it today. According to this interpretation, Jesus believed he was bringing to conclusion the tradition and the history of one religion—Judaism—and not, as it turned out thanks to Paul and the disciples, replacing it with another one altogether. And of course this thesis leaves no place for Jesus' divinity.

The early church tried just about everything in its struggle to codify its teaching about who Jesus Christ really was, and what He accomplished. The resolution of the christological problem gave rise to four main church councils, at Nicea, Constantinople, Ephesus, and Chalcedon, the first in A.D. 325, the last over a century later, in A.D. 451. So while individual Christians must have known all along what they believed, it was four hundred years after Christ's death before an official doctrine of His divinity and His participation in the Trinity was established and accepted by all official Christendom. And now that rapprochement is under fire as "the myth of the incarnate God."

Three of the four great christological passages in the New Testament (there are none in the Old Testament, of course) are from the Epistles: Phil. 2:5–11, Col. 1:15–23 and 2:9–10, and Heb. 1:1–4 and 5–14. The fourth passage is the justly famous introduction to John's gospel:

In the beginning was the Word, and the Word was with God, and the Word was God. . . . And the Word became flesh and dwelt among us, full of grace and truth; we have beheld his glory, glory as of the only Son from the Father. . . . No one has ever seen God; the only Son, who is in the bosom of the Father, he has made him known. (John 1:1–18)

Danny Akin suggested that Paul's analysis of the christological puzzle in Philippians is the better starting point for all deliberations. The passage reads:

Christ Jesus . . . though he was in the form of God, did not count equality with God a thing to be grasped, but emptied himself, taking the form of a servant, being born in the likeness of men. And being found in human form he humbled himself and became obedient unto death, even death on a cross. Therefore God has highly exalted him. . . . (Phil. 2:5–9)

The manifest difficulties of that passage are a harbinger of the difficulties posed by the whole question. The key word would seem to be "emptied." The concept established at Chalcedon is called the Hypostatic Union, the declaration that God, by emptying Himself from the person of Jesus, remained fully God yet became fully man at the same time. The details of this admixture are now recited by Catholics in the Athanasian Creed (which most Protestants could accept as well, if unofficially).

But if the whole idea of Christianity is the *divinity* of Christ, why the need to emphasize His humanity also? The answer to that question lies in soteriology, the theory of salvation and atonement. In 1096 the Italian prelate Anselm wrote the immensely influential *Cur Deus Homo. Why* did God become a man? That question, Anselm proposed, is logically antecedent to how He became a man. And the answer—grossly simplified, of course—was Paul's formulation: since sin entered the world through one man (Adam) it must be atoned for through the work of one man.

If Jesus were God only, the atoning act would have been a sham. And if He were man only, well, you have nothing at all. But the theory that He was *both* runs into serious problems immediately. If Jesus was God, why does He go off several times by Himself to pray—why does God need to pray? Why does He cry at the tomb of Lazarus before raising him from the dead—why does God cry? Why does He call out from the cross, "My God, my God, why hast thou forsaken me"—why would God beseech Himself? Why does He challenge a follower, "Why do you call me good? No one is good but God alone" (Mark 10:18). And why in Matt. 24:36 does He make a clear distinction between His own knowledge and the superior knowledge of God?

One of the earliest and still quite popular, if unacknowledged, answers to these challenges was docetism—the recognition that "fully God and fully man" is indeed difficult to grasp, that it has no more real intellectual content than the idea of the squared circle or the mixing of oil and water (John A. T. Robinson's metaphor). Of the two conflicting qualities, from the docetist viewpoint, divinity must certainly overwhelm, even eradicate, humanity. Docetists argued that Christ was fully and only God, walking on earth *in the form of* a man, not much differently than the gods of the Greek pantheon were sometimes portrayed in that literature. Or perhaps he was just a phantasm, and not really a bodily presence at all. In any event, for some docetists and their heretical kin (there were several related heresies), Christ's "emptying Himself" was, in effect, faking it—faking the prayer, the tears, the anguish on the cross.

A legitimate reading of many biblical passages, including those just cited, does indeed produce a picture of either a man seeking his God or God faking being this man. Some passages work frankly against any Christology that proposes the divinity of Jesus. Acts 2:22–23 is one of the main ones. The Apostle Peter is addressing a crowd: "Men of Israel, hear these words: Jesus of Nazareth, *a man attested to you by God* with mighty works and wonders and signs which God did through him in your midst, as you yourselves know—this Jesus, *delivered up* according to the definite plan and foreknowledge of God, you crucified and killed by the hands of lawless men" (emphases mine).

It's easy to interpret this passage as testifying to God's adoption of Jesus for use in His divine purposes. This doctrine of adoptionism was another popular heresy in the early centuries. Peter seems to believe that Jesus was a special man because He was chosen for a special role, but a man not qualitatively different at birth from Moses, David, or John the Baptist.

The doctrine of adoption slides easily into Arianism, yet another early heresy that taught that Jesus was a special creation of God—neither God nor man, but something perfect in between, a demigod, we might say today, on a special mission to earth and mankind to ransom our souls from the original sin of Adam. The founder of this doctrine, Arius, feared that the idea of Jesus as an incarnate God would devolve into polytheism in the popular mind.

Athanasius, the bishop of Alexandria, was a chief defender of the Hypostatic Union against the various Arian heresies. The politics of the period were vicious. When Athanasius refused to set aside a conviction of Arius for heresy, a kangaroo court of Arians found Athanasius guilty of sacrilege, the practice of magic, dishonest dealings in grain supplies, and murder. The emperor Constantine supported the Arians and ordered Athanasius into exile. Then he was reinstated. Then he was exiled and reinstated four more times, over a period of almost thirty years. He finally died back in the good graces of the church.

A version of the Arian heresy survives today with the Jehovah's Witnesses. One of their missives reads: "While Jesus is often called the Son of God in the Bible, nobody in the first century ever thought of him as being God the Son." Most liberal Christians today might agree with this statement, but some of them go way beyond the Witnesses in offering yet another alternative heresy, wherein they are joined by all unbelievers, by definition: the denial that Jesus was God at all. He was merely man.

While the basic believer might say that if Jesus was divine the rest is quibbling, and if He wasn't divine, forget it, the whole thrust of academic, liberal Christianity is to deny that either/or proposition and to claim that Christ's actual divinity is not necessary in order for His life and His death to have profound meaning for us today. These thinkers have no problem with the idea spurned by Paul in his first letter to the Corinthians, that hope in Christ may be "for this life only." In the vernacular, theirs is a Christology not of *substance* but of *agency:* The issue is not who Christ was in fact, but what He *does* as a catalyst for the believer; Christ is the Son of God because He helps me; He doesn't help me because He is the Son of God.

The thrust of the most liberal Christologies is that Jesus Christ's divinity was the tortured creation of the establishment church and was not in fact shared by Jesus' own contemporaries, not even by His disciples, and probably not even by Jesus Himself. It is noted that none of the christological passages come from the first three Synoptic Gospels, the "original" Gospels, but only in the later Gospel of John. Judaic monotheism would never have tolerated the idea of an incarnation, the argument goes, and therefore the Apostle Paul and the author of the late Fourth Gospel, John, must have picked up the idea from Greek-speaking Gentile converts. It is they on whom we can blame this myth of the incarnate God.

Albert Schweitzer was a key popularizer of this scenario, mainly in his book *The Quest of the Historical Jesus,* published in 1908, based on the premise that Jesus considered Himself not as divine but rather as the (self-appointed?) culmination of the apocalyptic atmosphere of first-century Palestine. Jesus read the laws and the prophets, focused on the messianic prophecies of Isaiah, chapter 53, and concluded that God wasn't going to work anymore through the old covenant with His chosen people. He, Jesus, would force God's hand and inaugurate the kingdom of God with His radical call to all mankind. And He was surprised on the cross when nothing happened. Thus His cry of anguish.

The latest rage on the seminary campus (but not on the Criswell campus) is process theology, developed by the theologian Charles Hartshorne and others from the philosophy of Alfred North White-head. Process proposes a brand new Christology altogether, based on a new definition of God that strips Him of His long list of adjectival superlatives and reenvisions Him as a deity with mind and will, yes, but restricted by the same processes of change and growth that bedevil human beings—processes that are deemed fundamental in the universe. God is interdependent with His world, not a perfect and separate reality above it. A paper in the Criswell library traces the history of process theology beginning with Heraclitus, famous for his remark that a man does not step twice into the same river, through Hegel, of course, and concluding with Whitehead. In addition, the tradition of "natural theology" in Judaism has developed a similar concept of the Godhead.

Norman Pittenger, a process theologian at Cambridge, outlines a Christology that could logically follow from this new formulation of God: Christ is not an "intruder" from the divine realm but an "event" of paramount importance in the cosmos, as proved by its "remarkable fertility, its extraordinary effectiveness, and its capacity to enrich and 'enable' those who accept it." This event disclosed to man what *man*, not God, really is, "a living, vibrant, dynamic creature moving toward becoming a fulfilled, realized, actualized, personal instrument for the Love which is God."

Process theologians argue that their idea of an evolving God is consistent with Scripture, and in fact is a good explanation for the apparent changes in God's nature, or, at the least, changes in His program for mankind, changes between, say, the peremptory "Thou shalt not" tone of the Ten Commandments and the more gentle "Blessed are the meek" benedictions of the Beatitudes.

Evangelicals dismiss process musings as the tortured evidence of a hidden presupposition—antisupernaturalism. Keep the language but throw out all the meaning. However, as Danny Akin acknowledged in his Systematics class, the Hypostatic Union as a solution to the christological question is also difficult to comprehend, and certainly not provable. It is, in the end, simply mysterious to the human mind how Jesus could be suffering man and at the same time and in the same body the omniscient, omnipotent God. Christians must simply accept this as a matter of faith (shades of neoorthodoxy, it seems to me). Akin said that the Criswell students would find that they have a predilection for either a *systematic* or a *biblical* Christology and theology. Systematics will produce a tighter system, he stated, but at the expense of "forcing adjustments" for some of the text. Biblical theology, because it does not force these adjustments, leaves more tension and ambiguity. The resulting system will be loose. As I would have guessed, Akin opts for a biblical Christology. He launched into one of his characteristic admonitions to the students: "Remember, guys, you do not have a monopoly on the truth, and you can learn from people you do not agree with. Don't believe we as evangelicals can learn only from ourselves." He proceeded to cite a series of books on Christology, one by B. B. Warfield, the godfather of inerrancy but an evangelical who accepts evolution, and another by Rudolf Bultmann who wanted to demythologize Christology along with other doctrines. "Bultmann's book is excellent," Akin added by way of teasing some of the more theologically aware students, because Bultmann is persona non grata in conservative Christian circles.

"There are good questions without good biblical answers," Akin concluded, "and so I will not answer them. We have to leave God as more mysterious than we sometimes want Him to be. To argue about speculative matters that aren't addressed in the Bible is silly."

CHAPTER 12

On one biblical issue there's not much dispute: Jesus and the authors of the New Testament cast a pale eye on human sexuality (not so in the Old Testament: the infamous Song of Solomon). As I was preparing to leave home for Criswell a friend asked me, "What I want to know is, how in the world do they handle sex?" He presumed that there must be some difficulties in aligning biblical injunctions about sexuality with a pop culture dedicated to sexual titillation, if not gratification. Sex is the touchstone of Freud's psychology, which sees neurosis as the patient's failure to achieve a mature genital sexuality. Freud's doctrinaire view has been modified by post-Freudian schools, but no therapist denies the importance, if not the primacy, of a reasonably functioning sexuality. The New Testament does so.

I got an early introduction to the subject in one of the first chapel services at Criswell. Chapel is held on Tuesdays and Thursdays, sandwiched between the second- and third-period classes, in the small chapel of the First Baptist Church across the street. Attendance in chapel is monitored; six absences (lowered to four the following year) required an explanation to the dean. This regulation would seem to be unnecessary; the students should attend chapel joyfully. The fact that not all of them do says a couple of things. As Danny Akin told me, some of them shouldn't really be at Criswell anyway; they don't have the real calling. He was referring to his two freshman roommates in 1977. "Those guys were irresponsible," Akin said. "We got our electricity turned off, our gas turned off. One of them dropped out, one graduated but isn't in the ministry now. He works for a bank. I don't think either one should have been here, really. They came for the wrong reasons."

Also, most of the students are young, and even Christians can be slipshod and rebellious. Apparently some of the professors can be, too. Later in the term Paige Patterson held a no-holds-barred fireside chat during chapel, and one intrepid student asked him about the attendance of the professors at chapel. They're supposed to be there, too. I hadn't been keeping track (by that time, I wasn't going every day myself), but apparently some of them had been lax. A deathly quiet settled over the student body. The question had taken some nerve but I wasn't surprised. I knew there are some real commandos at the school. Patterson joked about putting the questioner under "divine protection." Everyone laughed nervously. Then Patterson agreed with the student's point and said that he, too, had been "grieving" about this matter. He agreed there had been "just a shade of laxity" on the part of some faculty. So let us pray for them, Patterson said. He then concluded with the observation that compared with any other seminary faculty he knew about, this group stood out.

The main purpose of chapel, other than communion with God, is exposing the students to quality preaching brought by guest pastors, for the most part, but on this day George Davis, dean of undergraduate studies, delivered an urgent message from the text of Paul's first letter to the Corinthians: "What? Know ye not that your body is the temple of the Holy Spirit, which is in you, which ye have of God, and ye are not your own. For ye are bought with a price; therefore, glorify God in your body and in your spirit, which are God's" (1 Cor. 6:19–20).

Davis's subject was sexual purity. He began by frankly acknowledging the recent spate of "fallen preachers." I assumed he was referring to Swaggart and Bakker, and he was, but he also referred obliquely to a case unknown to me, the imprisonment of a preacher from nearby Garland on five convictions of sexual assault. The man had pastored one of the twenty-eight outreach churches sponsored by the First Baptist Dallas. Later in the term I was told that this fallen preacher had become obsessed with pornography.

A three-page document was handed out: "Fifteen Principles for Maintaining Sexual Purity," a straightforward, unashamed assault on the subject. Neither Davis's sermon nor the document were fire-and-brimstone warnings. Instead I heard a frank admission of the temptations for the Christian and specifically the Christian pastor, and practical advice for dealing with them.

The fifteen principles enunciated by George Davis are:

1. Understand that the Holiness of God is the ultimate basis for sexual purity, with a citation from the First Corinthians passage.

2. Remember that character weaknesses, if not dealt with, are likely to repeat themselves in one's children, citing Abraham's lies to his wife, followed by his son Isaac's lies; also David's failure to maintain sexual purity (2 Samuels, chapters 11 and 12), followed by the sexual sins of his sons Amnon and Absalom.

3. Recognize the destructive nature and devastating consequences of sexual sin, with three citations from Proverbs, including Prov. 5:3–5: "For the lips of a strange woman drop as a honeycomb, and her mouth is smoother than oil, but her end is bitter as wormwood, sharp as a two-edged sword; her feet go down to death; her steps take hold on hell."

4. Carefully guard your mind with the famous admonition from Jesus in Matt. 5:28, the admitted violation of which, in his *Playboy* interview, got Jimmy Carter into trouble: "Whosoever looketh on

a woman to lust after her hath committed adultery with her already in his heart."

5. Realize that the temptation to sin sexually may occur *at any time* in your adult life, citing 2 Tim. 2:22, in which Paul is warning Timothy, who is between the ages of forty and forty-five, to "flee youthful lusts"; and "Satan is like a pirate—he waits until the ship is worth more before he attacks."

6. If married, establish and maintain a healthy physical relationship with your spouse. Hebrews 13:4: "Marriage is honourable in all, and the bed undefiled; but whoremongers and adulterers God will judge." Also, "When a man is totally in love with his wife, it protects him from any other woman."

7. Avoid pornography and other sexually stimulating materials such as video, movies, TV, and the like. Matthew 6:22–23: "The light of the body is the eye . . . if thine eye be evil, thy whole body shall be evil." And Davis noted that he had heard of a traveling salesman who, in making motel reservations, would have the management remove the TV from the room. Davis himself always takes with him on trips a picture of his wife.

8. Share your struggles and weaknesses with your spouse. "If prominent spiritual leaders who have fallen in recent months had taken this precaution, their ministries probably would not have been devastated."

9. Develop spiritual accountability with a close Christian friend of the same sex.

10. If you are married, do not develop affectionate friendships with members of the opposite sex other than your spouse (1 Tim. 5:2: "Treat . . . older women like mothers, younger women like sisters, in all purity"). Do not discuss problems in your marriage with members of the opposite sex. Such conversations are likely to lead to affectionate relationships.

11. If you work with a member of the opposite sex, make sure that your relationship is always on a professional basis. Make sure that your secretary does not look to you to meet her emotional

needs. Make sure that your wife is on a deeper level of friendship with your secretary than you are.

12. Maintain close contact with your spouse whenever you are away. Always carry a picture of your wife and family as a reminder of your commitment and responsibility.

13. Surround yourself with constant reminders of your wife and family.

14. Always make sure that counseling sessions are on a professional basis. If a man, never allow a woman to share "intimate talk" with you. Some pastors refuse to counsel married women without the husband being present.

15. Never talk about the personal and intimate aspects of your marriage with others.

You snicker, perhaps, but why? The more repressive stricture of celibacy for the Catholic clergy isn't deemed so humorous. Likewise, priests are caught coupling with other priests, with nuns, with laymen (laywomen, too), but these peccadilloes don't constitute an indictment of the entire denomination, as is just about the case with the sex scandals of fundamentalist preachers. The dual standard reflects, I suppose, the general favor enjoyed in the secular mind by serious Catholicism over the equivalent Protestantism. The reasons are manifest. Even though conservative Catholics are anti-abortion and increasingly threaten excommunication over the issue, they aren't out on the sidewalks with Operation Rescue. And with the exception of abortion, Catholics aren't generally associated with the stereotyped conservative politics of fundamentalists and evangelicals; many Catholic clergy are perceived as liberal or even radical on other issues. Catholicism has the tradition of a couple of millennia on its side, and it has the sophisticated moral and theological apologetics that Protestantism also has, but without the same recognition. Catholicism has the office of the pope, which is generally granted respect, while Protestantism is yoked in the popular mind to the televangelists. And, finally,

Catholicism is not evangelical, in the technical sense: the dressed-up people on your doorstep will not be emissaries from John Paul II. (However, a recent papal encyclical called on Catholics to step up their lax evangelizing.)

It's an intriguing double standard and it came to my mind as I was thinking about these Protestant injunctions from George Davis. At the conclusion of his talk Davis asked everyone in the chapel to bow their heads in prayer: "Close your eyes. Don't look around. If you will vow sexual purity, raise your hand."

I bowed my head and closed my eyes and I did not look around. I did not snicker. And I raised my hand.

"Why?" I asked myself moments later. My wife asked me, too, reading the first draft of this book. I raised my hand for two reasons. One, I have no problem with aspiring to sexual purity, anachronistic as that might be. Faithfulness might not be easy or even "natural" or without psychological repercussions, but this is not inherently damning; it has its rewards, and the opposite conviction, a diligent promiscuity, certainly has its own price to pay. Two, and more important, I wasn't interested in merely reporting on the people at Criswell College and their beliefs. On most subjects I share the cynicism with which my generation observes the world, but it's way too easy to live this way. For a change—for a challenge—I wanted to experience other, very different, lives as totally and genuinely as I could, as long as hypocrisy wasn't required. If George Davis had asked a show of hands from those who had accepted Jesus into their lives, mine would not have been among those raised. His request in this chapel service was relatively easy; the other more difficult one would come later—and often.

I didn't look around in the chapel so I don't know whether all the students raised their hands, but I was certain that few if any declined—and not just because their dean was watching. After a brief time at the school I was already convinced of the authenticity of the people I had met—the genuineness of their religious emotion. Of course people do quit or transfer or flunk out—about 40 percent of any entering class, some of whom, as Akin acknowledged, shouldn't have been there in the first place. (The national average for all schools is at least 50 percent.) So there must have been some fakirs at Criswell, but I had not met them yet. The students I knew weren't going through the motions and I wasn't, either. The evangelicals at Criswell ask that people who claim to be Christians know what they believe, and why. They invite the believer to take his faith seriously. They shouldn't be faulted for being vocal about what that faith can be legitimately understood to decree. If you resent the Bible-toting proselytizers who go door-to-door, you don't like the Christianity of the Bible.

One excuse the nominalists do have is that many, perhaps most, churches are in fact set up to avoid the issue, to make it easy to say, "Sure, I'm a Christian." The whole idea of the sacramental religions is to insulate the individual from too many demands of faith. The Catholic church must have realized long ago that most people aren't interested in and don't have the talent for devout religious faith. Paul Tillich admired Martin Luther's "courage to be" in a direct encounter with God, as opposed to an encounter mediated by the "collectivist" system of Roman Catholicism.

Most of the people at Criswell have the talent for religious faith—or, in their language, they are chosen. I'm not chosen, apparently, but I, too, intended to take the Christian faith seriously and give it all the emotional investment I honestly could. If one day in class or chapel I was knocked down by the truth of the proclamation—if I was chosen—then so be it. I wasn't seeking this, but I wasn't trying to fight it, either. That's why I yielded up my ingenuous presence in the chapel service and raised my hand in a vow of sexual purity my own wife queried.

~~~~~~

The subject of sex was raised again one day in the library. Dave Porter, an earnest young man determined to do right in all matters, the Criswell student whose apartment I sublet when he moved in with a friend in order to save money, told me he was having second thoughts about the summer job he had lined up at Wet 'n Wild, a popular amusement park between Dallas and Fort Worth. The job would require dealing with barely clad girls and young women and Dave didn't know whether this was the right thing to do, whether it would be too difficult to look the other way all the time. He had often prayed that God would help him to avoid lascivious staring. Stuck in traffic behind a bus with a sexy ad on the back, Dave would drop the visor and turn away. Then he realized that instead of blaming himself for his normal sexuality he should recognize that it's healthy in itself. Only thoughts and actions outside marriage are immoral.

A main biblical reference on this subject is Paul's instruction to the Corinthians:

It is well for a man not to touch a woman. But because of the temptation to immorality, each man should have his own wife and each woman her own husband. . . . Do not refuse one another except perhaps by agreement for a season, that you may devote yourselves to prayer; but then come together again, lest Satan tempt you through lack of self-control. I say this by way of concession, not of command. I wish that all were as I am myself [celibate]. But each has his own special gift from God, one of one kind and one of another.

To the unmarried and the widows I say that it is well for them to remain single as I do. But if they cannot exercise self-control, they should marry. For it is better to marry than to be aflame with passion. (Cor. 7:1–9)

Some verses later Paul amplifies:

I want you to be free from anxieties. The unmarried man is anxious about the affairs of the Lord; but the married man is anxious about worldly affairs, how to please his wife, and his interests are divided. . . . And the married woman is anxious about worldly affairs, how to please her husband. (1 Cor. 7:32–34)

Paul concludes that it is well to marry your betrothed but better to refrain. It's important to know the liberal perspective, as noted in my Oxford Annotated, that these particular instructions were delivered by Paul in the context of his warnings that the appointed time for the Second Coming had grown very short.

But the young church took these and other Pauline passages, and the general tenor of Jesus' remarks, as testifying to the higher sacredness of the celibate life, and this became a subsidiary issue in the Reformation. The reformers allowed their pastors to marry. (Many Southern Baptists today are poor inerrantists when they look askance on the unmarried man; it is a sign of their anti-Catholicism. Danny Akin one day had to defend bachelorhood. Jim Parker is the only unmarried teacher at Criswell and he addressed the point in his jocular opening remarks in my Ethics class. "Still unmarried . . . by choice," he said with a grin, and paused. "Hers, not mine.")

In her book *Adam, Eve, and the Serpent,* Elaine Pagels puts much of the blame on Augustine for the morbid view of sexuality, specifically, and human nature as a whole, that has marked orthodox Christianity through the ages. Human sexuality is *proof* of the Fall, according to the reformed libertine Augustine. Without that original sin, sex between man and woman would be the straightforward mammalian coupling which is, it seems, without major hang-ups for the rest of the animal kingdom. Augustine, however, certainly did not initiate the church's perceived aversion to the beast with two backs. Origen, perhaps the most influential Christian theologian in the three hundred years between Paul and Augustine, reputedly the author of eight hundred books, is alleged to have castrated himself. Such rumors have followed other old-time churchmen, too.

Evangelicals are aware of their inheritance of what William James labeled the "sick-souled" outlook. In class one day Danny Akin said, while discussing one of Paul's many exhortations on sex, "I'm still surprised how many people have taboos and inhibitions about the value and the pleasure of sex within marriage." At another time he said it's not sinful to see a pretty woman and recognize her as such, but it probably is sinful to "drive around the block for another look." Everyone laughed. An analogy could be drawn with the Southern Baptist prohibition on alcohol. It is not sinful in itself; however, it too easily becomes sinful as an end in itself; therefore, abstain. And likewise with dancing among most Southern Baptists.

Akin said to me in his office, "Frankly, we're finding rampant immorality among fundamentalists. I'll be honest. It's starting to rear its ugly head." He was not referring to Criswell College. "In the past few years a large number of fundamentalist college students have fallen into immorality, and I think much of it has to do with their legalism. They couldn't bear up under the weight, spiritually or psychologically. They are repressing things that don't need to be repressed. Sex is said to be a bad thing: 'We don't talk about it, we certainly don't want sex education classes.' Well, I'm not necessarily in favor of those classes, although I'm not absolutely opposed to them, either. I believe the church should be much more open to talk about sexuality. We wind up damaging our young people with the old approach."

Many churches and Sunday schools are more open today. Dave Porter told me about a remark in a chapel service before I arrived at Criswell, to the effect that 10 percent of us (Christians included) admit to masturbation and 90 percent lie about it. In the early eighties, when Akin was a student at Criswell, a book titled *The Act of Marriage* was recommended to engaged and married couples. It was an explicit treatment of sexuality within a husband-wife Christian relationship. Ten years earlier, Akin said, that book "could not possibly have been recommended, and it probably would not have been written." And the Song of Solomon in the Old Testament is taught as a straightforward celebration of the joys of sex when consecrated by marriage.

Nevertheless, as Danny Akin acknowledged, sex is still often viewed by conservative Christians as basically dangerous. And of course homosexuality remains totally out of bounds for Southern Baptists and other evangelicals. It's a sin: Rom. 1:26, 1 Cor. 6:9, 1 Tim. 1:10, and the story in Gen. 19 about the town of Sodom, among whose residents' sins was homosexuality, and from whose name our word "sodomy" is derived. An avowed, unrepentant gay man or lesbian would not be welcome in evangelical congregations; the celibate homosexual who had renounced his or her past sin would be welcome. Or so I was told. Hate the sin but love the sinner.

In my Cultural Milieu class one student had acknowledged that pornography had been a significant problem for him in the past. One of the first guest pastors in chapel told us about the preacher who dropped out of the ministry and who, looking back, knew the exact moment when he fell: one night while spinning the television dial in a motel room he had seen a fleeting "pornographic" image. Over lunch in the Burger King across the street from the college, I asked Criswell student Kim Mayfield about any problems posed by her own good looks. I shall describe Kim as a statuesque blonde and leave it at that; I would have thought she would be considerably more provocative for the guys at Criswell than a poster on the back of a bus. (Shortly after I met Kim she had to drop out of Criswell for that term, unable to manage classes and her full-time job as a receptionist for an oil company, but she hoped eventually to get her degree in counseling and work in the mission field.)

Without wanting to embarrass her, I assured her that to outsiders there might be an inherent conflict between her beauty and her Christian morality. She looked surprised. It was not a problem for her. She said she had never really considered herself as an object of lust, but she did clearly see how the other women in her office were "chased all over the building" by the men. We talked about the role of women in the church. Two passages of the New Testament could not be more blunt in their assignment of a secondary, if not inferior, status for women in church matters. Paul wrote to the Corinthians:

As in all the church of the saints, the women should keep silence in the churches. For they are not permitted to speak, but should be subordinate, as even the law says. If there is anything they desire to know, let them ask their husbands at home. For it is shameful for a woman to speak in church. (1 Cor. 14:33–35)

And 1 Tim. 2:11–12 is the famous passage that blames women for all our problems:

Let a woman learn in silence with all submissiveness. I permit no woman to teach or to have authority over men; she is to keep silent. For Adam was formed first, then Eve, and Adam was not deceived, but the woman was deceived and became a transgressor. Yet woman will be saved through bearing children, if she continues in faith and love and holiness, with modesty.

I had thought that Kim and the other women in and around Criswell College might be defensive about their secondary role in the orthodox Christian scheme of things, but I didn't find this at all. They see no contradiction between their restricted role in the Baptist church and family life, and their absolute equality with men in the eyes of God. Glenda Eitel, the wife of missiology professor Keith Eitel, is a scrub nurse in a Dallas hospital and a veteran of years in the bush in Africa. She told me, "God set it up that men should be dominant, women submissive. It works better that way." Yet Glenda Eitel, like almost all of the women I met at Criswell, seemed to me as independent in demeanor as her secular peers. The women I met acknowledged that the changed times in the secular society have altered the views of some evangelical women, too, but they just don't see any contradiction with the biblical injunctions. Adriana Boyne, a Criswell student and a hard-shell Baptist who has grave doubts about the saved status of just about anyone who's not a Baptist, including Saint Augustine, doesn't believe a female should be elected president of the Criswell student body because the college is in effect a church. (This is a minority opinion; one year a woman came up one vote short of winning that election.) But Adriana told me, "Submissive does not mean inferior. It's one thing to be submissive, another to be a fool."

Adriana opposes abortion, as does Glenda Eitel and every other woman at Criswell, and every man, too. I knew this without asking. Abortion is a classic illustration of the power of nonnegotiable presuppositions: write another book, chapter, paragraph, or sentence on the subject but there's nothing really to talk about, nothing more to be said. Either the fetus's life or the mother's autonomy has the superior claim to the state's protection. The contemporary Christian perspective (both Catholic and evangelical Protestant) arises directly from 3,500 years of Judeo-Christian tradition regarding the secondary role of women in society; the feminist/abortion rights movement is a reaction to that tradition.

Which is the greater sin, abortion or bombing an abortion clinic? That question arose one day in Jim Parker's Ethics class. Barbara Wilson was a special guest lecturer in April, shortly after the massive march for abortion rights in Washington in which my wife took part.

Each of those actions is a sin, in Wilson's view. She cited Martin Luther King, Jr.'s, statement that "standing in the truth" requires nonviolence. "Stand in the truth and in love," Barbara said. "The only way we can win this is on our knees. Women will not respond to you if you're shouting 'Murderer!' through a bullhorn. I learned this when I stood on the corner at the Ruth Street Clinic and told a woman going inside, 'My name is Barbara Wilson. I've had an abortion. Could I talk to you?'

"She said, '*You've* had an abortion?' "

Asked about Project Rescue, the radical anti-abortion group that engages in civil and uncivil disobedience, Barbara replied, "I've really prayed about this and I've never been led in that direction. It is legal in our society to have an abortion."

While acknowledging, and acquiesing to, the patriarchal constraints imposed by the ancient Jewish culture and inherited by the first-century Christians who wrote the New Testament, Christians rush to point out the implicit message about the status and role of women as delivered by new covenant of Christ. In the fourth chapter of the Gospel according to John, Jesus pauses by Jacob's well to rest. His disciples have gone away into the city to buy food, for it is the sixth hour—noon. The disciples return and are astonished to find Jesus in conversation with a woman from Samaria. The message for today is clear, evangelicals say: Jesus quietly challenged the cultural norm of his day and granted full equality to women before Himself and God. Likewise, I was reminded several times that women were "first at the cradle, last at the cross." And the fact that a woman's testimony plays a key role at the Resurrection, in the context of a culture that did not recognize a woman's testimony in its courts of law, says a great deal about women's standing in the Christian community. (This detail about the testimony of females is also used to authenticate the Resurrection accounts, under the assumption that no Jewish author would make up the vital participation of a woman. He would try to hide it if he could.)

The first clause of 1 Cor. 7:4 reads, "For the wife does not rule over her own body, but her husband does . . ." and sometimes the reference is stopped at that point. Danny Akin made certain we read the concluding clause: ". . . likewise the husband does not rule over his own body, but the wife does."

In similar manner, Akin pointed out, a passage in Eph. 5 has to be read through in order to understand Paul's full message:

Be subject to one another out of reverence for Christ. Wives, be subject to your husbands, as to the Lord. For the husband is the head of the wife as Christ is head of the church, his body, and is himself its savior. As the church is subject to Christ, so let wives also be subject in everything to their husbands. Husbands, love your wives, as Christ loved the church and gave himself up for her, that he might sanctify her, having cleansed her by the washing of water with the word, that he might present the church to himself in splendor, without spot or wrinkle or any such thing, that she might be holy and without blemish. Even so husbands should love their wives as their own bodies. He who loves his wife loves himself. (Eph. 5:21–28)

In his Old Testament class Ray Clendenen drew attention to the designation of Eve as a "helper" in Gen. 2:18: "Then the Lord God said, 'It is not good that the man should be alone; I will make him a helper fit for him.' " Clendenen then directed the class to turn to Psalm 33:20: "Our soul waits for the Lord; he is our help and our shield."

The two words "helper" and "help" have the same root, Clendenen explained: "Woman is our 'help,' God is our 'help.' Woman is not demeaned by being referred to in the Bible as a 'helper.' "

It should not be surprising that the influence of female theologians in the history of Christianity prior to this century is minuscule. There's agreement among Southern Baptists that women should not preach in church or serve as deacons; the biblical injunction is too clear. There's disagreement about the role of women as teachers. There are female Sunday school teachers at First Baptist Dallas. Elizabeth Collins teaches English composition and literature at Criswell. Paige Patterson's wife Dorothy, holder of a master's and a doctorate, is adjunct professor of Christian marriage and family. Most of the professors, including Paige Patterson, Jim Parker, and Danny Akin, have no problem with women teaching the biblical and theological subjects, but some fundamentalists do.

Conservative pastors and scholars also disagree on the question of divorce. Danny Akin told his class, "There is no place for arrogance on this question." The apostle Paul writes that the man or woman married to an unbeliever should not seek a divorce because the unbeliever is consecrated through the spouse. However, if the unbelieving partner desires to separate, it should be so, Paul states, because "God has called us to peace" (1 Cor. 7:15).

Paige Patterson was asked a question about divorce during the fireside chat in chapel. The school does accept divorced students,

Patterson said. At the same time, he would counsel this person against choosing the pastorate as his Christian vocation. He cited the reference in First Timothy, chapter 3, that the bishop should be "the husband of one wife." Patterson reads this as forbidding a divorced and remarried clergy, but he acknowledged that W. A. Criswell interprets the passage as a prohibition of polygamy.

In any event, Patterson concluded, "Divorce is not the worst of all sins."

Dave Porter concluded his consideration of the job at Wet 'n Wild by turning it down.

CHAPTER 13

I heard in the hallways that a group of Criswell students were organizing a bus trip to Jacksonville, Florida, to attend a highly rated preachers conference. I asked Paige Patterson if there was any reason I couldn't or shouldn't go along. None whatsoever. Thirty-seven of us signed up for the trip, mostly students, a few spouses, and two elderly women from First Baptist Dallas who enjoyed going on these outings. At the appointed hour of six o'clock on a Thursday evening at a parking lot at Southern Methodist University we piled our blankets, pillows, and snacks onto the chartered sleeper bus and rolled east on Interstate 20. Our leader for the trip, Anthony George, who grew up in Jacksonville and was a member of the host First Baptist Church there, took the microphone at the front of the bus and offered a prayer of blessing. Within minutes a party atmosphere erupted. Everyone joked and played around; pop Christian songs were carried in good tune. I thought nothing about this frivolity—I certainly didn't consider it inappropriate—until the return trip home four nights later when it became an issue in a remarkable postconference encounter session.

The bus had seats facing foldout tables, all of this converting into double-decker bunk beds. After the initial excitement of the departure lost steam and everyone settled down, I ended up at a table with Van Freeman, Jerry Zucha, and Wayne Grier. Freeman was a senior about to graduate and, he hoped, go into evangelism, although he knew this wouldn't be easy because there are already about one hundred evangelists working in Texas, and that number or more in most of the states of the Deep South. Nevertheless, that's what Van felt called of the Lord to do.

Zucha was a gregarious, plump sophomore who lived with his wife in a nice house on a lake southwest of Dallas, part of the package that came with his job as youth pastor at a Baptist church in nearby Tool, Texas. Wayne Grier was a freshman from Georgia, and almost thirty years old. Wayne is perhaps the most transparently guileless individual I have ever met. He and I subsequently spent quite a bit of time together. I went down to his house south of Dallas and had lunch with his family (three kids with a fourth on the way) several times, and some of the details of the story of his life amazed me. I would not have guessed that Wayne Grier and his wife Renee had been through some brutal times.

Wayne's father worked for General Motors for thirty-three years, raising three children. All the Griers went to Sunday school and church in Woodstock, Georgia, right on Allatoona Lake. It's still there: about forty people in Sunday school, fifty or sixty at services. Wayne was saved when he was about twelve years old, and by seventeen he knew he was being called into the ministry.

"I didn't hear voices or see lightning or anything, I just knew it in my spirit," he told me. "It was time to quit playing. So I made that commitment while I was still in high school. I had never preached, never even taught Sunday school class. Scared to death to speak in front of anybody. I think it was January 18, 1976— Super Bowl Sunday, I remember that, but I don't know who played—when I told the preacher I knew I was called. He gave me three weeks to prepare my first sermon."

That evening service was packed because folks knew Wayne was making his debut. He remembers what his text was—James 2: faith without works is dead—but he doesn't remember what he said. He doubts that he used notes because, he explained, "In some of those country churches the use of notes was tantamount to liberalism." Wayne also doubts that it was a very good sermon: "I probably told them everything I knew, which was very little. I didn't know what faith was, or 'works,' either. I'd never studied the Bible."

He got through the sermon and preached some more but did not become a child prodigy in the mold of Paige Patterson. Wayne's wife Renee was a member of that church, and her brother was a pastor there. When Wayne and Renee first met she was only fifteen, and her parents wanted her to wait until her sixteenth birthday before dating Wayne, so they waited. In 1976 Wayne graduated from high school and got a good-paying job with the Atlantic Steel Company, where he remained for nine and a half years. Renee graduated from high school in 1977 and married Wayne the following year. She was eighteen, he was not quite twenty. They broke up after a year and a half.

"When it happened," Wayne said to me, "I really started looking at myself. What had I done wrong? I paid to go to counselors—some of them church counselors, all of them Christians. I met with pastors. Some gave me good direction, some bad direction, which I'm glad I didn't follow, such as the idea that God has an *A* plan for everybody and a *B* plan. If your *A* plan doesn't work, God expects you to go to plan *B*. I just couldn't find where that fit with Scripture. What I saw in Scripture was that God has an *A* plan for you, and if you get off, He wants you to get back on the *A* plan. So my whole idea was to reconcile our marriage. That's all I thought, dreamed, and ate. I was totally broken, to the point of weeping and sobbing. I couldn't even eat. It got worse and worse.

"I started going to a mission church, whose pastor had just

graduated from Southwestern Seminary. He was a friend. He stuck real close. He gave me some books on husband-wife relationships, and I started seeing the errors I had made. I was just completely ignorant, really. I wrote Renee some letters and told her that the things I had done wrong I repented of. But she just said we were not getting back together, period, forget it. But the first time we went to court on the divorce, it was thrown out on some technicality. I thought this was God answering my prayers. But Renee just refiled—properly, this time."

Renee also went off to college. Communication was cut off. After a good deal of trial and error, Wayne was told about a specific prayer for his situation.

"It's from the book of Hosea, one of the Minor Prophets. I don't think Hosea would appreciate that designation, but that's what we label him. When Hosea's wife Gomer was living in harlotry, God placed a hedge of thorns around her and prevented her lovers from having anything to do with her. And Gomer therefore came back to Hosea, who was using this story as an illustration of Israel's leaving God and then returning.

"According to a seminar I attended, there had been a lot of results from that prayer. So I began to pray for a hedge of thorns to be placed around my wife, for Satan to be bound, and for her way to be miserable until she turned and began to seek the Lord, to see what He really wanted her to do. I started praying that prayer in March, but the divorce went through sometime in April. I kept on praying.

"I was hurting so bad, I wanted help so bad. I really felt I just couldn't bear all this. I was totally miserable, but really finally learning how to depend on the Lord. When a lot of people would say, 'Listen, it's no use, you're not going to get back together, it's over with, you might as well go find somebody else,' I knew that isn't God's way. God is a God of reconciliation. If I married someone else, according to Scripture, I'd be committing adultery. God's way is reconciliation. In Second Corinthians He tells us He's given to us a ministry of reconciliation. The Bible is the backbone of everything I do. I knew that if I wanted to be happy I was going to have to do it God's way.

"I loved Renee more than anything and I wanted her back and I tried to let her know. I wrote letters. My pastor and his wife even went up to her college to meet her and talk with her. That was not productive. I was living with my parents then, teaching some in Sunday school, but doing very little preaching at all."

The divorce went through, but within a couple of months Wayne received word through a friend that Renee wanted to see him.

"I found myself sitting across from her in a restaurant—the first time we had talked sociably in nine months. There was tension, though. It was so thick you could just about cut it. There were no smiles or friendly exchanges. I tried to be as gracious and kind as I could, kind of like a little puppy dog, wanting things to work out, but they didn't seem to be working out. Renee finally said she didn't even know why she had called me, we weren't going to get back together. But she did agree to let me come up the following Saturday for the whole day. She had heard some folks say that God would forgive me, which He will.

"I went back to Rome on Saturday and Renee and I went shopping around the college. She went back to the dorm that afternoon and I stayed around, too, hoping she would come by. On Sunday morning I went to church. I recall very well when I left the church and returned to the hotel room I wept so hard I had to bury my face in the pillow because I was afraid the people in the next room would hear me. I seemed so close to getting her back, but not really. It was kind of like a bird that has flown away. You don't know whether it's going to come back or not.

"That was in June. It was some time before I heard anything else from her—maybe the last part of the summer. All this time I was still praying the hedge of thorns. Consistently praying. Then I got word Renee wanted to see me again. I went up there and found out that she was really having a hard time, too. I could see her breaking, see her softening. She was also getting ready to leave school. It wasn't what she wanted. She was totally, totally miserable. Distraught."

I felt rather strange listening to—*recording*—Wayne's recitation, the most personal and revealing of all the stories I heard at Criswell College, but he had no compunctions about telling it to me or anyone else, because he believes people can learn from it. Aggressive, quiet, shy—it makes no difference: any evangelical will be happy to tell you his or her Christian testimony, including some of its most private and perhaps embarrassing moments, in the hope that you will comprehend the sustaining grace and forgiveness of Jesus.

Renee quit college and moved back in with her parents. That was late in 1980—a year after the divorce. Wayne was determined to achieve reconciliation, but his first goal, he assured me, was "to make sure that my relationship with God was the best that it could be. My first priority had to be to turn my heart back toward the Lord, and if He wanted Renee and me to get back together, then okay. If He did not bring us back together, then I had to accept that also. I got to the point where I'd given my will up on the thing, but I still believed it was God's will for us to get back together. Malachi 2 tells how God hates putting away, hates divorce. I knew God's will. I was praying for *when* God brought us back together, not *if* He would.

"But back to the thickening plot. Sometimes late at night at my house the phone would ring and nobody would say anything on the other end. One night I was lying in bed praying, praying, praying, 'God, would you please let Renee call over here?' And the phone rang and I picked it up and nobody responded on the other end. And I hung the phone up and called Renee's house and let the phone ring one time and I hung up. She called back.

" 'Was that you?'

" 'Was that *you*?'

"We did this frequently and it got on my parents' nerves. They didn't know what was going on. Her parents definitely didn't know what was going on.

"On her birthday in December, about fifteen months after we had first separated, we went out to eat in Atlanta. Our parents didn't know. Her family was heavily supporting her in her actions since the divorce. I would not have been a welcome sight around their house. I bought her some diamond earrings—not real expensive things, but women love diamonds. I'd asked her scores of times to consider remarriage. That night I asked her again and she said she would. We would see each other a little, but not a lot.

"During that same period I had taken a contract on a house. On Christmas day I took her out there, then we went out a couple of more times. Late in January I began to ask her when we could get married, but she still wasn't willing for her parents to find out about it. We finally set the date and my pastor canceled other plans for that night—a Friday night in February. Friday the thirteenth, as a matter of fact. No superstition for me. Kind of like a slap in the face for Satan. We had the ceremony in the pastor's house, went up to Chattanooga to spend the night and I called my parents when we got there. They were elated. Renee had left a note for her parents, and some Scripture with it, with the reasons she had to do it.

"We came back home Sunday afternoon and my parents were tickled to death, and then the moment of truth came. We had to go get some of Renee's things. The atmosphere when we went over there was less than pleasant. But over the years it has eased considerably. That remarriage was in 1981, and we've been married for eight years now, almost nine, with the three children and the fourth on its way.

"In 1984 I began pastoring a church in Dallas, Georgia. I had a supervisor at the plant who had told me that as long as he was there I didn't have to worry about getting off on Sunday. But then the union rules made me 'bid up' to a job that required working three Sundays out of four. I said I couldn't do it. The company people said they had to go by the union contract. The union said the same thing. So I was fired because I wouldn't work those Sundays. But the company people told me that when I went to look for another job I should have that employer call the executive office directly for a reference.

"The Lord took care of us. About three months later I wound up with a job with the postal service, not making quite as much money, but not as many hours, either. We were doing very well—we were paying our bills. Then the next year I was asked to leave my church. We had a church discipline problem I wanted to address. I had discovered some . . . immorality."

Wayne didn't want to elaborate but in this day and age we get the idea: something to do with sex or money or both.

"Some of the deacons told me probably the best thing for me to do would be to go ahead and leave. They were afraid it would cause a split, or give the church a bad name. That left me with just the post office, and that put some strains on the marriage. About six months later I decided the Lord was wanting me to get an education. I didn't have any education. One of the staff members at the First Baptist Church in Atlanta, where we were attending at the time, had been a student at Criswell and he told me it would be a good place to sharpen my skills. It sounded like the kind of place I wanted to be, a conservative school. So I packed up and moved. I was here for two and a half months without the family, in the fall of 1988. If I had known it would be that long without them I probably would not have come. That was devastating. I'd never been apart from them, really. I knew it just wasn't right for my wife and children to be 780 miles away.

"But the Lord worked it out. I'd got to the point the week before this house opened up when I'd said, 'Lord, if something doesn't come through real soon I'm going to have to go back home.' I've found that's true a lot of times. We have to get—or *I* have to get—to the point of desperation, to where I can't depend on myself anymore, before God will actually come through. A fellow at school is a member of this church, and he knew the church had two pastoriums, one of them empty. He mentioned me to the pastor and I checked it out and it looked good—three bedrooms, two baths, a pretty nice house.

"Right now I've got three years left for the B.A. I'd like to get the M.A. That's not necessary in order to pastor, but some of the things I've already learned have been well worth my time. But the greatest ministry we have in our lives—something we really enjoy doing—is talking with people who are going through the same thing we went through. Living here in Texas we've been called by people from Georgia we don't even know but who have heard what we went through: 'My spouse has left me. What do I do?' But this testimony—this story, as you might call it—is something a lot of people don't know about. When we think back about it there's still pain there, it hurt so bad. It's just been in the last couple of years that Renee has really been able to talk to me about what she went through during those times, because it hurt her.

"So. We've been down the road. And we've seen that God was faithful."

CHAPTER 14

≈≈≈≈≈

A sect, a cult. Isn't that what we're talking about here? Evangelicals certainly don't consider themselves as such, but from the perspective of the secular world that's what any kind of biblical Protestantism has become in our time (again, Catholicism, even devout Catholicism, has a different image). But thirty to sixty million adherents, depending on the survey? A *large* cult, that's all.

What in the world was I doing there, forty-one years old, an agnostic at best, atheist more likely, riding on a bus with kids half my age (most of them) to a Southern Baptist preachers' revival, facing five days and nights of Christian captivity? As Wayne Grier, Van Freeman, Jerry Zucha, and I exchanged small talk (Wayne told me his testimony later, one afternoon at his house) I kept my eyes and ears on the rest of the bus. Everyone was talking about Jesus, the Bible, and faith. Once or twice someone would bow his head and lead one or two other passengers in Christian prayer. And

I entertained the thought—not for the first time, granted, but seriously—that this was all a terrible mistake: the trip, the college, the book. So what if my motives were noble, leading me to this exercise in empathy that required raising my hand in the chapel service? That changed nothing. If I wanted to figure out these people, that was impossible. If I wanted to figure out my own unbelief, that was equally impossible. How and why do Southern Baptists, Trappist monks, Hasidic Jews, and atheists believe so devoutly their mutually contradictory faiths? If William James never tried to answer that question, I certainly won't. We don't know why we believe or feel anything, other than those emotions dictated by blood. Where's the free will on the major matters? As Jim Parker told me, his education wasn't the reason he became a Christian; it was the reason he remained one. Danny Akin's mother is a saintly woman, her brother was a complete naysayer: same family, same education, everything the same but the self, for which there's no accounting.

James never mistook the psychology of religion for psychology *as* religion; he didn't pretend to explain religious states and attitudes, he only described them. I think he would have approved of the quote excerpted for the cover of my paperback edition of *The Varieties of Religious Experience:* "I believe that no so-called philosophy of religion can possibly begin to be an adequate translation of what goes on in the single private man."

Freud dismissed religion out of hand as infantile wishes—"Life is not kindergarten"—while his co-giant in psychoanalysis, Jung, believed that religious faith plays a key role in many healthy as well as unhealthy lives. James agreed with Jung, deriding "medical materialism" and the "bugaboo of morbid origin": perhaps the Apostle Paul was having, on the road to Damascus, an epileptic fit rather than a vision of Christ. It doesn't matter.

While readily conceding that religion is essentially a monument to our egos—the concept that I am important to the divine, somehow—and holding no orthodox belief himself, William James nevertheless believed that "there is more" and that the religious attitude is the best and only way that many people have of establishing some connection between their personal destiny and the cosmic scene. Is Freud or God at work in man? We do not know and cannot know, and James the pragmatist doesn't care: "Religion comes to our rescue and takes our fate into her hands. . . . When the outward battle is lost, and the outer world disowns [us, religion] redeems and vivifies the interior world, which otherwise would be an empty waste. . . . This enchantment is either there or not there for us. . . . If it be the only agency that can accomplish this result, its vital importance as a human faculty stands vindicated beyond dispute."

However, in his essay "The Will to Believe," often printed as an introduction to *Varieties*, James also suggested that there are, for any culture, live faiths and dead ones. The live faiths are those that the general public can even feasibly believe. Of dead options there are dozens. From this perspective, religious belief is just as culturally biased as our choice of games and foods.

But still, for James, if a given religious revelation is genuinely *believed* by the individual and is somehow productive in his life it is, by definition, alive and not dead. If it works in the field, we have no grounds for judging it as anything but *pragmatically* true. Michael Polanyi's *Personal Knowledge* is a potent extension of James's position—a defense of *personal* knowledge. He writes, "We owe our mental existence predominately to works of art, morality, religious worship, scientific theory, and other articulate systems that we accept as our dwelling place and as the soil of our mental development."

First we believe, Polanyi argues. We are all brainwashed and our diverse faiths are all equal and true as they function in our lives, and this is all that matters. Only after these presuppositions—evangelical Christian or orthodox Jewish or pagan or whatever—have established our individual "happy dwelling places" do we then think and know and behave.

If the individual and his culture generate a religious belief that denies the legitimacy of all other beliefs—and this is the way it has usually turned out—then so be it. It is a necessary contradiction. Those on the outside of any particular system will claim to understand, or at least to recognize, the psychology of what's really going on, while those on the inside—the particular believers—find all such judgments profoundly irrelevant and, of course, fatally mistaken:

> For the word of the cross is folly to those who are perishing, but to us who are saved it is the power of God. . . . Since, in the wisdom of God, the world did not know God through wisdom, it pleased God through the folly of what we preach to save those who believe. For Jews demand signs and Greeks seek wisdom, but we preach Christ crucified, a stumbling block to Jews and folly to Gentiles, but to those who are called, both Jews and Greeks, Christ the power of God and the wisdom of God. (1 Cor. 1:18–24)

Jesus freaks. Until that night on the bus I had forgotten that slur from the sixties. Politeness now generally precludes using the term, but that's what these students at Criswell are, and they'll tell you so: flat freaked-out in their love for Jesus Christ. I hadn't known any official Jesus freaks back in the heyday of that nomenclature, so these people at Criswell were my first exposure. The odd thing was they didn't seem all that freakish. The professors certainly weren't; the students, younger, less mature, less thoughtful by definition, were more freakish, in some cases, but that's all. Wayne Grier's belief in the efficacy of the prayer from Hosea about the hedge of thorns is far out from any perspective, but Wayne himself isn't at all; down at the post office I'm sure they consider him a thoroughly regular guy. I consider him a thoroughly regular guy, and I know him pretty well, although he's losing touch with baseball due to the demands on his time of family and school.

But what if Wayne *were*, in appearance, a "religious nut"? Am I supposed to sneer automatically at the rare lives spent with the Old Testament or the New Testament or any other Holy Scripture while lauding those tens of millions immersed in *People* and *TV*

Guide, Money and *Vanity Fair*? I can't do it. In fact, one of the pleasures for me at Criswell was the temporary isolation enjoyed from those four magazines—nothing personal; I choose them at random—and the culture they create and convey.

I have already reported that "liberal" surprised me as an appropriate word for the atmosphere in some of the Criswell classes. I was also surprised by the unadorned, joyful piety of the place—in the chapel, in the classrooms, and on this bus to Florida. Joyful, I realize, is a dangerous word. I haven't read or employed it myself in ages, and the reason is obvious: we're so busy having fun in this culture there's no time for joy. The word has the subtle connotations of a happiness that moves beyond its own private sphere: joy to the world. Along with Christianity itself, that concept is definitely passé in both pop and high culture today. It makes sense that the only place you might find true joy now would be in a subculture that isolates itself from a society that doesn't know what the word means. One point you have to give the Bible, Old and/or New Testament, is its ingenuous projection of the honesty and clear-headed confidence, the equipoise, that must underlie any true joy in the world. Those qualities in people go a long way when you're spending almost all your time with them. I certainly don't encounter such equipoise often in the secular world—never, really—but I sensed it at Criswell at times. My panic subsided. I stayed on the bus.

Squeezed into our upper bunk, Van Freeman and I discussed the New Age movement, John 14:6, 1 Cor. 1:18, ourselves, and other weighty matters. It was after midnight and everyone was under Anthony George's instruction to sleep, but I heard other quiet conversations on all sides. The bus was dark. Outside was dark. We roared along alone. Finally the other conversations died out and Van and I had to get some sleep ourselves. By way of conclusion he said to me, "Mike, the problem with the lost is that you want to approach God on your terms, not on His." This is patently true. God may have left man, may not exist at all, but man has certainly left God. Then Van said something out of the blue.

He said, "But you know, Mike, Christians have loneliness and hurt, too." I did not pursue the matter. It wasn't my business, nor was it news.

———————

Breakfast was a scruffy affair somewhere in Alabama following a makeshift morning hygiene. After we were rolling again, Anthony George got back on the microphone and addressed us. Apparently someone in the group had been rather rude inside the restaurant—where, indeed, we had waited a long time for service. Everyone was tired, but Anthony reminded us that we must always be courteous and behave in a brotherly way. There was never an excuse for bad behavior. Also, word began to spread that some of the people didn't have enough money to eat regular meals. This didn't surprise me. Many of the Criswell students have essentially no money but live week to week, month to month, on the earnings of part-time jobs, contributions from local churches, individuals, friends, whatever. But this near-destitution apparently never causes concern. Time and again students told me that they had given themselves to Christ and he would take care of their financial needs. He was in fact obligated to do so. In the Sermon on the Mount, shortly after dictating the Lord's Prayer, Jesus says:

Therefore I tell you, do not be anxious about your life, what you shall eat or what you shall drink, nor about your body, what you shall put on. Is not life more than food, and the body more than clothing? Look at the birds of the air: they neither sow nor reap nor gather into barns, and yet your heavenly Father feeds them. Are you not of more value than they? And which of you by being anxious can add one cubit to his span of life? And why are you anxious about clothing? Consider the lilies of the field, how they grow; they neither toil nor spin; yet I tell you, even Solomon in all his glory was not arrayed like one of these. But if God so clothes the grass of the field, which today is alive and tomorrow is thrown in the oven, will he not much more clothe you, O men of little faith? Therefore do not be anxious, saying "What shall we eat?" or

"What shall we wear?" For the Gentiles seek all these things; and your heavenly Father knows that you need them all. But seek first his kingdom and his righteousness, and all these things shall be yours as well. (Matt. 6:25–33)

I don't know how Dietrich Bonhoeffer reconciled this famous lilies-of-the-field passage, one that fits well enough with the rest of Jesus' teaching, with Bonhoeffer's own dismay with a Christian faith used as "a redemption from cares, distresses, fears, and longings, from sin and death, in a better world beyond the grave." Bonhoeffer found a more authentic Christian faith for our times (and for his own situation as a condemned man) in Mark 15:34, with Jesus crying out on the cross, "My God, my God, why hast thou forsaken me?", but this is not the position of the evangelicals I met in Dallas.

Wayne Grier told me, "Right now, Renee and I have zero savings. Zilch. But the money always comes in from somewhere. Someone sends us a check in support. I get some at the beginning of every semester from our church. We've had to count pennies to get bread. It's not fun; we don't enjoy it, but we're used to it. We're obeying the Lord, we're doing what we know we ought to be doing, and it's His responsibility to take care of His children. That doesn't mean we just kind of lie back and not do anything. I work. Right now I'm trying to get back on with the postal service, get another job, get with a church, something."

Also on the bus trip was Craig Walker, whom I had met in one of Danny Akin's classes. Craig is open, friendly, and without connivance—in this regard, rather like Wayne Grier. He was a senior at Criswell and a pastor at a small church on the east side of Dallas, which I would visit later in the term. His wife Debby was also on the trip to Jacksonville; she teaches their three children in their home. When Craig was first a student at Criswell he worked in a body shop in Dallas. Then he was robbed and didn't have the money to replace his tools. He didn't know what he would do but he felt God was calling him elsewhere. Sure enough, and as had always happened since he became a Christian, things fell rapidly into place. Within days of quitting the job, the call came from the search committee at South Mesquite Baptist Church, a small congregation in a suburb east of Dallas. The problem was that the committee was looking for someone with an M.A. and Craig didn't even have his B.A. But he interviewed, preached, and got the job. Earlier, when he had moved from South Texas to Dallas to attend Criswell, he and Debby couldn't sell their house but decided to walk in the faith anyway. The payments on the house were mysteriously taken care of until it was finally sold. Craig told me about a friend who was thirty thousand dollars in debt, and when that man began to pray on the subject, *his* large debt began to be anonymously paid off.

Craig is aware of the danger of "praying for money." He knows about the Christian television shows that promise tenfold, hundredfold return for every dollar donated to the Lord, if the check is made out to the order of that television ministry. But he and the other Criswell students see no relationship between that kind of thievery and their own conviction that God is taking care of their basic finances, or would do so, if necessary. Craig explained, "This has nothing to do with money. It has to do with honoring God and putting complete faith in Him."

The Apostle Paul said that all things are permitted but many should be shunned for the sake of the unsaved, because these practices are stumbling blocks to belief. There is no greater stumbling block than wealth. People who haven't read their Bibles in years assume that wealth is condemned throughout; we remember Jesus' admonition that it's easier for a camel to pass through the eye of a needle than for a rich man to get to heaven. But in fact the Bible is ambiguous if not contradictory on the subject of worldly goods, especially so if one contrasts the Old and New Testaments.

The reference to the camel follows Jesus' confrontation with the rich young ruler who was prepared to follow Jesus in every commandment but one. Told that he must sell all he has and give to the poor, the man "went away sorrowful; for he had great possessions." Jesus then turned to his disciples, exclaiming, "How hard it will be for those who have riches to enter the kingdom of heaven!" But a similar situation produces a different message in the nineteenth chapter of Luke. Jesus has arrived in Jericho and, after seeing the tax collector Zacchaeus perched in a sycamore tree for a better view of Jesus' procession through town, asks to stay at the man's home. The Jews in Jericho grumble about this because as tax collector, Zacchaeus is considered a sinner. At his house, the tax collector pledges to Jesus to give away 50 percent of all his goods and to restore fourfold whatever he had obtained by fraud. Jesus accepted this penance and assured the man's salvation.

Why wasn't Zacchaeus instructed to give away everything? I found an analysis of this question in an article in the *Fundamentalist Journal* titled "How Money Talks to Christians."

The author points out that a number of rich men in the Old Testament drew God's favor. Abraham was wealthy and assured of even more as he followed God's bidding. After Job had faithfully endured his trials, God doubled his holdings. In God's instructions for the tabernacle in Exodus, He specified the use of gold thirty-nine times, along with other precious metals and goods. The article asks rhetorically, "If God had despised wealth, as He does sin, surely He would have refrained from using so much of it in the place where He would meet with His people."

And Proverbs 15:6 reads: "In the house of the righteous is much treasure: but in the revenues of the wicked is much trouble."

However, Proverbs 11:28 reads, "He that trusteth in his riches shall fall," and Psalm 62:10 reads, "If riches increase, set not your heart upon them."

The author concludes that riches in the Old Testament are sanctioned if linked with righteousness. However, it is still foolish to rely on riches, or be controlled by them. And it is as possible for a poor man as for a rich man to be covetous.

What then about the New Testament, and Jesus' admonition about the rich man? The author directs our attention to the conclusion of that story. His disciples, astonished at the import of the analogy with the camel, exclaim, "Then who can be saved?"

Jesus replies, "With men it is impossible, but not with God; for all things are possible with God" (Mark 10:26–27).

And Paul (if indeed it was Paul; the Oxford Annotated doubts it) writes in his first letter to Timothy, "As for the rich in this world, charge them not to be haughty, nor to set their hopes on uncertain riches but on God who richly furnishes us with everything to enjoy (1 Tim. 6:17)."

In short, evangelicals conclude from the Bible that riches in and of themselves certainly cannot obtain salvation, but God in His autonomy can grant that salvation to whomever He chooses. Presumably He would do so in those cases in which the wealth is held with the right attitude, as suggested by the Old Testament references. This issue of wealth was the subject one morning in Cultural Milieu, and Luis Pantoja came down hard: "Rich or poor in this culture, we are all victims of the idolatry at the heart of the situation, the idolatry of wealth and satisfaction. We are completely blind to this."

His argument took a turn that surprised me: "Concern for mankind and the environment become secondary to keeping the machine going. Prosperity is the goal in and of itself. What the poor want is to be rich! And this is slavery! The rich try to ease their consciences by doling out money. Money becomes the means of righting the wrong, and this is impossible. It's a vicious circle. That's my harangue for the day."

The discussion continued in the following class and Pantoja asked about wealthy Christians. Everyone in the class knew that one particularly wealthy Christian at First Baptist Dallas, Ruth Ray Hunt, is the school's most generous angel. The consensus was that the wealthy must be made aware of their accountability before Christ. One student brought up the particular example of rich doctors. Pantoja referred to an idea once offered by Paige Patterson to the effect that the school hire three full-time doctors as a way of solving its own medical insurance problems. Then he joked,

"If we don't watch out we'll end up as a commune around here, growing our own food."

Then he asked seriously, "How many people in here have more money than they really need?" There were over forty in attendance that day, and six of us raised a hand. "Okay," Pantoja continued, "what is required in this instance? Think about it. What is our accountability before God?"

A profound accountability was the unspoken answer. From the back of the class a student shouted, "The church won't take care of the poor because folks won't tithe, brother!" and everyone laughed, because, I assumed, he had expressed the truth.

Charity for the poor is cited again and again as mandatory for wealthy Christians—"But if any one has the world's goods and sees his brother in need, yet closes his heart against him, how does God's love abide in him?" [1 John 3:17]—but Paul also enjoined, "If anyone will not work, let him not eat. For we hear that some of you are living in idleness, mere busybodies, not doing any work. Now such persons we command and exhort in the Lord Jesus Christ to do their work in quietness and to earn their own living" (2 Thess. 3:10–12).

The unbeliever might say that all this is fair enough but beside the point. The big stumbling block is wealthy pastors. Danny Akin expressed the opinion of what seemed to be the great majority of students in his New Testament class when he said one morning, "It's wrong for a minister to become rich. Folks, people stumble when they see ministers getting rich off their ministry. If you want a fancy life-style, fine, just don't be a minister." (If you're a teacher at Criswell, there's little threat of becoming rich. While the school maintains a salary scale competitive with seminaries, this is far below the scale at a state university. A new professor at Criswell with a Ph.D. earns in the low twenties.)

The class then exchanged stories about evangelists driving into small towns in their big sedans, and the students were unanimous in their disapproval. A series of students then decried the "begging" of the televangelists. The question came up about First

Baptist's gift to W. A. Criswell of a Mercedes-Benz on the occasion of his fortieth anniversary with the church. By general agreement at Criswell College, if not in fact, W. A. Criswell is a wealthy man thanks to long-term real estate investments. Apparently not everyone in the congregation was happy when the church gave him that car. Akin said, "If the church wants to give W. A. Criswell a Mercedes, fine. It was an honor from them."

Was it an appropriate honor? Judging from some grumbles I heard, some students thought not.

The question of wealthy churches was addressed most powerfully and most succinctly one morning in chapel. Students who had been on the mission trip to Cameroon over the Christmas holiday were speaking of their experiences, and the theme of the day seemed to be the contrast between the faith of these people and the jaded formulaic worship all too common back in the States. As evangelist Vance Havner admonished, Christians have become keepers of the aquarium rather than fishers of men. A young woman I did not know stood up and, in a pale, trembling voice I could barely hear, paid tribute to the generosity of the Cameroonian people, true "first-century Christians" who owned almost nothing yet offered most of that to the missionaries. She compared the struggling churches in Africa with the hypothetical campaign in an American church to raise $300,000 for a new chandelier. She was almost in tears as she managed to say, "We will be held accountable for that before the Lord Jesus."

And then she said: "I learned a lot about myself on the trip. We all did. I saw covetousness, greed, selfishness, pride. I'm being candid here. And I saw how much we need our Savior."

CHAPTER 15

〰〰〰〰

Many Southern Baptists believe that First Baptist Jacksonville may be the new Baptist Vatican, in large part due to the dual pastoral leadership of the avuncular Homer Lindsay and the intellectual Jerry Vines. On the bus I heard all about the great preachers we would be hearing—Wayne Grier is a particularly keen judge of homiletic styles—and no contrast could be greater, I was assured, than between the two pastors of the church. Lindsay preaches in a homey, rambling, good-natured manner—in the style of W. A. Criswell in Dallas, or at least the elderly Criswell I had observed. Vines, on the other hand, is famous for his elegantly crafted epistles. His sermon "A Baptist and His Bible" before the 1987 Southern Baptist Convention greatly helped his election as the president of the convention the following year.

With a membership of 19,000, the congregation of First Baptist Jacksonville has already outgrown the auditorium that seats 3,500.

The building is a new structure similar to other modest Baptist auditoriums in that only the cross on one exterior wall declares it unequivocally to be a church; no soaring steeples.

The excitement was building on Friday evening as the Criswell contingent walked through the glass doors of the building. The place was alive. Inside the wide, shallow, two-tiered auditorium a full-scale orchestra tuned up for the evening's music. I found a seat right up front next to a music director from Alabama who was highly impressed throughout the service by the professionalism of the orchestra and choir. He was awed by their practice sounds. Indeed, the Christian music from the stage for the entire weekend was Broadway quality, and the audience let the performers know it after every number, by cheers and applause or amen's, as appropriate.

Delegates milled around and greeted friends. Forgetting the import of the interior decoration—the baptistry with glass sides extending over the stage area and, above that, an overhanging garden near the ceiling—the general sense of the Baptist auditorium that night was no different from that of a highly charged political gathering of some sort. Average age: forty. Blacks and Hispanics: few and far between. A steady procession of preachers moved past Drs. Lindsay and Vines, hoping for a quick word with the famous pastors, and most of them seemed to receive one. Someone on the bus had noted that the two men have sometimes employed bodyguards—Vines especially, in his role as president of the Southern Baptist Convention. When I queried the need for bodyguards by Christian pastors I was reminded that Jesus had some, too, and they helped him escape dangerous situations several times. I didn't see any obvious bodyguard-types lurking just behind Jerry Vines that evening, but maybe they were somewhere.

Homer Lindsay finally called the session to order and proceeded to call out state by state the enrollment for the conference. Alaska: nine; New Jersey: three; New York: five. My new friend the music director leaned over and whispered, "Those are missionaries!" No one from Massachusetts had registered. Only ninety-one of us were from Texas, which I thought disappointingly low, since one bus from Dallas accounted for over one-third of those.

We sang hymn number 266, "Nothing but the Blood of Jesus," the refrain of which goes, "O precious is the flow that makes me white as snow/No other fount I know, nothing but the blood of Jesus." We were four thousand very happy Southern Baptists that evening. I was one with them. The robust hymns were hard to resist, and I didn't try.

Homer Lindsay introduced the evening's program: "What we're trying to do tonight is set the tone of this conference. We have about a thousand people here who have never been to one of our conferences before. We're just delighted to have you here, and we've been praying for weeks that you would be encouraged and helped and would leave here not only motivated, but with the tools to equip you to do whatever God has for you to do. That has been our prayer, that God would really bless you during these days. We have our combined orchestras, our eight o'clock orchestra, our gospel orchestra, our chancel orchestra, and our senior high orchestra all put together—almost a hundred in all, and they're going to play a special for you in a minute, but first let me introduce the first four testimonies. These men tonight are all deacons. Looking over our deacons, trying to select ten men to give testimonies, it was really hard to narrow it down because we have so many soul-winning deacons. But these are ten soul-winning deacons. And I have twice written them and asked them not to take over five minutes!"

Everyone laughed. Lindsay said, "They were gonna put me a bell over here but I don't see it. I'll probably just jerk on your coattails if you go too long."

Following the orchestral interlude the first of the deacons addressed us. "My name is Steve Luxemberg—"

Homer Lindsay interrupted, asking the bearded Luxemberg to step up onto the stage where the crowd could see him and where the pastor could reach his coattails.

"—and you may be wondering what a nice Jewish boy from Brooklyn is doing in a First Baptist Church. I'm here to testify that Jesus is alive—"

"Amen!"

"—and that he can save *anybody!* When Dr. Lindsay asked me to share my salvation testimony, I was a little bummed out. I wanted to share soul-winning testimonies. So if I slip a few in during the next four minutes and forty seconds . . .

"I was born and raised in Brooklyn, New York, in an Orthodox Jewish family. I tried religion. I was bar mitzvahed in an Orthodox Jewish synagogue in North Miami Beach, where my parents had moved, where the rest of the Jewish people from New York go. I then tried a little bit of everything this world has to offer—sex, drugs, rock 'n' roll. I experienced what the streets have to offer, what money has to offer, and they never satisfied my soul. I ended up in the service and drifted around the world, trying traveling and other cultures and seeing the sights—everything this world has to offer—and this never filled the void in my life.

"My uncle was the first person in my family to become a Christian—unless you go all the way back to my great-great-great-grandfather . . . Nicodemus. I guess he was the first one."

The crowd laughed and applauded. Nicodemus was the Pharisee who came to Jesus by night and addressed him facetiously as "Rabbi." The ensuing conversation is recorded only in John's gospel, and it contains one of the most beloved of Christ's promises, known universally among Christians by its chapter and verse, John 3:16: "For God so loved the world that he gave his only Son, that whoever believes in him should not perish but have eternal life."

Luxemberg continued: "After the military service I ended up with a company in Jacksonville, and I worked with some Christians from this church and they were faithful to witness to me throughout the day and share Scripture with me—things I really didn't understand—while we played Ping-Pong during breaks and lunch. I was aggressive in turning them down. But I finally came to visit this church one time, maybe just to get 'em off my back, and then I made the First Baptist Church mistake . . . I filled out the visitor's card."

Everyone roared.

"And they came to my door and they never stopped coming to my door and they didn't give up on me and Jesus didn't give up on me. A pastor's wife led my fiancée to the Lord—my fiancée who was about to marry a Jewish guy. A few weeks later we were married and a week after our honeymoon, July 25, 1982, while opening up wedding presents I got this big, red Baptist Bible—from this fellow I worked with who was so faithful in witnessing to me. I sat on the couch opening up this big, offensive thing and I started thinking about it and it all came into the light and I realized that Jesus was the Messiah and I said yes to Him and He said yes to me.

"My life changed. It was difficult at first, with my family. I lived a closet Christianity like Joseph of Arimethea for a long time because I didn't know how to tell my mom and dad. I knew that when my uncle had been saved he was no longer welcome in their home. But you know when Jesus is in your heart He's just gotta come out. We went to Fort Lauderdale to visit and I shared with my little sister, and in 1983 she became my sister in Christ. A year later my brother came to visit and said he needed what I had, and he became my brother in Christ. In 1985 Mom finally broke and became my sister in Christ. That just left old hard-core dad. They moved to Jacksonville to be close to us and Mom got baptized in this church, and through a series of circumstances, from hearing the truth in this church, in 1986 my father was finally set free and became my brother in Christ.

"The Bible says, 'Though the Israelites number as the sands of the sea, only a remnant will be saved.' To be part of that chosen remnant encourages me to know that Jesus is for everyone and there's no hard cases."

George Contois spoke next: "It all started when I was about eleven years old. Smart-aleck kid, sitting in the woods smoking cigarettes with a couple of pals when somebody broke out a pint of booze. Unfortunately I not only tasted it, I liked it. And it opened the door for thirty-five years of misery and discontent and a chain of Satan that grew stronger and stronger."

Contois wept as he told how he "stole from that wonderful woman, my wife, day by day for twenty-five years.

"We went through it, we hung in there, we fought, we battled, I lost her love, I lost the love of the kids. And then one day one of the kids came over—she was married at the time and her TV broke down. 'Dad,' she said, 'I want to turn on a program.' Well, I had my usual Sunday morning hangover and I didn't really care what she did. I was just trying to read the paper and wanted to be left alone in my misery. So she turned on the set and I was listening to this pretty religious music and then the music stopped. And he hit the pulpit."

Laughter as Contois pointed to Homer Lindsay.

"My daughter had turned on the services from this church. Sermon of the day: 'Responsibilities of the husband toward the family; drinkin' in the home.' And I looked over the paper at my daughter and said, 'I really don't need to listen to this.'

"And she said, 'Yes you do.' I put the paper back over my head. I was a good Catholic from New Jersey. What do I want with Southern Baptist preachers? So I tried not to listen, but the words came over that paper. Around that paper. And when he was through I told my daughter, 'Thank goodness he's gone, next week get your television set fixed and don't come back.'

"Next week Abbott and Costello rolled over into First Baptist Church again and I was mixin' a drink and I was too lazy to get up and change the channel. And he came back. The next eight months I listened to pastor Lindsay preaching. Looking back I would say that was God's hand on my miserable ol' life. I just listened. I cheered 'em on. I told the deacons as they left the front row, 'Go get the cash!' And then one day my wife and daughter decide they're going to visit the church. They came home telling me about the love in this place, the fellowship, the preaching, the music. And they told me they had filled out the visitor's card.

" 'You don't build a church like that ignoring people who come to visit!' I said.

"Tuesday night, here they were. Knock on the door. I open up in a bathrobe, bourbon in one hand, cigarette in the other. Homer's heroes. I never had an enemy in my life I didn't like so I invited 'em in. That rascal, talking through the cigarette smoke, opened God's Word, went through Romans, went through John, and he witnessed and he witnessed and somehow they got out of me a promise to come down here. My wife never let me forget it. Reluctantly I came. We sat back up there somewhere. Pastor Lindsay started his preaching. And then something happened. . . ."

Tears welled in Contois's eyes. He paused.

"The world started to change around me. My wife and I were within penstroke of a divorce. After all that time we figured that was it. It's done. Our house was about to be put up for sale. But God's spirit started to move. . . ."

He paused again. "Every time I give my testimony I never get through it. . . . Pastor Lindsay got to that precious invitation and said, 'Maybe there's a husband and a wife here today and you oughta just join hands and come forward and accept Jesus into your life.' And I looked at that precious woman and said, 'You know. We don't need a divorce. We don't need the booze. We need Jesus in this marriage.'

"And that's exactly what we did. And from that time Jesus has been in our home. He brought the love. He restored the marriage. He's used me in some marvelous ways. I take no credit for it. It's all His. He's allowed me to be a deacon of this church, allowed me to serve these men behind me, allowed me to teach a Sunday school, and allowed me, up to this day, to see almost three hundred souls come to Jesus. Thank you."

The other testimonies that followed Luxemberg and Contois that Friday evening were also powerfully conveyed. Then the next day the theme was extended in the first seminar I attended, on soul-winning, conducted by a former military man and insurance seller.

"Evangelism is not taught," Tom Crisp told the packed class-room, "it's caught. It's a disease you have to be infected with. Soul-winning has to be total surrender! This is a supernatural God and this is a supernatural ministry."

Crisp cited Rom. 8:31, ". . . if God is for us, who is against us?" So Tom Crisp worries about absolutely nothing—the same as-suredness that drives the Criswell students through financial crisis after financial crisis. And as always, this soul-winner refuses any credit for his deeds. The Lord does it all. Specifically, the Holy Spirit must move the sinner.

"You can be the best soul-winner in the world," Crisp assured us, "with just forty verses of Scripture." He reminded us of the quite beautiful story of Jesus and the woman at the well. "What was the first thing Jesus did?" Crisp asked rhetorically. I was probably the only one in the room who didn't know the answer. "He asked her about the water. *Start where they are!*"

A man he had once witnessed to had just a single question for Crisp: "In one word, what is sin?"

And Crisp had answered: "Unbelief."

I was getting the impression that no one could ask any question of Crisp that could trip him up.

He continued: "Now remember! Our message is not on trial. We are not on trial. The *listener* is on trial. Suppose the listener says, by way of outright prevarication or mere hesitation, 'Yes, I know Jesus Christ.' I reply, 'I know Ronald Reagan. I know the gover-nor. I know the mayor. I've seen them on TV, I know them. But they don't know me. You say you know Jesus. Fine . . . *but does Jesus know you?*' "

Crisp is very, very good.

Suppose someone claims outright to be an atheist. It happens, not often, but it happens. Crisp told us how he might proceed with this intrepid soul:

" 'What kind of atheist are you?'

" 'Well, what kinds are there?'

" 'Two. Practical and practicing. Practicing is like Madalyn Murray O'Hair. Practical has half the story and wants to know the other half. Which are you?'

" 'Practical.' "

We erupted with laughter, appreciating how neatly the evangelist had tricked the erstwhile atheist into inviting the enemy in for cocktails, so to speak.

Proselytizing, evangelizing, getting decisions and winning lost souls for Jesus Christ: one moment you are going to hell and the next to heaven. Of all the imponderables in Christianity, this instant salvation is just impossible for the skeptical, even for many semi-Christians, to accept. This is where evangelicalism and unbelievers really part the way. But there the doctrine is in the New Testament, time after time. Nor is there any denying the impact of conversion and true belief on the human being; no denying, explaining, or, sometimes, coping with it.

Consider the mechanics of conversion. If we're stuck with presuppositions and deductions from them, as we are, how then do we ever change them? William James said that conversion is the gradual or sudden process wherein the divided self, feeling itself to be unhappy, inferior, and wrong, becomes unified and right with the world, and therefore happy. This conversion is a wholesale transformation within one's "habitual center of personal energy." In a conversion, everything changes. What was dead becomes alive. Religious conversion makes falling in love seem like child's play. Setting aside the issue of "soul" altogether, and restricting the definition of "mind" to being nothing more than the structure and functioning of the brain, the mechanics of a wholesale conversion are still impossible to grasp. Conversion must be like starting over, a transformation that lies in a twilight zone way beyond explanation. Even Einstein's mind could tolerate only one such revolution (relativity, yes, but he could not make the quantum leap). No wonder most of us can't change at all.

In the Saturday convocation we heard pastors Lindsay and Vines dealing with straightforward matters of running a church and writing sermons. Being a good soldier for Christ and running a real church in the real world are two different matters entirely. The contradictions can run men out of the Southern Baptist ministry. Fifteen hundred leave every year. Homer Lindsay and Jerry Vines tried to convince their students at the conference that there doesn't have to be any contradiction. If you are truly right with the Lord, everything else can and will fall into place—one of the lessons Wayne Grier learned in his long saga with his wife Rene. Not even the family can be put before Jesus, Lindsay said. "But," he added in his slow, peaceful drawl, "you will be right with your family if you're right with the Lord."

In Christian thinking, this axiom follows as the night the day because, again, the Lord will take care of his faithful. If He doesn't appear to be doing so (in the example of Job, say), He has His reasons. A church doesn't just fall apart on the pastor; the pastor fails the church.

"Feed the sheep and they'll come to the pen," Lindsay urged. "If you love Jesus and go after the lost, there won't be any church fights. I'm not interested in being 'one of the boys'; I'm God's man! Only three things bring down ministries. Laziness, sex, and money." Lindsay has no sympathy for any pastor embroiled in any of the three. On the positive side, you only need two things to have a great church, and they're plentiful and free: Jesus and lost souls. Nothing brings a church together like soul-winning. Evangelism is the heart and soul of a church. Evangelism is the barometer: this is dogma among conservative Southern Baptist preachers. If you truly love Jesus and have truly given your life to Him as He demanded, this conviction will tell, most of all, in your evangelism. Lindsay concluded his exhortation with nuts-and-bolts advice about organizing the search for prospects, compiling excellent literature, and keeping the automobile in good condition.

Jerry Vines spoke eloquently about speaking eloquently. Preach without notes, he said. This is important not in and of itself, he added, but primarily to assure that you have attained "total saturation" in the heart. The preacher's sermon, just like every Christian's heart, must be born and born again. See what you say and say what you see. And spend your mornings in Bible study, Vines advised, thanking W. A. Criswell for the advice: give God the best hours of the day.

~~~~~~~

Because many of the students in the Criswell group couldn't afford motel accommodations, and because Anthony George knew people at the church, he had arranged host families for all of us. My host for the weekend was Kenny St. John, a youth pastor at First Baptist Jacksonville and a most dynamic guy. We had met the evening we arrived on the bus but didn't have a chance to converse until late the following evening—Saturday—at the home he shares with his wife, daughter, son, and brand-new Rotweiller puppy.

St. John is a few years younger than I. He was a street kid, an addict, a loser-in-the-making, by his own ready confession, before he found Christianity. He listened quietly as I filled him in on my beliefs and doubts and purposes at the conference. I added a thought I had scribbled down just that day. Scientists often use the word "beautiful" to describe their equations and theories and will even dismiss certain ideas on the instinctive appreciation that they don't have enough beauty and elegance. Christians must be expressing the same emotion when they talk about the transparent truth of Christianity, which is beautiful for them as an explanation of the world and their place in it. It is Polanyi's "happy dwelling place." For others, mathematics is such a dwelling place. Literature can be one. Anyone who loves the English language understands that Shakespeare is and will be the greatest author in the language. The outsider doesn't understand how this clearly illogical assertion can be made. It can't be, logically, but it's true and we know it. So it is with Christians and the intuitively perceived beauty of their absurd faith based on the historical death of a Jew on a cross who thereby atones for the sins of, and declares a philosophy of love for, all mankind. If you're a Christian, this formulation is beautiful; if you're not, it's an equation way over your head.

St. John was not impressed. He gave credence to the emotion but not the conclusion. His answer went like this, and I paraphrase: You, Bryan, are open to faith because there's that God-shaped vacuum in your heart; you're open because you should be. But why should I be open to you and your humanism, or whatever it is, any more than I'm open to a man advocating murder and incest? I'm not open to your "faith"—as opposed to your humanity—because you have nothing to offer me, and you know it.

Well put, Kenny. I have difficulty remembering all the places I've lived and all the jobs I've quit. Most people can't operate this way. St. John was right: I have no business proselytizing for my own rootless romanticism, and so I don't. I might even agree with the conservative argument that people and society would be much better off with biblical Christianity—if only they could believe it were true.

CHAPTER 16

~~~~~~

On Sunday afternoon Dr. John Phillips spoke on the Second Coming. Phillips is renowned among evangelical Christians as a writer and teacher. He's British and sounds it: his cadences are clipped and grammatical and learned. He makes an excellent showpiece for the evangelical faith except that I, for one, kept envisioning T. S. Eliot in his stead. Phillips looks somewhat like Eliot.

Because the main auditorium was overflowing I sat in the cafeteria along with Craig and Debby Walker. The Walkers introduced me to their host and hostess for the long weekend in Jacksonville, who apparently had been informed of my story and status because the lady asked with the brightest, frankest eyes I have ever seen whether I felt the Holy Spirit moving within me yet.

Phillips started off with the story of the lady from the church in Florida who called him in March or April, wanting him to change his speaking engagement from November of that year. Phillips said he couldn't do it.

" 'But we want you to come before September.'

" 'Why?'

" 'Well, the Lord's coming.'

" 'Hallelujah, I believe that, but what's that got to do with September?'

" 'It's the Feast of Trumpets.'

" 'What's that got to do with it?'

" 'The Lord's coming on the Feast of Trumpets and we want you to come before that.'

"Well," Phillips said as the crowd chuckled, "I tried to get some sense into the lady's head but didn't do much good. I went in November anyway. As a matter of fact, just after the big day that didn't happen I called her up. And I said, 'Hey, how come you missed the Rapture?' "

Phillips then began his carefully considered exposition of the timing of the Second Coming by directing our attention to Matt. 23:29, in which Jesus laments over the fate he forsees for Jerusalem in the "woe to the scribes and Pharisees" declamation. Jesus proclaims that the crime these Jews are about to commit—the murder of Jesus Himself—is so heinous in the eyes of God it outweighs all the righteous blood ever shed on earth. And then Jesus says, "Truly, I say to you, all this will come upon this generation."

A literal generation, Jesus meant, and he was right. Within that generation the hills surrounding Jerusalem were black with crosses, and on every cross a Jew. When the Romans finally captured the city they massacred a million citizens and deported so many of the survivors that the arenas and slave markets of Rome were glutted and the bottom fell out of that market.

The expression in Greek for "generation" occurs sixteen times in the gospel, another nine times with an adjective such as "wicked" or "adulterous." In every case the meaning of a literal generation is clear.

Now Phillips directed us to Matt. 24:32—the parable of the fig tree: "From the fig tree learn its lesson: as soon as its branch becomes tender and puts forth its leaves, you know that summer is near. So also, when you see all these things, you know that he is near, at the very gates. Truly, I say to you, this generation will not pass away till all these things [darkening of the sun and moon, stars falling from heaven] take place. Heaven and earth will pass away, but my words will not pass away.

"But of that day and hour no one knows, not even the angels of heaven, nor the Son, but the Father only."

Phillips explained that the phrase for "generation" in this verse is the same as used in chapter 23, "so it's difficult to see how it means anything other than a literal generation. Yet no one knows which generation but the Father. There's no use setting dates for the Rapture. There's no use saying that because Israel became a state in 1948, and a generation is forty years, therefore the Lord's got to come in 1988. Obviously that ain't so. Pardon my American. We don't know how long a generation is and we don't know exactly when God starts the count anyway. But we do know we are mighty near the end. I believe 'these things' are beginning to be."

Phillips proceeded to explain why. "There are three trees in the Bible that symbolize the nation of Israel: the fig, the olive, and the vine. The vine represents the Israel of the Old Testament, up to the denial of Christ. The olive tree represents Israel after it finally accepts Christ, in a time yet to come. And in between that time when the Jewish nation rejected God and then repented and accepted Christ, Israel is the fig tree. As Paul wrote to the Christians in Rome, the Jews had lost their position of religious privilege.

"For two thousand years, if God had had anything to say He said it in Hebrew. He spoke to a Jew. But after Calvary and after Pentecost, if God had anything to say He said it in Greek. He began to speak a Gentile language."

But eventually the Jewish nation will accept Jesus as Messiah and the great prophecies of the Old Testament will be fulfilled. In the meantime, Phillips advised and Jesus warned, learn the parable of the fig tree. Jesus performed only one "judgment miracle." He cursed the fig tree. "That lonely fig tree by the side of the road was a picture of the Jewish nation to which he had come, utterly barren toward God and with nothing for Christ except a cattle shed in which to be born and a cross upon which to die.

"Jesus withdrew his blessing from Israel in the eight terrible curses of chapter 23. And then he told the parable, that when we see that fig tree coming to life, that's the sign that He was coming back to earth. Watch the fig tree. And my friends, you and I have lived to see the budding of the fig tree. Spring is here, summer's on the way! The rebirth of the state of Israel simply tells us that Jesus is on the way. The clock that God stopped at Calvary has started to tick again. It won't be long before it's chiming out the hours. Jesus is coming again."

And then Phillips brought the audience to a rapt silence as he outlined the quite mysterious survival of the Jewish people, contrary to the law of assimilation. "The scattered remnants of conquered nations finding their homes in other countries are simply absorbed and they disappear as a separate people. That's an observable law of history, and it works for all people except the Jewish people. It doesn't work for them."

We have Italian-Americans, German-Americans, African-Americans—but no Jewish-Americans; instead, American Jews. A family may be able to trace their North American ancestry back three hundred years, but that family is still . . . Jewish.

"The Jew," Phillips said, "has remained a gulf stream in the ocean of mankind. He has preserved his national identity not just for two or three generations, but for sixty. And not just in one or two countries, but in a hundred. That is a very great mystery. The only explanation for that mystery is God, and the fact that God has a future for this people as outlined in His word."

I acknowledge the mystery. However, the Jews are not alone in this tenacity of identity. Gypsies are always gypsies first. And we do not refer to our own native Americans as Indian-Americans, but rather as American Indians. So the issue might not be so much God's selection as man's rejection.

Phillips continued: "Along with the mystery is a great miracle. The Jew cannot be assimilated. Neither can he be exterminated. There have been countless attempts in history to exterminate the Jewish people. Their history has been one of continuous persecution. Anti-Semitism is endemic in all Gentile societies, but from time to time it becomes epidemic."

Phillips related the statement of the chief British prosecutor at Nuremberg: "He described how human hair was baled for commercial purposes, how human fat was rendered into soap, how tattooed human skin was made into lamp shades, how gold was extracted from the teeth of the corpses and melted into ingots and shipped to the Reich bank."

Phillips was almost whispering now. " 'Mass murder,' the prosecutor said, 'had become a state industry . . . with by-products.' "

The audience in the cafeteria and I'm sure in the church auditorium was absolutely silent. "And yet," Phillips continued, his voice rising, "the Jews today are a greater force in this world than they've ever been before. And I tell you, as I study the entire prophetic picture, I've come to the conclusion that when the Soviet Union finally rolls its armies southward to attack Israel it's gonna get a mauling on the way, before it finally gets to the frontiers. Jews aren't gonna stand back the second time and let it happen again. And they've got the technology to make the Soviet Union wish she hadn't started. And then when they cross the frontiers, God's gonna step in and finish the job.

"Here are a people that can't be assimilated and they can't be exterminated and, my friends, now they've gone back to the promised land a third time. The first time was after the sojourn in Egypt, and they gave the world the Bible. They went back again from Babylon and in the process of time they gave the world Jesus. And now they've gone back a third time, and they don't know it yet but they're getting ready to give us the millennium.

"It's an amazing thing, when you stop to think of it, that a nation uprooted, scattered in a hundred countries for hundreds upon hundreds of years, should suddenly come back to life in our generation."

Phillips told the story of the miraculous rebirth of the Hebrew language after a death of two thousand years. "It was the idea of a Jew by the name of Eliezer Ben Yehuda. He was a Russian-born Jew on the way to Palestine between the two world wars, and he announced to his Russian-born bride on board the ship that he intended to speak to her only in Hebrew when he got there. And he was so impatient he began to fulfill his pledge right then and there. He had only one purpose for living, and that was to resurrect the dead Hebrew language. He wanted to have twelve children, one for each of the twelve tribes of ancient Israel. He had eleven. He was absolutely furious. Those were the first children since the days of the Romans to be born into a home where only Hebrew was spoken. He sent his kids out into the streets to pick fights with other kids in Hebrew. And in the end he won.

"Here's a language that had been dead for two thousand years. No word in it for anything in modern society—no word for automobile, steamship, spark plug—anything. So what did they do? They went back to the old Hebrew roots, and constructed coinages, and they did that until those old Hebrew . . . roots had put forth their . . . leaves. And a dead language came to life. It is an extraordinary thing."

And the great mystery and the great miracle have the great message. The tree, Jesus said, would put forth leaves, not fruit. It would be reborn in exactly the same status as it was when it was vanquished. And indeed, Phillips said, Israel is probably the most Christ-rejecting nation on the face of the earth today. "It's got its leaves, but it doesn't have any fruit yet. And that's what Jesus said would happen. He foretold that just before His coming the nation of Israel would be back in the land as a nation in unbelief."

And when these things transpire, Jesus promised, "this generation" will not pass away. Not the generation he was speaking to, but the generation he was speaking of.

"I submit to you, my friends," Phillips concluded, "without any desire whatsoever to fix any dates at all, that the generation of which he was speaking is our generation, and I refuse to throw out the baby with the bath water just because some idiot set a date last year. Jesus is coming again, and we can confidently expect it will be in our lifetime! As God injected the church supernaturally at the beginning of this historic era, He is now about to eject it supernaturally out of history, and leave the nation of Israel in the land, alone."

Phillips, like most but not all evangelicals, is a premillennialist, believing that the fairly imminent Second Coming of Christ will precede the one thousand years of perfect peace on earth promised by Scripture. But first this current Church Age will conclude with seven years of worldwide Tribulation. Postmillennialists believe that Jesus' coming will follow the millennial peace, which will have been inaugurated by the work of the Christian church. And there are amillennialists, who don't believe in any earthly millennium.

The main technical passages on this issue of the Second Coming are the final three chapters of Revelation, which declare the period of one thousand years of peace and evoke images of worldwide battle and the ensuing arrival of the New Jerusalem. Revelation 20, the main source for Second Coming considerations, begins:

Then I saw an angel coming down from heaven, holding in his hand the key of the bottomless pit and a great chain. And he seized the dragon, that ancient serpent, who is the Devil and Satan, and bound him for a thousand years, and threw him into the pit, and shut it and sealed it over him, that he should deceive the nations no more, till the thousand years were ended. After that he must be loosed for a little while. . . . And when the thousand years are ended, Satan will be loosed from his prison and will come out to deceive the nations which are at the four corners of the earth. . . . (Rev. 20:1–8)

Evangelical inerrantists allow for allegorical interpretation of some of the symbolism, numerology, strange beasts, and general obscurity of the Book of Revelation. For example, the reference to the "four corners of the earth," which is also employed by Isaiah and Ezekiel in their Old Testament prophecies, is of course deemed metaphorical. Nevertheless, the Ryrie Study Bible adopts the view that Revelation is a fairly straightforward set of prophecies. My Oxford Annotated Bible introduces Revelation as "an inspired picture-book, which, by an accumulation of magnificent poetic imagery, makes a powerful appeal to the reader's imagination."

Either that or it makes the modern reader wonder what kind of men were these first-century proselytizers for God. Can we understand them and their surrealistic worldview at all? The Book of Revelation is impossible for any but the most committed to pay any attention to today (although it has furnished artists through the ages with a plenitude of fantastic images). In line with my recommendation that the potential Christian not begin his study of the faith with Genesis, the first book of the Bible, I would irreverently suggest that the last book be removed from the canon altogether. It cannot speak meaningfully to most of us, including most Christians.

It goes almost without saying that any kind of literal Second Coming does not feature in the thought of liberal theologians, but it's vital to evangelicals and practicing Catholics (the doctrine is part of their Apostles' Creed), and it was also vital to first-century Christians. They wanted to know the timetable. Jesus' disciples asked him during his resurrection appearance when He would restore the kingdom of Israel, and He replied, "It is not for you to know times and seasons which the Father has fixed by his own authority" (Acts 1:7).

In the Gospels of Matthew and Luke, Jesus said, "But know this, that if the householder had known in what part of the night the thief was coming, he would have watched and not let his house be broken into. Therefore you also must be ready; for the Son of man is coming at an hour you do not expect" (Matt. 24:43–44).

In the liberal interpretation, Paul's early letters reveal that the apostle thought the final days were quite imminent—within weeks, months, a few years, perhaps, but definitely not decades, generations, centuries, millennia. The seventh chapter of First Corinthians is most often cited in defense of this interpretation. The twenty-sixth verse reads: "I think that in view of the impending distress it is well for a person to remain as he is." Three verses later Paul writes,

I mean, brethren, the appointed time has grown very short; from now on, let those who have wives live as though they had none, and those that mourn as though they were not mourning, and those who rejoice as though they were not rejoicing, and those who buy as though they had no goods, and those who deal with the world as though they had no dealings with it. For the form of this world is passing away.

The Oxford Annotated Bible interprets this "impending distress" passage as a reference to the end of the world. The editors *want* it to be such, thereby impugning literal interpretations of the Second Coming. However, in Paul's letters to the Thessalonians, which are placed later in the New Testament but were written before the letters to the Corinthians, Paul is more equivocal: "But as to the times and the seasons, brethren, you have no need to have anything written to you. For you yourselves know well that the day of the Lord will come like a thief in the night" (1 Thess. 5:1–2). Then in a second letter Paul urges this congregation not to wait passively for the day of the Lord. The Oxford Annotated is silent on these passages, which don't support a failed prophecy of the Second Coming.

Evangelicals, of course, favor a literal Second Coming and must therefore explain the impending distress passage. One way to accomplish this is to translate "impending" as "present" (a legitimate interpretation, my Oxford Annotated concedes), and then to assert, as Ryrie does, that the *present* distress was "probably a particularly difficult circumstance through which the Corinthian Christians were passing."

Back in Dallas I mentioned John Phillips's lecture to Danny Akin, who was surprised and maybe even disappointed. Akin doesn't believe in any kind of date-setting. Luis Pantoja, however, told me that he, too, believes he will see the Second Coming in his own lifetime. Christians have always believed this, he said, and there's no harm in doing so. The people at Criswell told me that the Christian faith won't lose credence, or any more than it already has, if the centuries continue to roll by without anything happening, but this must surely be wishful thinking. The Christian faith is historical and eschatological; it depicts and demands a culmination in history. Without one fairly soon, and taking into account everything else going against it in modern times, biblical Christianity will struggle even more for credibility.

CHAPTER 17

~~~~~~~~~

On Monday afternoon evangelist Bill Stafford preached. A tall, lean fellow I judged to be in his late fifties, dressed in his gray suit and (I was told) trademark cowboy boots, Stafford is one of the wild men of the Southern Baptist evangelism circuit. "Wild Bill" he's called. The only way I have devised to portray his emphatic cadences is to employ a rash of italics and capitalizations.

"If every preacher here, including myself, could walk away from this conference *clean* and *godly* and *holy* and *repentant* and broken before God," he bellowed in the beginning, "I believe our churches would think they had new preachers. AMEN?"

"AMEN!"

Stafford then cracked a joke about his wild-and-crazy style: "When I get through I have to either duck or pucker. They gonna hit me or kiss me. *Amen?* I go into many churches that try to put me under pressure, to make me function in a different way. I won't let 'em. Back when I was pastoring, brother Homer, I'd have given all the world if a pulpit committee would have come by and just sat down in my auditorium. My people didn't think anybody else would have me! I almost paid one group to come by and just *look* like a committee. *Amen?*

"And brother Homer, I thank you for just letting me come here and preach. Hey brother, I feel like the mule at the Kentucky Derby. I'm not gonna win any races but I sure am running with high-class stuff! Amen? Hallelujah! That's how I feel! I'm just glad to be in the race! And man, you should have seen me when God called me! But, hey, I have fun being Christian. When God works me over it brings me to the joy of Jesus. I'm amazed—but anyway, let's go.

"I was just thinking here today, what if every one of us could get in a position before God to have that touch of God on us we need so desperately. God didn't bring you here to stir your emotions. He brought you here to meet with God. Amen? And if you meet God you'll never be the same preacher, you won't ever lead the same life, you'll walk out of here a different person and things that were not really sin to you a week ago will be sin when you leave here tomorrow. Amen? Because you can't walk with God without putting off, putting off. The more you *put on* Jesus the more he *pushes off* the things of the world, the things of self, and fills your life with the replacement of Jesus Christ. He's *everything.* Amen?"

Stafford proceeded to relate the story of conniving Jacob from Genesis, chapter 32, when Jacob, after wrestling all night with the angel, was renamed and annointed "Israel" by God. The title of Stafford's sermon: "God's Transforming Power."

"What God really wants every one of us to do is to go through fresh metamorphosis. . . . The Christian life is a life of *change.* If you think you've arrived, you're dead. Amen? A man who thinks he's spiritual is not. He just *thinks* he is. Amen?"

No response from us.

"Well, hang in there now. I know preachers are the hardest

people in the world to confront. We want our *members* to change, but not us. Tell that lousy deacon how to live. No! I want to get on *your* case. That deacon is not your problem. He's merely your *excuse.* And I tell you what. God's gonna leave him there till *you* change. Amen! In other words, you gonna take the test until you pass it. Man, I had some deacons in my church, I would to God He would have moved 'em, but if He had, I'd have been dead as a hammer. I stayed alive just to see what God could do in spite of 'em! Hey, they'll make you see God! They'll make you pray! They'll *drive* you to Jesus! The very thing you're praying to take *out* He put *in*—to *drive* you to the lamb of God!

"You see, we forget God's dealing with nobodies. Everything we are He had to make. The only good thing about us is how much Jesus controls us and lives through us. God's not interested in but one thing: How much of me can He control? And pour through me the totality of Himself? Listen, when I leave a place, if you can't remember my name, wonderful. But if you remember the Jesus and the God and the Holy Spirit and the glory of God, I will have accomplished my task in lifting up the lamb of God. God don't work with good folks. He works with bad folks, with nobodies, with losers.

"Somebody said we only got one nature. I got news for you. You've got a nature lying in you that is just as sinful and ungodly, and if you don't let Jesus overcome you with the glory of Himself you'll be worse than a Jacob, and so will I, without the mighty power of God ruling in my life. And we'd better get to believin' that. Amen? Somebody said that's negative preachin'! I said, 'Yeah, but it'll give you that *positive* life!' It's somebody else *soaring* you by the power of God! Jesus! *Jesus! JESUS! Plus* and *minus* nothing.

"That's what it is."

He paused and the audience grabbed a moment's resuscitation. Just listening to Stafford is hard work.

"So that's my introduction, so let's go. Adrian Rogers said I'm the only preacher he knew who didn't need a runway. I'm airborne

CHAPTER AND VERSE   213

by the time I get there! When I hear preachin' like I've heard here it brings me to Calvary, brings me to the cross, wipes me out before God and makes me want to say, 'Oh, God, could you do something in our lives today, bring every one of us preachers broken before the cross to where we'll know liberalism isn't really our enemy. The devil is our enemy. And we're gonna march in revival until God shakes us back to our first love, and we shake this country for Jesus Christ.'

"Well, that's a few things I was brewin' on over there. That's off the cuff—"

He shot his cuffs out of his suit jacket.

"—I didn't have that written down."

The audience in Jacksonville knew that brother Stafford would have nothing written down. Stafford was all he was cracked up to be by Wayne Grier. However, the Protestant denominations that revere preaching (Catholics never have, to the same degree) must be careful because Paul warns *against* preaching with "eloquent wisdom, lest the cross of Christ be emptied of its power" (1 Cor. 1:17). Southern Baptists reply that the eloquent wisdom of their great preachers doesn't deter them from, but rather directs them to, the cross. Stafford's country preachin' was the sort that I love but most unbelievers revile. Jimmy Swaggart became an embarrassment but he was and still is a superb stump preacher. But the best of this kind of preaching does nothing for the lost. It's mainly fuel for the faithful. It can't convince or convict a single soul, not for the long haul. Darrell Gilyard might refer to Stafford's work as *white* rousology.

Religious faith is emotion, certainly, but surely there has to be some element of deliberation in it, too. Jerry Zucha told me on the bus that guest evangelists can sometimes work against a church. They come in and whip up the emotion but then comes the morning after. "They hit and run and leave you saddled with the church," Zucha said. And for the likes of me, even for the likes of the Christians at Baylor University, as Jim Parker pointed out, the connotations of this kind of preaching are all backwoods and redneck—fundamentalist, not evangelical. I compared Bill Stafford with the courtly presentation of John Phillips. The audience on Sunday had been listening carefully to Phillips and thinking about what he said. On Monday they were cheering for Stafford as a hero of the pulpit.

"I guess what I'm trying to do is overcome my emotions," he continued, "because what I really feel like doing is crying and bawling and squalling and saying, 'Oh, God, we don't need another sermon!' We need to get before God and say, 'Don't let me leave here until I start living out what I already know.' To me, that's what I'm feeling in my heart. Preachers, for God's sake, I can't waste any more time. I'm too old to care anymore. I'm tied to Jesus and Momma—Amen! That's my *wife,* not my *momma.* Amen! I just want to see the Holy Ghost, heaven-sent, gully-washer, the moving of God to break us down like a shotgun before God, to where the only way we can get back together is the Holy Ghost put us back together. . . .

"Now, I'm tryin' to get to my sermon. Pray! If you don't I *am* gonna be here till five o'clock! But anyway—"

A few voices shouted out that that would be okay with them.

"That's just five votes, boys. I need more than that!"

The house convulsed with laughter. But then Bill Stafford did get serious and spoke more calmly, generally without joking, about the preacher who talks the talk but doesn't walk the walk and the folks in the pews see through him.

"Is Swaggart real? Is Bakker real?"

You could feel the silence now.

"Who's really real? Who'll stand up and live out the reality and the truth!? Every *day* it's broken, every *day* it's weeping before God, every *day* it's the touch of God I've got to have. And that overrides everything else in my life. How can we expect our people to be real when we're not? Whenever I've got those impure thoughts, when I won't admit my temptation, and I won't admit the Jacob in me, and I won't admit the ungodly stuff that is still rising up in me at times, that I've got to get before God and say, 'Lord,

I will *not* preach unless you *clean me up* and let me walk out *full of God,* to have the annointing of God on me. I want to have a touch of God, to where the people will be *shocked* and *amazed* at the presence and the power of God. I believe that.

"Let me tell you something, friends. You'll never have a ministry that'll touch lives and churches and people until you come to the place where you're so sick of preaching sermons without the touch of God you'll say, 'God, I'll never preach again until I preach with the touch of God on my life!' We must get sick of that! Amen? We must get sick of it!"

With regret I cut pages and pages of Stafford's oratory; not everyone loves this stuff as much as I do. I appreciate it as pure talent, pure theater, while others dismiss it as pure manipulation. I rejoin the sermon at a more pensive moment: "Let me say something. Don't feel sorry for the preacher who has walked through the *deep, deep* pits of despair and problems and depression. If I could tell you—one of the greatest preachers in America today doesn't know many weeks when his wife is not in deep, dark pits of deep, *horrible* depression—but friends, remember one thing, don't feel sorry for that preacher. Feel sorry for the *other* preacher who God *ignores.* When God's through with a man and knows He can't use him anymore, He just ignores him. He doesn't bother him. He doesn't put him through any trials. . . . He's through with him. I'd rather die than walk out of here today *knowing* that this would be the end of my ministry. I live in that constant fear—not of what God might do, but that there might come the proud moment where I might cross that line to where God would say, 'I'm gonna leave you alone. I'm not messin' with you anymore. I'm just gonna let you stay with yourself.'

"And I'm afraid that's where many of us are. . . . You're gonna hurt till God heals you. When God heals you you're gonna be glad you hurt."

Stafford had been preaching for twenty minutes. He paused and looked out at us carefully. "Boy, it's gettin' tough. I know it's afternoon. I know it's your nap time, preacher, but hang on just a little longer, would you? Man, I don't mind you sleepin', but don't let your *head* fall so *far* so *fast*. That's what upsets me."

That sally woke us up.

"Adrian Rogers said something one time I thought he was crazy till he explained it. He said, 'Our greatest enemy's not communism. Our greatest enemy's God.' Boy, I had to think a minute. What do you mean? He said, 'What you've got to realize is that the Bible says 'God resisteth the proud.' Whoa, I got to thinkin'. Of all the areas in me, I've got pride as big as Jacksonville, ego big as Florida. Ladies and gentlemen, if you're gonna walk with God, He's got enough out there to keep you reduced, and just about the time you think you're topping out, you can't go any further, He'll pull the rug out from under you so you got to do it again. Amen? You say that's bad. No! That's *good!* That keeps you on *fire*, that keeps you depending on *God*, that keeps the *glory* in your life. Amen? And God knows, if there's one thing we preachers need it's to quit fearing denominations and quit fearing churches and quit fearing deacons and get in a relationship with God to where when you walk in that pulpit you *reign* like a *king* because you've been with the Holy God. And I wanna tell you, when you wrestle with the Man from Glory, when you've had a Holy God ahold of your case, these little puny fights in the church are garbage!"

Stafford told the story about the letter he got from a search committee while he was an evangelist, and he got down to the bottom of the long list of questions in the letter and there it was: "Do you have dignity in the pulpit?"

"And you know what I put down there?" Stafford asked the preachers in Jacksonville.

" 'What you see is what you get.' Needless to say, I didn't hear from 'em anymore. You know what they wanted? They wanted Jericho preaching; pampering; don't preach straight to me; don't tell me how to get holy; just let me hang on to myself and my carnality, do what I want to do. Don't tell me about godliness and confessing sin, give me a *preacherette* with a *sermonette* so I can be a *Christianette* and dress like a *majorette.*' Amen? *AMEN!*'"

The evangelist softened his voice.

"Most of our battles aren't really with the devil. We just like to talk about it. Makes us sound spiritual. Devil don't have to bother with most of us. He don't bother with dead ducks. He just bothers fellas that's wantin' to walk with God, just want to walk with Jesus. Don't care whether their name's in the limelight or not. Constantly amazed at the presence of God. Never get over the fact that He loves me.

"People come up and say, 'I heard something on you.' I say, 'Oh dear sister, I wish you hadn't heard it 'cause I got a list of 365 things about how sorry I am. One for every day. Would you like to read the list? That way you won't have to listen to gossip. Just look at one item every day and say, "Look at how sorry he is."'

"It's easier to say no to the devil than it is to say yes to God. I don't have any problem with the devil if I'm right with God. My biggest struggle wasn't with the devil. My biggest struggle was obeying God. All these people running around about the devil. 'Oh, he's demon-possessed.' Probably not. He just probably said no to God so long God's just passing him by, and the self-life is totally dominating him, and he'll never count for God."

It must be remembered when listening to preachers like Bill Stafford that hypocrisy and sin do not surprise or even disappoint Christians. In fact, they're necessary. The problem with Christianity is Christians? That idea misses the whole point. The church is justified *because* people sin. The Resurrection and our salvation are necessary *because* we sin. Without it there's no church. The fallenness of mankind is nearly the first among the first facts of the Bible. The main purpose on earth of an evangelical Christian is not to be good or do good. In a very real way, it's too late for that. The only hope is to be saved.

On my first trip to Dallas the city was engrossed in the scandal involving Walker Railey, minister at the First Methodist Church downtown, just around the corner from First Baptist. Railey's wife was strangled in the garage of their home in circumstances worthy in their staginess of an episode of *Murder, She Wrote*. *The New York Times* and other national newspapers followed the unfolding investigation in Dallas as it closed in on the pastor himself as the main suspect and also revealed his affair with Lucy Papillon, the daughter of a Methodist bishop.

Railey told the police he was at the library of Southern Methodist University at the time of the attempted murder, but he couldn't prove it and he couldn't explain a discrepancy between his story and the time of a telephone call from his car to his home, which he apparently didn't realize had been logged in at the central office. Any number of circumstances led to the widespread assumption around Dallas of Railey's guilt. He took the Fifth Amendment before the grand jury. A civil case found him responsible for the crime but he remains unindicted today, living near Los Angeles and working in a clerical position in the aerospace industry while his wife lies in a probably irreversible coma in Tyler, Texas, and their young daughter and son live with friends. The former minister still swears his innocence but few in Dallas believe him.

On that visit to Dallas I asked Gerald Cowen, professor of Greek and New Testament at Criswell, about Railey, and what he thought of the zealous and continuing coverage in distant papers. We were seated in the Burger King near the school, where Cowen had caught me by surprise by offering a brief prayer before we ate our sandwiches. Subsequently I was surprised only when this did not happen, which was almost never (in Jim Parker's company, mainly; he sometimes prays silently when he's dining in restaurants).

Cowen looked at me sharply, "Where were the stories in *The New York Times* about Paul Tillich?"

"What about Tillich?" I asked.

"About his womanizing," Cowen replied. (Indeed, Tillich's wife discusses in her autobiography her husband's philandering and fondness for pornography.)

Tillich. Bakker. Swaggart. Railey. No matter how lengthy the list of fallen preachers grows—and the clergy knows a lot better than the press how long it really is—no matter how gleefully the outside world recites that list as evidence of hypocrisy within Christendom sufficient to cast doubt on its very legitimacy, orthodox believers reiterate that sin is just another word for unadorned human nature. The church has always had scandals. Paige Patterson's book on First Corinthians is titled *The Troubled Triumphant Church.* The greatest saints have the greatest awareness of sin. Jacob, one of the heroes of the Old Testament, the subject of Bill Stafford's sermon, was a sinner. The prophet David set up the death of another man in order to obtain his wife. Vance Havner, a famous preacher from another era, was asked how it felt to be a saint of God with temptation under control, and he replied, "I pray every day that I don't become the dirty old man I might become at any moment." The great Billy Sunday said he believed in the devil for two reasons: first, the Bible said so, and second, he had done business with him.

Among evangelicals, there's a certain odd gratification when preachers do succumb. See?! We *must* have Jesus Christ. In Romans, Paul speaks of sin as almost an irresistible alien force. In the middle of a lengthy discussion he writes, "For I know that nothing good dwells within me, that is, in my flesh. I can will what is right but I cannot do it. For I do not do the good I want, but the evil I do not want is what I do. Now if I do what I do not want, it is no longer I that do it, but sin which dwells within me" (Rom. 7:18–20).

One of my bigger puzzles at Criswell was this expressed preoccupation with one's own sinfulness. The psychology of orthodox Christianity certainly flies in the face of all the secular therapies that advocate self-esteem, self-actualization, and a hundred other bromides, all emphasizing the "self-life" that Bill Stafford excoriated. William James had this to say about these secular therapies: "Many people are simply incapable of operating under an ethos of rigidity, eternal vigilance, and the like. Their machinery refuses to run at all when the bearings are made so hot and the belt so tight."

For these people, in James's opinion, a nonmoralistic relaxation is the ticket: "Mind-cure with its healthy mindedness sets lose the springs of higher life, which had been sealed up by church Christianity. . . . Protestantism has been too pessimistic as regards the natural man, Catholicism too legalistic and moralistic." However, James expressed sympathy with the Catholic observances of confession and absolution as healthy-minded purgatives of sin, something approaching today's "I'm okay, you're okay." The Protestant obsession with sin and its doctrine that sin can be atoned for but never erased during a lifetime borders on unhealthiness, in James's view. But in his evenhanded way he mainly considered the two different approaches to sin to be another proof that the two takes on Christianity are irreconcilably opposed, manifestations of two different types of personality.

I asked just about everyone with whom I talked at Criswell about this expressed preoccupation with sinfulness that needs to be set right before God. Often enough it was presented as the driving force behind the faith, but I never felt the answers got below the surface. I'm not sure they do. I know I didn't feel any overwhelming sense of guiltiness and anguish coming from them. Dave Porter, the Criswell student who finally decided against taking the job at Wet 'n Wild, had battled with his sexuality, but so does everyone else. Dave didn't seem essentially all balled up. At Criswell, try as I might, I simply couldn't find many people I would label as sick-souled, and I was on the lookout. Proportionately, I know many more such individuals, people who seem essentially crabbed in their spirit, in the secular world beyond. But then again, the Christians at Criswell have been washed in the blood of Jesus. Perhaps I should have known them before they were born again.

Bill Stafford asked, "How *badly* do you want to change? How *badly* do you want to be full of God? How *badly* do you want to walk with the power of the Holy Ghost? How *badly* do you want to walk in the pulpit and people see Jesus only? How *badly* do you want to be mightily touching lives and winning souls and weeping over a lost world? HOW BADLY? If you do, grab hold. One of the most beautiful things I've ever read in the Word of God is when a sovereign God whom I believe was this angel of the Lord in heaven"—the angel in the Genesis story of Jacob is often considered a Christophany, a preincarnation appearance of Jesus— "looked at Jacob and said, 'Turn me loose.' Well, my *soul* he could have gotten loose if He wanted to. But Jacob was doing what God wants every preacher, every man of God to do in his life, grab hold and don't turn loose until God touches you with the fresh annointing of God to be the man He purposed you to be. Amen? And Jacob held on, and you know why? Because he knew that otherwise he would have to be Jacob the rest of his life.

"I've been a preacher in a church twelve years. I've been an evangelist almost twenty years. And I believe one of the biggest problems in America is unbroken preachers."

Jacob, after he was broken by the angel, was renamed Israel. The angel touched him in the hollow of the thigh and Jacob limped off into the sunset. Bill Stafford concluded the story and then sang in a surprisingly warm baritone: "He touched me . . . Ohhhhh Jesus touched me . . . He touched me and . . . made . . . me . . . whole."

Our applause was rapturous. Homer Lindsay grasped the microphone and said, "It doesn't get any better than that."

Jerry Falwell spoke on Monday night. I admit I have never admired the man. He's not even a good speaker. Falwell's demeanor is one I think of when reminded of the line from the rabbi who said some years ago, "When I hear the term Christian America, I see barbed wire." That's a harsh denunciation and certainly unwarranted. For one thing, the rabbi was wrong because, as John

Phillips had made very clear Sunday afternoon, the Jews are special to conservative Christians. Israel had no stronger political ally than Falwell's Moral Majority before he shut it down. It has an ally today in Criswell College.

I have read that Falwell in private conversation is an open and engaging man. In Jacksonville, he came across as narrow and self-serving. He also got off on the wrong foot by repeating a joke that evangelist Junior Hill had told earlier in the conference, and better. Most of the time Falwell talked about the importance for a preacher of putting one's family first, the value of his private jet for allowing him to return home most evenings, the glorious achievements of Liberty University in Lynchburg to be topped off one day when the football team is competitive with Brigham Young and Notre Dame.

The auditorium was standing room only that evening—Falwell remains a major figure in the pantheon of conservative Christianity—but if I read the audience correctly, it was somewhat taken aback by the tone of Falwell's speech, which was all wrong. Compared with the other preachers and evangelists at the conference he stood out clearly as what he is first of all, in my opinion: a politician.

Junior Hill, a giant of a man with modest demeanor, had delivered a cogent address earlier in the day on the problems of faltering, failing, disgraced, and discouraged ministries. He started off with this joke: "I asked a pastor the other day, 'Sir, how is the work going?' and he said, 'Well, pretty good. I believe this church I'm pastoring now is dying *slower* than any church I've ever pastored.'

"Now doesn't that just bless your heart?" Hill called out. "We have a generation of *discouraged* pastors. You may be one of those men of God who came to this conference thinking if I don't get something, I can't go on. I can't go on!"

This discouraged pastor got no sustenance from Jerry Falwell.

But then came triumph, the grand finale for the revival. In the darkened auditorium at First Baptist Jacksonville spotlights lit five trumpeters on the balcony above the stage. Banners held aloft proclaimed HOW GREAT THOU ART. A huge flag emblazoned JESUS was draped above the choir. The massed orchestras filled the space with hymns. The audience cheered wildly. I was standing in the balcony with Scott Cain, a student at Criswell whose eyes were filled with tears. Earlier Scott had told me, "If we're not offering something more than the world, if being a Christian is not a joy, we're wasting our time." His faith is certainly a joy for Scott, who has a youth ministry program he takes to high schools. He lost his scholarship at Dallas Baptist University because he refused to play in the band at the Napoleon Hill Gold Medal Awards dinner at the Fairmont Hotel—an "Eastern mysticism-type" affair, Scott told me. He was accused of withdrawing from society. "Far from it!" he replied. He was holding out for the truth.

Jim Parker was a professor at Dallas Baptist at the time and lost his job as a result of the affair. The president of the school was W. Marvin Watson, LBJ's chief of staff for a while, then his postmaster general. Watson wanted a course taught at DBU on the Napoleon Hill "Think and Grow Rich" seminar, which Parker considered strictly New Age, neopagan crap, utterly inappropriate for a theologically conservative Baptist university. He believes Watson considered the material appropriate because it was endorsed and underwritten by W. Clement Stone, the Chicago insurance magnate and a Christian. Parker introduced a faculty resolution opposing the course. On a secret ballot, his position won an overwhelming victory. Then his contract was not renewed. That was 1986, and he moved over to Criswell the following fall.

~~~~~

On my last night in Jacksonville, Kenny St. John and I settled down for a long talk. He acknowledged that when we had first met three nights earlier, he had been holding back. He wasn't certain of me or my mission. I had felt the same way about him. When he realized that I was approaching evangelicalism with clean intentions, he relaxed. I told him about being approached by Philip

Martin during the Sunday night invitation. Philip had offered to help me walk the aisle. He was a freshman at Criswell, clean-cut, earnest, nineteen years old, from Tennessee, and he, like St. John, was in trouble with alcohol and drugs before he was saved. Then he became one of the Green Berets that Paige Patterson had advised me about.

I had been wondering how many times I would be obliged to refuse Christ on that trip to Jacksonville. Twice a day, at least, for four days. It often happens that a family member or friend will be asked to help, or will offer to help, a hesitant convert make the public decision and walk down the aisle. That evening I realized that someone from Criswell really *should* offer to walk with me. Within moments Philip was by my side, patting me gently on the back, asking me if I wanted him to walk down there with me. I just shook my head.

After I told St. John about the episode he looked directly at me. "You have been shown the way to be saved, haven't you?"

"Oh, yes."

"Do you want to get down on your knees right now and invite Christ into your life?"

"I can't do that, Kenny. You know that."

But he *didn't* know that. None of them do. People with that kind of Christian conviction are not kidding us. They do believe that everyone might indeed get down on his knees and accept Christ. They've seen too many people say no to Christ for too many years before suddenly one moment bursting forth in faith. The more adamant the non-Christian, the more certain are Christians of that person's susceptibility. Christians know rejection. They expect it. They understand it. And they are never surprised to see it succumb.

Late the next afternoon we were heading home to Dallas, exhausted after five days and nights of nonstop Christianity. After our dinner stop Anthony George got on the microphone and suggested that we take turns sharing our experiences from the conference. A strange mood soon set in. Night had fallen. The bus was dark. The seats had already been folded into the bunk-bed position, ready for sleeping, so people and bags and bedding were strewn everywhere. Fatigue, enforced closeness, leftover elation from the preaching and music and seminars, excitement about going home at last—all these rubbed away most of the inhibitions. The session that followed reminded me of the marathon encounter groups I used to help monitor when I was a drug counselor.

Some of the early speakers confessed to the impure motives that had taken them on the journey to Florida in the first place. They had gone as a lark, now they wanted to confess their guilt. Others referred to unnamed sins for which they needed to repent. Everyone felt that the trip had had a mighty impact on his or her faith. I listened and then decided to take my turn. I believe I can safely assert that I had the serious attention of everyone on board. Kenny St. John had told me that several of the Criswell people had come up to him over the weekend asking what to do about me. They knew I enjoyed some kind of quasi-official observer status at Criswell, but did that mean I shouldn't be officially witnessed to? St. John also said they were somewhat confused by me. I seemed like a nice guy. I listened politely and seriously to everything everyone said. I asked questions. I answered questions. I was different from the usual lost person they encounter in that I wasn't defensive or angry. They weren't sure how to approach me. Maybe they didn't know how to explain me.

On the bus I decided to help them with that latter issue. "Some of you know my story—my testimony," I began. "Others don't. I think I should make it clear now." And I did. Then I turned to the subject of the conference, a gathering of conservative Christian pastors and their wives, people with whom I shared neither faith nor, perhaps, politics nor many other cultural affinities, but whose company and hymns and preaching I had enjoyed. I said that I would never forget Adrian Rogers's sermon on Monday night. Rogers is a former president of the Southern Baptist Convention, a tall, elegant man with appropriate pulpit demeanor. He is beloved of Southern Baptists and it's easy to see why. His text that night was Genesis, chapter 22, the story of Abraham and Isaac. Even pagans who haven't read the Old Testament in decades know this story in which God has decided to test His man.

" 'Abraham!' And he said, 'Here am I.' He said, 'Take your son, your only son Isaac, whom you love, and go to the land of Moriah, and offer him there as a burnt offering upon one of the mountains of which I shall tell you' " (Gen. 22:1–2).

And Abraham prepared to do so. He "took the wood of the burnt offering, and laid it on Isaac his son; and he took in his hand the fire and the knife." They went to the place where God had directed them. Isaac asked his father where the lamb was, which he believed was to be the object of sacrifice. Abraham answered, "God will provide himself the lamb for a burnt offering, my son." But when they got to the place and built the altar and laid the wood, Abraham bound his son Isaac in place on the altar.

"Then Abraham took forth his hand, and took the knife to slay his son. But the angel of the Lord called to him from heaven, and said, 'Abraham! Abraham!' And he said, 'Here I am.' He said, 'Do not lay your hand on the lad or do anything to him; for now I know that you fear God, seeing you have not withheld your son, your only son, from me' " (Gen. 22:10–12).

Then Abraham looked around and there was the ram, its horns caught in a thicket. He slew the animal and sacrificed it as a burnt offering. As Adrian Rogers narrated the conclusion of the story, he spread his long arms low and wide in front of him, and then brought them slowly upward and closer together as he said, "As Abraham and Isaac had started up one side of that mountain, the ram started up the other."

Say what you see; see what you say. Jerry Vines's instructions to the conference on the art of preaching were perfectly embodied by Adrian Rogers. A chill had run up my spine. It was a magnificent moment in the pulpit. Rogers saw Abraham, he saw Isaac, he saw that ram and its destiny on that mountaintop, and he saw God. He almost convinced me to see, too. I told the people from Criswell that I wasn't totally impervious to the beauties of Christian faith, and I wasn't. I'm not. I thanked them for taking me along and concluded with the promise that if I ever did walk the aisle as a Christian, in whatever kind of church, wherever it might be, young Philip would be by my side. (He subsequently left Criswell.)

Then I crawled into my bunk and listened to some other confessions. Soon I realized that one young woman two bunks away was crying, and continued to, as others on the bus spoke, for what seemed half an hour. The tears were pouring out. Finally she took the microphone but was so emotionally wrought she could barely speak. Her name was Cheryl Baker and this was the hardest thing she had ever done, she said, and hesitated.

"And it concerns Mike Bryan."

I had been lying down. Now I sat up. Cheryl said she was burdened by the weight of my lost soul. Something about my testimony had shivered through her like an arrow. She had been weeping all that time for me. She finished talking, walked back down the aisle past me, we hugged as best we could, and she went on to her own bunk. Someone else began speaking. I didn't hear a word of it. I was frantically trying to understand how someone I had met only a few days previously, with whom I hadn't exchanged fifty words all together, could break down under the weight of a stranger's forlornness, as she perceived it. In Cheryl's heart and mind and world there's only one way to heal any hurt or help any need, and she knew I hadn't accepted that way. If I hadn't realized it before, I certainly did that night on the bus heading home to Dallas: take away the church services, the fine preaching, the indoctrination, the group dynamics, harangues about sin and guilt, take away John 14:6, Revelation, chapter 20, the resurrection appearances, and the entire Bible, even, and you are left with the true heart of the Christian faith and all the others, which is simply the human heart itself. That's hardly profound but it's a fact easily forgotten. Remembered, it tempers my own more dismissive moments.

CHAPTER 18

C lasses at Criswell College let out at one o'clock. One afternoon shortly after my return from Jacksonville the doorbell rang at two. Young Philip was standing there, Bible in hand. This would be an official session, I realized, and it occurred to me that my position at the school might be different, post-Jacksonville. At that time I was staying with friends in Dallas. I had just located my furnished apartment—Criswell student Dave Porter's old place—and I invited Philip to drive over with me so I could handle the paperwork on the sublease. When we got back to my friends' house we sat in the car and talked. I didn't think I should invite him into their house, and I also admit I was a little embarrassed by his presence. Those friends thought this book the worst of all my ideas. The husband, a recently converted Catholic who accompanied me to a service at First Baptist and stared around at the scene, a far cry from his dour Jesuit services, considers Paige Patterson the arch-devil. He turned down my suggestion that the three of us have lunch or dinner one day. I hadn't asked Patterson if he wanted any part of that, but I was pretty sure he'd have been delighted to participate in the colloquy. That's his raw meat.

"Why?" I asked Philip. Why do you evangelize? First, he is commanded to do so by the Bible. Second, he said, "If you feel the way I feel, you just naturally want to share it."

How does Philip feel? Saved. Possessed with a conviction I cannot comprehend. Maybe there's an analogy with falling in love, I don't know. Paige Patterson drew an analogy with a woman's experience of delivering a baby. He told me: "Being in on the preparations for that baby does give a level of comprehension on a psychological and spiritual level, but that still comes short of experiential knowledge, which is ultimately the final form of knowledge, as far as I'm concerned. And short of a conversion experience in which a person discovers the release of the freedom of being forgiven, and the gratitude of his heart that comes from being forgiven, and coming to have a genuine love for people who have not found the Lord, that is another world.

"I think by the time you finish here, Mike, you will come as near to comprehending and grasping that as anyone can come, short of experiential knowledge. You'll never grasp the intensity of it, the mandate of it, the compelling nature of it, but you will at least see us for what we are, see us as folks who have lots of problems and difficulties and failures and foibles like anybody else, but who do intensely believe, to the point where most of us are willing if necessary to hazard their lives for it. That much you can get."

Obviously my talk on the bus had led at least some of the students to believe that I was about to make the Christian leap of faith, even though I hadn't told the Jacksonville group that Philip would be by my side *when* I walked the aisle. I had said *if,* with no intention of implying the occasion was imminent or even likely, but the distinction wasn't interpreted that way.

Sitting in the car I said to Philip, "You know, you guys are a minority, certainly so as you define real Christianity."

He acknowledged this as true, but, again, the proof or logic or

whatever that the evasive outsider demands is the proof that Philip
disdains. Many are called but few are chosen. . . . Narrow is the
way. . . . Foolishness to the Greeks. Philip told me about the pain
he sometimes feels for not doing enough, for not preaching well
enough, for not talking about the Lord with enough people every
day.

This was the emotional trauma that had so overcome Cheryl
Baker that last evening on the bus. Shortly after Philip's visit I was
able to arrange dinner with Cheryl and her boyfriend Denny
Gorena. Cheryl isn't a student at Criswell; Denny is the student,
and the two had plans to be married (and eventually did). Cheryl
worked at a Dallas church as the pastor's secretary and head of the
outreach program. She was baptized and saved when she was eight
years old, but in 1988, when she was twenty-one, she began to
realize, thanks to "some things happening in my personal life,"
that she didn't have a truly personal relationship with Jesus Christ.
Her job at the church, she realized, was just a job. At about that
time the pastor gave a series of sermons on the Book of Revelation,
and Cheryl became frightfully aware that her destiny on the day
of judgment was not assured. She wanted to get this straight. She
knew what she had to do, and she was ready, but she was also
worried what the people at the church would say. Would they feel
she had been hypocritical before? Then one Sunday the preacher
read Psalm 29, and with the very first verse—"Ascribe to the Lord,
O heavenly things, ascribe to the Lord glory and strength. Ascribe
to the Lord the glory of his name; worship the Lord in holy
array"—tears poured from Cheryl's eyes, and she cried for the rest
of the service. At the invitation, she walked forward and accepted
Jesus Christ as her personal savior. And of course she had worried
for nothing. She was welcomed with hugs and kisses. This happens
all the time: people who are believed by one and all, including
themselves, to be saved, suddenly realize they are not, really. It
happened while I was at Criswell with Amy Kerr, the first student
I met at the school, in Danny Akin's New Testament classroom.
It had happened years before to George Davis, who gave the early

chapel talk on Christian sexuality. There's no stigma whatsoever attached to this turn of events. You can carry on for fifty years as a faithful evangelical Christian and then decide it hasn't been sufficiently real all that time, but now it is, and when you announce this fact, it will be fully accepted. Professions of faith are seldom doubted. The genuineness of that profession is your problem; everything will come out in the wash at the end of the world.

When I had delivered my little talk on the bus I had triggered Cheryl's own memories of vivid fear for the state of her soul. That's why she had been crying. Still, she was genuinely concerned about me—but more concerned, I would assume, about her father and brother, who are not active Christians.

We nonbelievers make it hard on ourselves, Cheryl told me. "The answer is Christ," she said. "The Bible says so."

"The Bible says so!" This truth screams out in their heads. When someone replies, "So what?"—and this is the implication of any rejection—they look on with pity. Often they will cite the fourteenth chapter of John's gospel, a depiction of the Last Supper. Jesus' disciple Thomas asks him, "Lord, we do not know where you are going; how can we know the way?"

Thomas is confused because Jesus has just said that He was going ahead to prepare a place, and would return for them, and they would know the way. Jesus replies to Thomas in the famous sixth verse, "I am the way, and the truth, and the life; no one comes to the Father, but by me."

This verse evokes as well as any in the New Testament the chief power of Christianity: the simplicity that is the whole secret of the faith. Know Jesus Christ in your heart and you understand everything that matters. What other religion, faith, philosophy, or psychology can match Christianity in this regard?

Truly, there is felt by all human beings a yearning for a simple truth. Much has changed in two millennia; this hasn't. (The New-Agers of my acquaintance seem to be a contradiction in this regard: they say so many different things, using language that says so little.) Christ on the cross answers all the needs of the heart and relegates all questions of the mind to their proper subservient place. For the earliest converts to the new faith, the Old Testament did not offer this degree of simplicity, devolving as it did into that legalism of the Pharisees against which Jesus rebelled. And that devolution began quite early in the tradition, as witnessed by the laboriously detailed instructions (seven columns' worth) for building the ark of the tabernacle, the sanctuary in which God would dwell in the midst of his people. This was a tribal god and the issues resolved by his worship were social and political. The Messiah the Jews were seeking throughout the last millennium before Christ would be a political figure, and this of course is a main reason most of them rejected the candidacy of Jesus, who called them to a diametrically opposed, intensely personal salvation. Those Jews who did accept the call of Christ considered the salvation thus delivered vastly superior to any offered by the old faith. What are the justices of the world measured against the eternal love of Jesus Christ—God Himself—for *you?*

Christianity wagers everything on our acceptance of the power of a single *person* to define and change lives. Theoretically Christianity teaches the Trinity. Theoretically a relationship with the Holy Spirit is vital. I heard this message the entire term at Criswell, but I'm still certain that the concept and meaning of the Holy Spirit is nothing more than distant theology for most Christians. The Holy Spirit might mean something to Cheryl Baker and the Criswell students and staff; I don't imagine it means much, if anything, to average Southern Baptist church-goers. How could it? Week after week they are pounded with exhortations to develop a personal relationship with Jesus Christ, Jesus Christ, Jesus Christ—but then once a year comes a sermon about maintaining a similar relationship with a concept called the Holy Spirit. It won't take. From what I saw at Criswell and other conservative churches, evangelical Christianity calls for the worshiping of Jesus Christ, and that's it. Christ alone is the source of this faith's compelling attraction; the whole idea of the Trinity, though fundamental to the theology, is functionally irrelevant. One Pentecostal sect does in fact worship the deity of Jesus alone; Christo-unitarianism, this might be called. Tens of millions of other Christians might as well join that group.

God? God is a list of superlatives, and despite all the preaching that He is a personality, most believers and unbelievers alike think of Him as a force of some sort. The Holy Spirit? Some references in the Bible. But Jesus Christ? He's the man-God who walked on earth and resurrected *Himself* from the dead—"the greatest man who ever lived," a relative of mine said one Christmas. It's people we are mainly interested in, and the religion that invested everything in one person—monotheism *personified*—is either a stroke of shrewd human genius or God's final truth.

~~~~~~

I asked Cheryl Baker, "Why do we reject Jesus?"

"Because you want to live your own lives. You don't want to give anything up. You don't want to live for Jesus."

That was as concise and accurate an assessment as I heard at Criswell. At some point I asked Paige Patterson why we don't believe. "A chorus of reasons," he replied quickly, and with a nice irony. "One, satanic deception. The Bible makes it very clear that Satan has blinded our eyes."

He must have noticed my eyes glazing over. "Well," he continued, "we do believe such a malignant spirit exists in the universe. We hate to think we can explain all the evil that exists in the world on the basis of man by his lonesome.

"The second reason you don't believe is human pride. It's a fortuitous coincidence of the English language that the middle letter of both sin and pride is the same letter, and the one that it happens to be. Coming to Christ is basically a terrible injury to one's pride. You have to say, 'I'm a good-for-nothing, rebellious sinner, and furthermore I realize there's no way I can possibly help myself, and so I'm going to place all my faith on a first-century Jew who led a small uprising in Palestine, got himself crucified, and I believe rose from the grave.' That's pretty outrageous. There's not a lot of room for human pride in that sort of deal.

"It has always been easier to lead folks who are less genteel to Christ. The bigger the sinner, the easier it is to lead him to Christ. With a moral, genteel north Dallas slick, it's hard."

Danny Akin said in class one day, "We must acknowledge that intellectuals aren't going to fall over themselves in a rush to embrace Christianity in the twentieth century. They are idolators of their knowledge."

We (intellectuals and the rest of us) are also victims of our times. We don't want to see ourselves as playing some kind of role in the storybook vision of the world taught by Christianity. It stands to reason that acceptance of the radical self-surrender called for by Jesus Christ will be on the wane in purportedly egalitarian, democratic societies. That sacred vision and this social culture don't fit together; a secular outlook may be the inevitable consequence. The greatest of all the stumbling blocks many people have with biblical Christianity may be its inescapable message that we are part of some experiment played out for the pleasures and purposes of God. Consider the introduction to the Old Testament story of Job. His travails are the result of a bet, in effect, between God and Satan. To the lay reader this is certainly the sense of the dialogue. My friends don't care to worship any god who toys with mankind for the sake of wagered bets, but their refusal is made easy because they don't believe any such god exists. The people at Criswell have no problem with the story of Job or its hierarchical vision of the world. They are honored to be a part of the show. They are astonished that the holy God of this incredible cosmos has chosen *them* as individuals to be saved.

And thus we arrive at the issues of predestination, omniscience, omnipotence, theodicy (the technical term for reconciling God's omnipotence and goodness with the existence of evil; "the problem of evil," in the vernacular). We speak now of Calvinism, and these issues were brought into sharp focus at Criswell on February 6, the day that Luel Pantoja died after a lengthy struggle with cancer. Luel was the eighteen-year-old son of Luis Pantoja, professor of my Cultural Milieu class at the school. I had not known about the illness at all, but most of the students did. Luel was a student at the Christian Academy on the eleventh floor of the building that housed Criswell College.

Memorial services were held in the auditorium of the church. W. A. Criswell spoke first, and his text was Second Corinthians, chapter 5, which begins:

For we know that if the earthly tent we live in is destroyed, we have a building from God, a house not made with hands, eternal in the heavens. . . . So we are always of good courage; we know that while we are at home in the body we are away from the Lord, for we walk by faith, not by sight. We are of good courage, and we would rather be away from the body and at home with the Lord. (2 Cor. 5:1–8)

Luis Pantoja stepped behind the pulpit. He spoke quietly of his son's illness, of the recent trip he had taken to the Holy Land, of how Luel had devoted the last year of his life to witnessing for the Lord. On the very last days in the hospital, Luel spoke to the staff at every opportunity about Jesus Christ.

"The answer of prayer is life," Luis Pantoja said of the Christian way, "and the answer of prayer is death."

He told the audience that he was wearing his son's watch, because Luel was now in a place where he would not need it. It was midafternoon in Dallas, Texas, but Pantoja said in closing, "Good *morning* to you all."

Most of us in the audience had tears in our eyes; some were weeping openly. Luis Pantoja was not, and I marveled at his composure. So did Paige Patterson, who spoke briefly and acknowledged that under the circumstances most of us—himself included—would not have had the strength or the courage to speak as calmly and as eloquently as Luis Pantoja had.

After Patterson's brief remarks, he told us that he had asked and received permission from the Pantoja family to proceed with the traditional conclusion of a Southern Baptist worship service, the invitation to accept Jesus Christ as Lord and Savior. Patterson asked for bowed heads and closed eyes. He told anyone who that day wanted to accept Christ into his or her life to raise a hand. "Only you and this minister will know of this statement," he said, and I wondered whether he was looking at me. He might have been, since I was perhaps the only person in the audience whom he knew to be lost.

"In a gathering of this size," he continued, "there must be a few who feel the need to make this commitment." Two people apparently raised their hands. I came within an eyelash of raising my own. What happened is this: Luis Pantoja's marvelously courageous tribute to his son had, for me and I would think many others present, struck to the heart of the problem. Forget death; consider life. The world's demands are not mortised to fit neatly with our own needs; quite the contrary. To use the Christian terminology, we are fallen and do suffer and do need help, whether from ministers, priests, books, shrinks, family, friends, whatever.

The semester before I went to Criswell I had taken an evening class at Rice University in Houston. The subject was atheism, a refresher course for me, in effect. We reviewed Nietzsche, Marx, Freud, and the others, and near the end of the course the teacher cited the British philosopher Anthony Kenny and his book *The God of the Philosophers*, in which Kenny asks whether it is ridiculous for agnostics to pray. In partial answer, he notes that it would not be deemed ridiculous for the sailor stranded in the middle of the Atlantic Ocean to fire shots from a pistol, hopeless though it might be that those shots would ever be heard. Is it absurd, Kenny asks, to draw an analogy with the spiritually lost human being who doesn't believe in the traditional Judeo-Christian God, yet feels the urge in moments of acute sympathy or suffering to pray anyway? No, it is not absurd.

So I don't apologize for almost raising my hand. I wonder about anyone who would not *almost* do so. Who would not want to pray or do something by way of reaching out in moments of keen vulnerability?—Only the truly truculent materialist, to use Michael Polanyi's phrase from *Personal Knowledge*. I know a lot of these people and I can't believe they benefit from their stubborn refusal even to acknowledge weakness and yearning.

Shortly after that service for Luel Pantoja, Keith Eitel, professor of missiology at Criswell and teacher of my Religious Belief Systems class, acknowledged in his opening prayer in class that "the mind knows Luel is in a better place, but the heart still grieves." Nevertheless, Eitel cautioned, the Christian cannot pray for a contradiction between God's omniscience and His omnipotence. Eitel is a Calvinist. So is Luis Pantoja. All conservative Christians are, to some extent, Calvinists. That's a word that evokes non-Christians' disdain, standing as it does for the most rigid vision of God's kingdom. Danny Akin told me that when he first arrived at Criswell College and was introduced to Calvinism, he thought it was "the dumbest thing I'd ever heard of." Then he started reading his Bible. And it's true: the Calvinist interpretation of God and His creation is clear in the Scriptures and it's also logical, given the hypothesis—the presupposition—of the omniscient and omnipotent God. Official Calvinism now has five points, summarized in the acronym TULIP—Total depravity; Unconditional election; Limited atonement; Irresistible grace; and Perseverance of the saints—and people who have thought about these matters a great deal disagree on certain points. The Criswell faculty has three-, four-, and five-pointers, but, frankly, these distinctions aren't worth getting into. They do, however, require an explanation vis-à-vis the doctrine of inerrancy. Inerrantists want to forbid discussion of the literal truth of almost every word of the book, yet they allow for differences in the major conclusions derived from those words: Criswell professors score differently on the Calvinism scale; conservative Christians disagree on questions of eschatology deriving from the book of Revelation; Criswell and Patterson disagree on whether a certain passage of Scripture forbids divorce or polygamy. But inerrantists say that if you don't believe in the *accuracy* of Scripture first, it doesn't matter what you believe on the "derivative issues" because you can build any belief by picking and choosing exhibits from the Bible. Jim Parker drew an analogy with the United States Constitution, which is inerrant and authoritative for our earthly affairs, but is also interpreted in diverse ways in the real world.

The elaboration of Calvinism gets extremely technical—way over my head—and is utterly irrelevant for the average believer, for whom Calvinist theology boils down to this: if an omnipotent and omniscient God created the universe, He must by definition know everything that is going to happen in that universe or He wouldn't be omniscient, and He must cause everything to happen or He wouldn't be omnipotent. Jesus said not a leaf falls without the knowledge of God. In Exodus, Pharaoh's stubbornness in releasing the tribe of Moses is plainly stated as ordained by God: "But I will harden Pharaoh's heart, and though I multiply my signs and wonders in the land of Egypt, Pharaoh will not listen to you," (Ex. 7:3–4). And in Acts 2:23 Peter tells the men of Israel: "This Jesus, delivered up according to the definite plan and foreknowledge of God. . . ."

Everything is envisioned, if not ordained (there's a subtle distinction between these two, for many evangelicals): the fall of Adam and Eve, the rejection and crucifixion of Christ, the Holocaust, the long illness and then the death of Luel Pantoja. This the Christian can know. Why these things happen the Christian cannot know.

God is holiness and righteousness by definition. How dare the created judge the Creator, the sinful judge the pure? Ancient folktale or the Word of God, the Old Testament Book of Job remains the last word on the problem of evil: We must trust that in the long run—in heaven and hell—justice even we can understand will be served. (Which do we like better, the problem of absurdity in a godless world or the problem of evil in an ordained one?)

Another conundrum for Christians posed by Calvinist doctrine is prayer. If God has preordained everything, what is the logic of beseeching Him for divine intercession? Aren't we asking God to contradict Himself, or to change His mind, neither of which is possible, by definition? The orthodox Christian answer is that this is another mystery of the cosmos. Whatever the logic or lack of it that underlies orthodox prayer, the Judeo-Christian faith has historically required that God hear and respond to specific prayers. Prayer and even healing services are on the rise in all sorts of churches, not just in the more conservative denominations. Catholic and mainline Protestant churches are instituting them, too, and maybe they should. The logic may be questionable but the doctrine is right there in the Bible.

～～～～

A few weeks after the memorial service for his son, Luis Pantoja and I had a long conversation in his book-lined office at the college. I told him that his composure and eloquence during the memorial service were as meaningful a tribute to his Christian faith as any I could think of. I would never have been able to tell my friends, "Good morning to you all."

He replied, "Hope has never failed us. Hope is the *effectiveness* of faith."

Our conversation turned to Calvinism, to the election of individuals for salvation or damnation, to the fate of my own soul. In the evangelical Calvinist view, God must know who will choose Him and who will reject Him. More precisely, He knows whom He has elected and whom He has rejected, and there is nothing we can do about it. There are three main passages in the New Testament that address this issue. The main one is Eph. 1:3–4: "Blessed be the God and Father of our Lord Jesus Christ, who has blessed us in Christ with every spiritual blessing in the heavenly places, even as he chose us in him before the foundation of the world, that we should be holy and blameless before him."

That's it in plain language: God chose us before the foundation of the world—before the beginning of time.

Romans 8:28–30 reads:

We know that in everything God works for good with those who love him, who are called according to his purpose. For those whom he foreknew he also predestined to be conformed to the image of his Son. . . . And those whom he predestined he also called; and those whom he called he also justified; and those whom he justified he also glorified.

The problem posed by this doctrine is obvious: if the chosen have no choice, why evangelize them? They must choose Christ sooner or later; it is ordained. Also, how do we reconcile God's omniscience and arbitrary choice of the elect with the human freedom that we—including most Christians—also feel obliged to uphold? Einstein asked in a letter, "How is it possible to think of holding men responsible for their deeds and thoughts before such an almighty Being?" Therefore Einstein dismissed such a Being.

During a discussion on Calvinism and evangelizing in Danny Akin's classroom a student called out to general merriment, "Let's close school and go home!" Akin replied that he senses paradox, not contradiction, in the idea that God knows in a loving way what we will do, yet we have free will to do as we choose. What else can the Christian say? Paradox beyond our understanding, just as with the Hypostatic Union in christological theory, in which Jesus Christ is fully God and fully man. In Jacksonville, John Phillips drew the neat analogy of a chess game played between grandmaster and novice: "The professional exercises his sovereignty and you exercise yours. The problem is that *He* is a better player."

"Nobody knows who's chosen," Pantoja told me in his office. "The election is God's prerogative of action and revelation. This election doesn't concern us on earth. Our responsibility is the preaching of the gospel." A Calvinist of Pantoja's persuasion believes that an individual can be elected by God but not *yet* saved by his own choice of faith. This gives the evangelist his rationale.

Pantoja related his own attitude about the lost to that of Jesus Christ when he told the disciples: "And if anyone will not receive you or listen to your words, shake off the dust from your feet as you leave that house or town. Truly, I say to you, it shall be more tolerable on the day of judgment for the land of Sodom and Gomorrah than for that town" (Matt. 10:14–15).

Toward the end of our discussion Pantoja asked, "Is there any good reason to reject what I have said?"

All I could reply was, "Yes. I don't believe it."

Pantoja then said, "I have done my part."

I asked him about close friends he must have who are also not saved. I based this supposition on my reading of him as a man who circulates widely in secular culture: his Cultural Milieu classroom was infused with a pervasive, occasionally corrosive irony I thought came from the streets, and following one class he had asked me which of Woody Allen's movies I'd recommend. In his office Pantoja said he has about forty people for whom he regularly prays. "Honestly," he concluded, "from a theological point of view, I feel sorry for them."

He asked if I had ever heard of Pascal's wager. I had. Blaise Pascal was the seventeenth-century French scientist and makeshift theologian whose *Pensées* were admired by my generation. In addition to formulating the law that led to modern-day hydraulics, Pascal could be considered one of the earliest Christian existentialists, with his view that we cannot approach God through reason. A mystical faith is the only way. And yet his famous wager calls for coldhearted calculation. It has been formulated with different emphases, but in essence the wager argues that if Christianity is false, we have lost nothing important by adhering to it, while if true we have lost everything eternal by rejecting it. Likewise, and in the evangelizing sense Pantoja and I were discussing, if Christianity is false, Christians will have misled people but won't be held accountable for that behavior, while if it's true and they don't evangelize, they will be held accountable.

A couple of other times at Criswell I was asked why Pascal's wager didn't convince me to believe. If the Christians are wrong, what's to lose? Not much. If they're right, what's to gain? Everything. I conceded the logic but added the obvious reply that belief—faith—must come from some motivation beyond mere calculation, which would not be faith at all. It certainly wouldn't fool God. That's the problem with all conservative polemics that urge us to return to Christianity for the sake of morality and the social order. It's easier said than done. Faith is either in the air or it's not; it's either alive or dead. Or so I thought. Then Jim Parker surprised me one day when he said in a relevant context, "Faith is a minor matter. It's not the amount of faith. It's the focus. Remember Jesus: faith the size of a mustard seed can move the mountain."

Preachers tell the story about the man who is "trying" to become a Christian. The preacher then asks, "Have you ever *tried* to be an elephant?" They believe this settles the issue, but Parker doesn't. People do try to believe, he told me, and there's nothing wrong with that. Non-Christians, waffling Christians, detouring Christians all seem to believe that religious faith must be a consuming passion without qualification; if they don't have it, they don't belong. I had this same general notion but Parker assured me it is erroneous. Some people do believe with heart and soul, and never doubt. He's among them. Others—Christians, good Christians—don't have that conviction. It is not necessary. People do *try* to believe, and there's nothing wrong with that, Parker said. In fact, one behavioral school of thought proposes that behavior actually precedes and creates emotion. Act as though you believe and you may start doing so. But however you get there, Parker cautioned, at some point you do have to cross over from struggling for faith to a final, genuine acceptance of, and trust in, Jesus Christ. Doubt if you must, but trust nevertheless.

Once or twice I said to my Criswell interlocutors, "Hey, I'm just not chosen!" They were not amused. That's an easy cop-out and, in my particular case, also a falsehood, they believed, because why else would I be at Criswell. I must have been brought there by God.

And following the Jacksonville trip and my little talk on the bus, this opinion perhaps became more widespread.

~~~~~~

Young Philip Martin and Cheryl Baker were puzzled by my apparent lack of concern for the future of my soul in all eternity. "Eternal" is a word with an especially potent, literal meaning for Cheryl. Since her experience in church that Sunday evening she has been much more serious about her outreach work, because now she understands that what she does could affect someone's eternity. However, she also knows that no one's salvation depends on anyone else's personal witnessing. Young Christians often become burdened with the knowledge that if they don't share the gospel with an individual right now, that individual could die in a car crash the very next moment and be doomed to hell. Philip relayed this scenario to me while we were driving to my new apartment. He wasn't kidding.

In the final analysis, for some of the faithful, the purpose of Christianity is to deal with death. The question came up early and often at Criswell, and I told people that concern for my fate at death has never been an issue. I've always assumed it will be at that moment just as it was before I was born: nothingness. Not a knowledge of nothingness (a pretty good hell, that), but pure nothingness. Dorothy Sayers, the mystery writer and Christian apologist, despised this excuse for rejecting Christianity. She wrote that to have no interest in death is to have no interest in life. I'm living proof that's not true, so far.

One problem for the Christian faith today is that it has no meaning in biblical terms without this eschatological element— judgments for eternity—but in this ecumenical era many people don't have the stomach for that judgment. Hell is a major stumbling block; it isn't held in high favor by most theologians working today. Even many of the evangelicals at Criswell exercise caution on the subject. Young Philip finds it difficult to preach about hell, to tell someone he's going to hell. When I asked him bluntly about my own fate he hesitated . . . but, yes, I'm going to hell, and it hurt him to say that. It hurt him to *know* it.

If you accept the special revelation of the Bible, you're committed to the doctrine of hell. Neither the Hebrew concept of *Sheol*, used dozens of times in the Old Testament, nor its near-equivalent in the Greek, *Hades*, used eleven times in the New Testament, has fire-and-brimstone connotations, but the Greek term *Gehenna* (derived from Hinnom, a valley south of Jerusalem at which trash and dead animals were buried) is used twelve times in the New Testament in contexts that definitely denote a place of future punishment—hell.

Two images dominate these depictions: fire and separation from God. In almost all Christian denominations today, even the most conservative, the fire is downplayed. Jesus is the only authority who uses images of fire (Mark 9:43, 49), and Jim Parker explained today's evangelical interpretation that Jesus was speaking of fire metaphorically, in the manner in which we speak of a broken heart.

The contemporary focus is on separation from God. This phrase could be just another meaningless locution, but Parker emphasized that this is a quite real separation in a real place in another dimension of reality in which we retain our individual consciousness, certainly, if not our bodies. (The authors of the book *Heaven—A History* propose that concepts of the better place have also changed from the original, biblical concept. The original God-centered heaven has been replaced today by many Christians with a vision of a paradise of *human* relationships and activities. A member of my family told me she expects to greet the whole family there, including me.)

In a most diplomatic mood Paige Patterson commented to me one afternoon, "I hope when we come to eternity that we find we have misread the Bible some way. When the Bible tells me about heaven and hell and eternal condemnation for those who die outside Christ, I believe it. But I also hope I'm wrong. Absolutely. I could hope that even for the Hitlers and Mussolinis and Marxs and

Stalins of the world. I don't see how any man can obtain pleasure, without being a cosmic sadist, in someone else's suffering. I'd be delighted to discover in eternity that punishment is either nonexistent or temporal in its duration, and that there is some kind of purgatory, like our Romanist friends imagine. All I'm saying is that I don't see it on the pages of Scripture. The best as I can understand the Bible, for whatever reasons may be in the mind and heart of God, it seems that there is a place of eternal condemnation to which those outside of Christ must go. Of course you can understand that this becomes a motivating factor for us.

"One of the reasons we're motivated to do what we do . . . well, a case in point is you. You at one time said to me that you were surprised by our openness here. And I think I hinted, if I remember correctly, that you suspected an ulterior motive on our part— that we would have designs on you. Well, that's true. I thought you had an appointment here that God made for you in eternity. God sent you here for us to love and to pray for.

"The second point I would make is that we're dealing with a God who, on the one hand, is infinite love, but on the other is infinite justice and holiness, and he must abdicate his position as God if he is anything else, if *every* evil is not ultimately met and satisfied in some way. Now, God has provided two ways for justice to be done: one way is to accept, through Jesus' dying in our place, a justice we don't deserve. However, one of the sovereign decrees of God was that man should be free. So a man may choose not to accept God's first remedy for justice, in which case he chooses to accept God's second remedy for justice."

On my departure for Criswell, friends had asked whether I would "fight back." I said no. Why should I? My nonreligion doesn't propose that anyone who doesn't accept it is doomed to hell. If I did believe so, I would rethink my position. I agree with Paige Patterson: it would be a gross denial of the evangelical faith *not* to evangelize people and warn them about hell. After I had been at Criswell for a while friends asked if I wasn't insulted by being accosted all the time and condemned to hell. But I was not accosted, nor did I ever sense delight in my lostness. Students were in fact crying about it, in at least one instance. Nor was I overly concerned they might actually be right. I assured young Philip it didn't bother me to be living under his sentence of death, and so he shouldn't feel badly about my rejection. But he must.

One of the more interesting thoughts on hell that I encountered during my term at Criswell did not come from the evangelicals at the school. I had tracked down Don Pevey, the pastor at the Methodist church in Houston favored many years earlier by my parents. He lived with his wife in San Antonio, where he had moved quite a few years ago and where, after putting in several years as a district superintendent in the Methodist hierarchy, he had retired.

When I first reached him by telephone he remembered my father, whom he had not seen, heard of, or probably even thought about in at least two decades.

"Worked for an oil company, right?"

"Right."

Curious about this project, Pevey said he would be happy to meet with me, and subsequently we had a long conversation at a restaurant in San Antonio. Before we met I couldn't remember at all what he looked or sounded like, but when he walked through the door of the restaurant I knew who he was, and when he spoke I recalled the voice. He's a short, stocky man with the engaging warmth and friendliness every pastor should have, but a surprising number don't. He loves to tell stories; almost every point he makes veers into one. He told me a story when I asked him about Methodists and hell.

"I have a lot of trouble with heaven and hell," he told me bluntly. "I haven't got it all worked out, but let me tell you about the tremendous experience I had when my brother Bill died. He was an alcoholic. He didn't live anywhere. He just roamed. I only knew that he had died when I was notified because my name had been on some of his papers. He was buried in an unmarked grave in San Angelo, Texas.

"I started thinking. What has happened to the spirit of my brother? Is it even possible that this man who is not respected even by his own children—two wonderful children—could go to the same place on his death that my mother went—and my mother was a saintly woman. And I kept answering my question, 'I hope so.' Then I thought that if I could love my brother enough to forgive him for what he did to our parents, to his son and daughter, to my own family—because we had gotten him out of jail a couple of times, brought him to live with us—am I, Don Pevey, better than God?

"Can I love enough that I can forgive someone who has really hurt me and my loved ones, but God says, 'That's tough, he's gonna burn forever'? Or does God have a greater love still?"

Pevey believes God has a greater love still. When evangelicals respond, as they would, that this emotion is understandable but not biblical, Peavey replies, "Yes, but Jesus said of the priests and the Roman soldiers, 'Father, forgive them. . . .' Of all the blasphemies, the greatest is surely to kill the Son of God. And yet the Son of God said to the whole world, 'Forgive them, for they know not what they do.'

"So. I don't have an eternal hell."

Another Texas churchman with whom this subject arose was William Farmer, a professor at Perkins School of Theology, a branch of Southern Methodist University. After my departure from Criswell, Farmer made the small headlines in Dallas by affiliating with Roman Catholicism while also remaining a member of the Methodist denomination. (After I left Criswell a prominent Lutheran theologian, Rev. Richard John Neuhaus, quit his denomination in order to seek ordination as a Catholic priest.)

Definitely not an evangelical, Farmer is nevertheless an acquaintance and friend of Paige Patterson, and he has even spoken in chapel at Criswell College, where he angered many of the students by addressing a prayer to God the *Mother*. Perhaps there aren't too many *better* ways to anger evangelicals, for whom God is definitely a male personality—and fairly enough, because that's the way the Bible reads throughout.

Informed that I was writing about Patterson and Criswell College and Christianity, Farmer invited me to his office one afternoon. The place was a chaos of books, not surprisingly because he is a leading New Testament scholar and one of the world's experts on the Synoptic Problem. (I won't pretend this issue is critical to the thrust of this book, but it is an excellent example of the kind of biblical studies that many bright Christians—conservative and liberal—are devoting their academic lives to, so a brief explication is justified. When were the Gospels written, and in which order? That's the Synoptic Problem. In general, conservative scholars chose the earliest dates of composition for all four gospels, bringing their composition as close as possible to eyewitness accuracy, while liberals prefer later dates, allowing more time for the embellishment inherent in oral storytelling, and for the development of the liturgical formulas that help to diminish subsequent claims of strict factuality [inerrancy]. The possible dates range from A.D. 50 to 80. Traditionally, Matthew was held to be the first of the gospels, but most New Testament scholars now believe that the first one was written by Mark. William Farmer is a tenacious defender of the traditional order: Matthew was the first composition, after all. The debate is incredibly technical. Some of the illustrations used in articles on the Synoptic Problem, with arrows pointing this way and that between various groupings of verses, look like equations in organic chemistry, complete with catalysts and reagents.)

But in his office Farmer and I set aside the Synoptic Problem and talked about liberal and conservative Christianity in general—leading eventually to the status of hell in his theology. Immediately he expressed an admiration for Patterson and the evangelicals at Criswell, almost a defense of them. He suggested that *all* Christians would be wise to consider the possibility that there indeed ought to be some basic beliefs for the faith, as evangelicals insist but many nominal Christians deny with all their equivocations. Farmer considers himself "united in spirit" with evangelicals in their effort to "remove unnecessary barriers to sharing the Eucharist."

Farmer believes an inerrancy doctrine can be legitimately derived from Scripture, in those passages I've cited much earlier, just as he feels the oft-ridiculed Catholic doctrine of papal infallibility can be so derived from the "keys of the kingdom" passage in Matthew.

At the same time, Farmer is nobody's orthodox Christian. Was Jesus divine or merely a great moral leader, a martyr for his vision of a loving mankind? That, Farmer told me, is a "false issue." He accepts the idea that Jesus was the self-appointed Messiah who focused on the messianic prophecy of Isaiah, chapter 53, as the main guideline for his mission on earth. And his death works for the atonement of our sins, just as, say, Martin Luther King's does: in the political and moral realms on earth. Although Farmer understands this Christology is woefully unacceptable to Paige Patterson, he still has hope: "I think of Paige as a 'soft absolutist.' I don't think Paige Patterson believes I'm going to hell."

I didn't have to ask the president of Criswell College to know his answer to that assertion. It would be the same one he provided on a television program when asked about Ted Bundy and Mother Teresa. If at the end the serial killer genuinely accepted Jesus Christ as his personal Lord and Savior, he went to heaven; if the Mother of Calcutta does not, she won't.

CHAPTER 19

～～～

E very year missiology professor Keith Eitel and perhaps other professors at Criswell, including Paige Patterson, lead one or more groups of students into the mission field. In recent years Criswell teams have gone to El Salvador, Cameroon, Brazil, Mexico, Thailand, Costa Rica, Sri Lanka, Dominica, and East Africa. At the end of my term at the school I joined Eitel and fourteen others, mainly Criswell students, on a journey to El Salvador.

Overseas missionary work has high visibility and stature among evangelical Christians. The tiniest rural churches often send a few hundred dollars a month in support of a missionary working in some distant land no one in the congregation has ever visited. The general funds of the Southern Baptist Convention support almost 4,000 missionaries in over one hundred different locales. Eleven thousand volunteers are aiding the professionals. The total budget for the operation, including hospitals and schools, is $136 million—money which, it is claimed, actually reaches the field. Another 7,000 evangelical missionaries are supported independently or by other conservative denominations. And the other Christian denominations, including Catholic, send forth many, many more men and women. One count registers a total of 80,000 people as vocationally involved in missionary work. (And I have friends who were surprised to learn that anyone at all is still going abroad.) Although the numbers sound large, many times at Criswell I heard the cautionary, even critical, note that 95 percent of mission resources are directed at 5 percent of the world's people, and that within that 5 percent the same areas get the lion's share year after year.

Although the mandate for worldwide evangelism is a Christian development, or a Christian *emphasis,* Jews also evangelized in the ancient world. In the century immediately before and after Christ there were entire synagogues of Greek-speaking Gentile converts to Judaism, and some scholars believe that the Greek names of some of the Jewish persecutors of Christians indicates that these men were converts to the faith.

Nevertheless, the two wings of the Judeo-Christian tradition had, from the beginning, radically different conceptions of their respective covenants with God. Worship in the Old Testament was marked by exclusivity and social bonds. It was tribal. Jehovah could not be worshiped in isolation from the tribe and the homeland. When David was driven from Palestine, he said about the men who did it, "They have driven me out this day that I should have no share in the heritage of the Lord, saying, 'Go, serve other gods' " (1 Sam. 26:19).

Only through the new covenant brought by Jesus Christ did God deliver the mandate to take His gospel throughout the wide world. The message of one itinerant Jewish preacher, directed mainly to other Jews, somehow slipped the leash of tribal custody and, with the mighty help of the missionary Paul and his momentous decision to go west from Palestine instead of east as originally intended, established itself as a religion with a universal message.

Of course, neither Paul's decision nor the ultimate triumph of the faith were accidental or fortuitous in the eyes of believers. How other than providentially could a specific covenant between one isolated people and their God be modified into a covenant between all peoples and the one true God? Indeed, hints of the universalist scope of the final covenant are planted in the earlier communication. Isaiah wrote, "I will give you as a light to the nations, that my salvation may reach to the end of the earth" (Isaiah 42:6). Jeremiah expressed a similar prophecy, and the Minor Prophet Zechariah wrote in the next-to-last book of the Old Testament (as it is arranged by Christians; not so in the Jewish Bible):

Many people and strong nations shall come to seek the Lord of hosts in Jerusalem, and to entreat the favor of the Lord. Thus says the Lord of hosts: In those days ten men from the nations of every tongue shall take hold of the robe of a Jew, saying, "Let us go with you, for we have heard that God is with you" (Zech. 8:22-23).

Christians have long argued that the very success of their faith worldwide and its long tenure is a valid measure of its truth claim. As Stephen Neill writes in *A History of Christian Missions*, "The Jews believed themselves to be, and claimed to be, the people of God—a claim on the face of it so absurd that no one could be expected to pay it any attention, unless it happened to be true. And, after all, the Jews were right. The Old Testament, akin though it may be in certain details to other ancient Scriptures, is in reality not in the least like the sacred book of any other religion. It alone can be read aloud today to a modern audience, and be felt to be, on page after page, luminous, contemporary, and challenging. Like other ancient books it is marred by certain crudities, but among them all it alone can establish a claim to be a permanently valid message for the whole of mankind."

In Acts, Luke records the speech of the great liberal rabbi Gamaliel, who urges tolerance for the bold ideas of Peter and the other disciples and warns his own people, "Keep away from these men and let them alone; for if this plan or this undertaking is of men, it will fail; but if it is of God, you will not be able to overthrow it. You might even be found opposing God" (Acts 5:38–39).

That argument has been taken up by Christians ever since. The longevity of Christianity is now considered almost a proof of the faith, although not by Christians like Keith Eitel, who realize the problems with the argument. If the past successes of Christianity are viewed as proof positive, why shouldn't a continued waning of the faith be equally fair grounds for doubting the truth claim? Evangelicals say this eventuality will not diminish their claim, but consistency is not on their side when they do so. A second problem is more subtle. Christianity has held sway in the Western world for the better part of two thousand years but the world changed very little for the first fifteen hundred of those years. Very little. The moment the world did begin to change, orthodox Christian faith began to decline and has not ceased to do so. Viewed against a time scale that measures transformation within cultures and not numbers of years, the triumph of Christianity was actually quite brief.

All of which is beside the point for the people at Criswell. There were fifteen of us on the mission to El Salvador, where we joined a group from New Orleans that the school has worked with on many other occasions in the country. Therefore the Criswell mission program could be accused of contributing to the problem of a narrow focus, but in its defense, and in defense of the fact that most missionary resources are directed at a small percentage of the unsaved, a great deal of local support is required for missionary trips. It's not a matter of flying into the airstrip, Bibles in hand or in boxes. I learned this quickly in El Salvador, where we were delayed—detained would be too strong a word—at the airport. Without local support in the person of Steve Kern we might not have been allowed in the country. Steve, an associate pastor with the Iglesia Bautista Miramonte church in San Salvador, is the missionary who had organized our visit. At the airport he explained that large groups of young Americans are not greeted with open arms by the Salvadoran government. As likely as not, such groups have come to El Salvador to help the guerrillas. That's the opinion of the government. While we sat around in a hallway and grinned at our good fortune—some Third World excitement to start the trip—Steve met with the customs officials to convince them of our peaceful mission. When he signed a document assuring that we would not engage in any political action they finally let us through, but with only one-day visas, so we were required to spend the following day filing for our two-week extensions.

Steve assured us that the document he had signed was serious. We must not engage in political discussion of any kind with anyone outside the group. Seventy thousand people, out of a population of five million, have died in El Salvador in the course of the ten-year-old civil war, so respect for life has diminished, Steve said. A few weeks before our arrival, the attorney general had been killed in his car while surrounded by bodyguards. The army had recently caught urban guerrilla groups allegedly run by two women, one of them a Baptist. Stick together, Steve told us. Stick to business. And, finally, he urged everyone to keep in mind the notorious image of the Ugly American, and avoid all but the most polite, gracious, and modest presence in this people's country. That message is implicit in Jesus' ministry and, based on my acquaintance with the people at Criswell, I would have been astounded at any other kind of behavior on their part.

Salvadorans are known among themselves and other Central Americans as "guanacos," Joel Turcios told me on the way into San Salvador. Joel is a Salvadoran native who attends Criswell. The guanaco is a curious llama who always wants to know what's happening. Salvadorans therefore make a fine field of operations for itinerant evangelists. A crowd of the curious is almost guaranteed. Kern told us, "Don't worry about the language. If you have the love of Jesus in your heart, they'll really appreciate it. The gospel is seen positively in this country. We're seldom met with disdain, even by strong Catholics. Also, Salvadorans have always felt closely linked with the United States, as proved by the one million Salvadoran citizens living in southern California. The country applied for American statehood in the forties."

The revivals are generally more effective if an American leads the proceedings, with or without translation. The guanaco spirit of the people appreciates that someone has come a long way to speak to *them*. Keith Eitel told me our group would hand out almost 50,000 tracts over the ten-day period, and the street revivals would produce, if they met the precedent of other years, almost 1,000 decisions for Christ. Perhaps a raised eyebrow betrayed some doubt on my part. Eitel said, "There will be some insincerity, yes, but that isn't for us to judge. And people come to Jesus for a variety of reasons, as they did in the Gospels, and yet leave with eternal salvation." And he was quick to point out that of the people who had made professions of faith during the 1988 campaign, well over one half—700—were still in Bible study one year later. That's a very high percentage for continued participation.

Most Salvadorans are born into the Catholic faith, so the mission for the evangelicals in El Salvador, and elsewhere in Latin America, is not to introduce people to the Good News, but rather to convert them from one interpretation of that gospel to another—from the works/merit system of Catholicism, which cannot and does not guarantee eternal salvation, to the true, biblical message of Jesus Christ, which does guarantee salvation—the classic evangelical frame for the debate.

This Protestant message is meeting with great success throughout Latin America, in both the poorer and the upper classes. In 1978, 3 percent of the population of El Salvador was evangelical Christian. Today, they claim 20 percent (in Guatemala, 30 percent, highest in the Western Hemisphere and therefore the world). Common wisdom explains this conversion—stampede, even—to evangelical Protestantism in three ways. One, the evangelical message offers assured hope in war-torn, economically depressed countries; human rights workers in Latin America are routinely quoted as believing that evangelicalism, with its emphasis on eternal salvation, pacifies the lower class and thereby harms the necessary political agenda for social change; these workers accuse the CIA of supporting the evangelicals as a means of bottling up revolutionary fervor. Two, the message feeds on the disenchantment of middle- and upper-class Salvadorans with the perceived political agenda of the Catholic Church, expressed most vividly by the "liberation theology" of many Latin American clerics. Finally, evangelical worship services are more highly charged than Catholic services, and this is asserted to appeal to the Hispanic character. (Twenty million Hispanic-Americans have converted to Protestant denominations, usually conservative ones, and this trend is routinely attributed more to the differences in the worship services than to dogma; recently there has been a countersurge in charismatic Catholic services. Regarding this hypothesis of the stereotypical Hispanic character, I wondered how that nature tolerated over four hundred years of lackluster Catholic worship. A shortage of competition is part of the answer, certainly, but the issue must be more complicated than is usually presented in the press.)

The evangelical response to accusations of crass exploitation and manipulation is straightforward: man's extremity is God's opportunity. Dire circumstances are often necessary to make people see and understand the truth of Jesus Christ's message. Steve Kern told the Criswell group, "After living here four years, I'm convinced politics won't solve anything. People's hearts have to be changed." Capitalists propose that all economic and social good flows from private property rights; evangelicals might or might not agree with this (almost all do), but they must deny that any social structure can in any way "save" individual men and women, or mankind. They must deny the thrust of liberation theology. On the trip, I was reading Phillip Berryman's *Liberation Theology*, a good introduction to the subject. Berryman was a Catholic priest in the barrios of Panama for eight years, and then Central American representative for American Friends Service Committee for four years. He was present in the Catholic church in San Salvador on March 23, 1980, the fourth Sunday of Lent, when Archbishop

Oscar Romero delivered his challenge to the military to stop the killing and the repression of the peasants. "God's law, 'Thou shalt not kill,' takes precedence over a human being's orders to kill," Berryman reports the archbishop said in what turned out to be his last sermon. The following day he was assassinated—the most significant event of the civil strife in El Salvador.

Berryman asserts that while the main issue for Christianity in the Northern Hemisphere of the Americas is its sheer believability, in Latin America the question is what *type* of God is the true object of Christian worship. He continues:

Liberation theology is an interpretation of Christian faith out of the experience of the poor. It is an attempt to read the Bible and key Christian doctrines with the eyes of the poor. It is at the same time an attempt to help the poor interpret their own faith in a new way. To take a simple but central example, in traditional Latin American piety Jesus is almost always mute, indeed most often represented dead on the cross. Perhaps the fact that their society crucifies them and keeps them mute makes ordinary Latin Americans identify with such a Christ. Liberation theology focuses on Jesus' life and message. For example, in his initial sermon, a kind of manifesto, Jesus quotes Isaiah, "He has sent me to bring glad tidings to the poor, to proclaim liberty to captives . . ." and says that the Scripture is fulfilled in him. The poor learn to read the Scripture in a way that affirms their dignity and self-worth and their right to struggle together for a more decent life.

Moses is often cited as a paradigm for liberation activity. He led his people out of bondage in Egypt at the behest of God. The Old Testament depicts the issue as essentially historical, not cosmic. Berryman writes, "Biblical religion in general is a reaction against the mythological view, which sees things as they are now, both in the cosmos and in the human culture, as given and as part of an overarching divine order."

Berryman argues that conservative Christianity wants to return the faith to the realm of the cosmic only, while ignoring the strong elements of historical, political deliverance so manifest in the Old Testament and implied in the New Testament. Matthew, chapter 25, Jesus' great judgment discourse on the Mount of Olives, is one of their key exhibits in this regard. Jesus envisions for his disciples the scene when he returns as the Son of Man to inaugurate the kingdom of heaven on earth:

Then the King will say to those at his right hand, "Come, O blessed of my Father, inherit the kingdom prepared for you from the foundation of the world; for I was hungry and you gave me food, I was thirsty and you gave me drink, I was a stranger and you welcomed me, I was naked and you clothed me, I was sick and you visited me, I was in prison and you came to me. . . .' Truly, I say to you, as you did it to one of the least of my brethren, you did it to me" (Matt. 25:34–40).

Salvation is dependent on what you *do* for others. Liberation theology emphasizes Jesus' denuciations of the idolatry of wealth and power and anything else of this world, his frank appraisal that the meek shall inherit the earth, his universal siding with the poor, the outcasts, even the outlaws (the thief on the cross). In short, God has preferential love for the dispossessed of the earth. From this analysis, liberation theology concludes that a Christian faith commanding political action on behalf of the poor and the powerless *is* biblically grounded. Liberationists do not advocate armed insurrection, which is not biblically defensible by any stretch, but they do claim that Jesus Christ's message arose out of the facts of his own unjust society and can and therefore must speak to the facts of this unjust society. Isn't the celebration of the Eucharist by fascist colonels who enslave their people a perversion of the sacrament? Does anyone propose that *this* is the kind of remembrance Jesus had in mind for the Last Supper?

The Roman Catholic response to liberation theology was neatly summarized in a letter from Archbishop Ratzinger, keeper of the true faith in the Vatican (and formerly a liberal, a key player in

Vatican II). Ratzinger denies the economic argument that the poverty of one group of people is the result of the wealth of others. He also argues that the result of liberation theology in action is not liberation but subjugation under a different oppressive power, Marxism. He cites what must be, biblically, the basis of any and all salvation: Christian faith. There can be no ultimate salvation from a sinful world within that sinful world. Liberation theology, pushed to its extreme, implies that salvation and liberation can be achieved in tandem, and this is false. Berryman cites one sentence from Ratzinger's letter as summarizing the case against liberation theology: "One needs to be on guard against the politicization of existence, which, misunderstanding the entire meaning of the kingdom of God and the transcendence of the person, begins to sacralize politics and betray the religion of the people in favor of the projects of the revolution."

This issue of political action is ticklish for evangelicals. Luis Pantoja surprised me one morning in Cultural Milieu when he advised the class that an evangelical Protestant can be a liberation follower *if* priorities are maintained, and if liberation does not become an idolatry itself. In this way evangelicals contrive plenty of room for maneuver in the social and political arenas, but they also warn stringently against worthwhile goals that descend into idolatry. Political freedom is a legitimate goal but the ultimate freedom for a Christian, and the only one that will mean anything in the end is freedom from sin under Jesus Christ—the Ratzinger doctrine, more or less. Christians should dedicate their pseudo-freedom in society to bondage under Christ: "For he who was called in the Lord as a slave is a freedman of the Lord. Likewise he who was free when called is a slave of Christ" (1 Cor. 7:22).

There is no question that the Apostle Paul, perhaps operating under an assumption of the final days close at hand, urged acquiescence to the civil authority and the status quo. So did Jesus, and perhaps the main passage in this regard should be read into the record:

You have heard that it was said, "An eye for an eye and a tooth for a tooth." But I say to you, Do not resist one who is evil. But if anyone strikes you on the right cheek, turn to him the other also; and if anyone would sue you and take your coat, let him have your cloak as well; and if anyone forces you to go one mile, go with him two miles. Give to him who begs from you, and do not refuse him who would borrow from you. You have heard that it was said, "You shall love your neighbor and hate your enemy." But I say to you, love your enemies and pray for those that persecute you. . . . (Matt. 5:38–44)

The following chapter concludes, "Do not be anxious about tomorrow, for tomorrow will be anxious for itself. Let the day's own trouble be sufficient for the day."

Liberation theologians deal with these passages as best they can. Pantoja said that man has one relationship with God, another with our fellow men, and another with the earth. They are all important. The relationship to God must be primary, but within that relationship must come concern for the other two, because they are the creation of God.

"Does God approve of the industrial fouling of our atmosphere?" Pantoja asked rhetorically. No student spoke up in defense of carbon dioxide. Then a student suggested that North American Indians had a just cause for redress; he also questioned the internment of the Japanese in World War II, and Pantoja agreed with him. Someone else brought up the Palestine Liberation Organization, and sounded essentially sympathetic to its cause. Pantoja agreed that the Palestinian goals of self-determination and a homeland of their own are essentially sound.

"But given the theological and political reality," Pantoja continued, "what is wrong with Israel's behavior?"

In the Old Testament, the battles against the Hittites and other peoples as the Israelites fought their way back to Judea were, literally, holy wars overseen by God. I asked about the more recent Six-Day War. Disregarding for the moment who started it—the Arab nations—was the war justified? No one spoke. Then someone suggested that the rapidity of the Israeli victory might have betokened divine intervention.

"And American supplies," Pantoja murmured quietly.

South Africa: If the Palestinians have a right to a homeland, what about the Afrikaners, who also feel they have a covenant relationship with the land. "Is there any end to the subdividing of nations into ethnic and racial subgroups, once the principle of self-determination is accepted as sacrosanct?" Pantoja asked. Idolatry of state or race is too often the result of political action.

In a subsequent class he asked who had seen the movie *Mississippi Burning,* about the murder of the three civil rights workers in Mississippi in 1964. Not a hand was raised and a student quipped, "That's because it hasn't made it to the dollar movies yet!" The movie portrays the FBI agents as using questionable means to identify the murderers, and Pantoja admitted that while watching the show he was emotionally deceived into agreeing with the doctrine that "wrong is right in order to right a wrong."

My friend Manny Mateus asked whether slaves were justified in the use of violence. Opinions differed. The relevant passage is the famous one from Romans, chapter 13:

Let every person be subject to the governing authorities. For there is no authority except from God, and those that exist have been instituted by God. Therefore he who resists the authorities resists what God has appointed, and those who resist will incur punishment. For rulers are not a terror to good conduct, but to bad. Would you have no fear of him in authority? Then do what is good, and you will receive his approval, for he is God's servant for your good. Therefore one must be subject, not only to avoid God's wrath but also for the sake of conscience. For the same reason you also pay taxes, for the authorities are ministers of God, attending to this very thing. (Rom. 13:1–6)

As with other Pauline passages, it's necessary to again remember that, according to liberal exegesis, Paul at that time didn't think the world was going to last long enough to justify concern with worldy matters, including government and social justice. A few verses later, Romans 13 reads, ". . . you know what hour it is, how it is full time now for you to wake from sleep. For salvation is nearer to us now than when we first believed; the night is far gone; the day is at hand" (Rom. 13:11–12).

In Danny Akin's view these passages forbid active civil disobedience. Only passive disobedience is allowed. Jim Parker also cited Romans as teaching that taxation without representation was *not* sufficient cause for the American Revolution. Pantoja said that some evangelicals have teamed with secular liberals on an agenda to weaken the power of the defense establishment. What did the Cultural Milieu class think? What does the Lord require of us? We were slow to respond, then a student said there's nothing wrong with defense, but it shouldn't come before our faith in God. He noted that Billy Graham wrote in his book *Angels, God's Secret Agents* that dead Allied pilots had shot down German war planes, proving that God can and does work with military means. Another student noted that God often used Israel's enemies in Old Testament times to humble his stiff-necked people. (The war in the Persian Gulf began months after my departure from Criswell College. I was informed long-distance that most students and faculty supported the war. But would the Iraqis have been justified in deposing Saddam Hussein themselves? Not if Romans 13 is interpreted strictly. Then again, since Hussein is a Muslim. . . . The issues are complex.)

Pantoja asked, rhetorically, "Could you stand before your congregation and say that we Americans have become idolatrous in our national defense?"

A student I had not heard speak before did so now, haltingly. I couldn't prove it, but I felt that perhaps he spoke for a good many of his silent classmates. This student doubted whether things would ever get better before Armageddon—a political pessimism that goes hand in hand with premillennialism. In fact, things should get much worse with the approach of the end times.

I suggested that a decline into idolatry is exactly what had happened with the Moral Majority. What group in America was more guilty of idolzing a flag, a nation, an economic system? By this point in the term I wasn't surprised that the class more or less agreed with me. One of the black students said that democracy is just as evil as communism and socialism because it, too, is driven by human pride. Then he surprised everyone by referring to the candidacy at that time of Texan John Tower to be George Bush's secretary of defense: "And now we're trying to put into office a former alcoholic and a womanizer!" He quoted Daniel that the day had indeed arrived when men of immorality are ruling over us. "We should stick to our mission," he concluded. "Evangelism."

Pantoja: "Can we use our mission of evangelism as blinders against the world around us? People accuse us of being single-minded about this narrow mission."

Another student: "We're not winning the world because people see us as so narrow, and not relevant enough."

Pantoja: "Redemption is a right relationship with God, which includes a right relationship with our fellow men, and with our world and our environment. We can be too narrow."

Student: "Secular man sees Christians who claim to have the truth yet hide in their crystal cathedrals. A lady on the *Donahue* show said, 'You people are more interested in a man who died two thousand years ago than with a man starving on the streets today!' First-century Christians saw no relevance to the Old Testament covenant; people today see no relevance to *our* covenant."

Is a man ever justified in lying for the sake of a human life involved in a political situation—a Jew running from the Nazis, say, or an American slave? "Would Christ ever lie in such a situation?" Pantoja asked.

One student was offended by what he considered the impious tone of the question and exclaimed, "Of course not!" According to the Bible, Pantoja said, you should tell the truth and leave everything else up to God. Ephesians 4:25: "Therefore, putting away falsehood, let everyone speak the truth with his neighbor, for we are members one of another." One student said quietly he would lie to save someone from injustice, and leave his punishment up to God. I should have mentioned the Huck Finn story, but I didn't recall it. Huck knew that Providence required him to tell the truth to Miss Watson about the whereabouts of Jim, his pal the runaway slave. So Huck writes the letter to his aunt and pretends to feel good about fulfilling his God-given duty. "I knowed I could pray now," Huck says. But then he gets to thinking about Jim and their good times on the big river. He reconsiders his letter: "I studied a minute, sort of holding my breath, and then says to myself: 'All right, then, I'll go to hell.' "

He tore up the letter.

On the ride into San Salvador from the airport, I discussed these issues of liberation theology and political action with Mark Graham. Mark was not a student at Criswell, but instead sold advertising time for a radio station. He was present on this trip under the sponsorship of Keith Eitel, who had met him in a church in Richardson, Texas. Mark was wearing one of those classic evangelical T-shirts: the name JESUS CHRIST is embossed in the fancy script known worldwide as the trademark of a certain nonalcoholic beverage, and below in block letters is the punch line HE'S THE REAL THING. Mark was aware of the political conflict in Latin America and agreed that the peasants' plight should be changed, but it was not an issue for him personally. Mark's only interest, he said, was "to bring the good news that Jesus Christ loves the poor people as much as He loves me."

CHAPTER 20

‿‿‿‿‿

Iglesia Bautista Miramonte is a major institution in San Salvador. It was founded in 1970 as a Bible school by one Bruce Bell, who had been invited to San Salvador by a missionary to set up a Baptist church among the rapidly growing professional and middle classes in the capital. The church now has about 2,500 members plus another 2,000 in outreach churches. To accommodate the membership and guests, the church has one morning and two evening services on Sunday, and the same schedule for Sunday school.

The daughter of an army colonel works at the church; her brother was assassinated in the parking lot six years ago. The new church campus on Alameda Juan Pablo II, across the street from a sports field recently converted into a hospital, was endowed by the Dallas-based LeTourneau Foundation, which was funded by the patent holder on some earth-moving equipment and distributes to worthy causes 90 percent of all corporate profits. Lettered on the white stucco wall of the main auditorium of the church is the motto EL SALVADOR AL ENCUENTRO CON DIOS (a play on words: "El Salvador's/the Savior's encounter with God") and three biblical references, Matt. 12:6 and Psalm 16:11 and 88:2.

The campus, including a Christian academy, seminary, and bookstore complete with translations of Billy Graham, Pat Robertson, and others, hooks in a ninety-degree angle around a housing project. Behind the complex and across a ravine is a slum inhabited mainly by victims of the earthquake that struck San Salvador on October 10, 1986. New cinder block flats are being constructed, but they aren't yet ready. In the far distance is the Catholic church that was blessed by the pope during his visit in 1983.

On our first morning in the country, waiting for some matters to be taken care of at the church and prior to our trip to the visa office, I talked with Dennis Piercey, a sophomore at Criswell, while watching the household activity in the squalor across the ravine. Dennis accepted his duty to preach the gospel "after fighting God's call for six months." One night, reading the Bible, he gave up the struggle. "If that's what God wants, so be it." Dennis has warm and yearning eyes, and it's easy to understand when he says that he has always had "a burden for people"—a standard term evangelicals use to connote a deep sympathy for the lost, and a passion to save them. Keith Eitel joined us, and the discussion veered into the difference between North American and Third World Christianity. Eitel lived in Africa for six years before moving to Dallas and has been all over the world on mission trips. He admits his preference for the "realism" in the faith he encounters overseas and misses in America. "First-century Christianity" is the phrase often used to describe the sense of urgency and authenticity that, relatively speaking, marks Christian faith in Third World lands. The last Great Awakening was the series of religious revivals that swept through the North American colonies in the mid-eighteenth century. Many evangelicals believe the next Awakening will be in the Third World.

Power went out during lunch at the Hotel Ritz Continental, for the first of many times on the trip. The urban strategy for the guerrillas at that time, six months before the major battles fought later in 1989, was confined to the bombing of power lines and generators, causing random power outages in isolated sections of the city. For whatever reason, the guerrillas do not give the evangelizing Protestants much trouble in San Salvador itself. They have received a couple of written threats, and occasional verbal abuse, but nothing else, and sometimes they go, as we would, to known guerrilla and sympathizer hotbeds. Outside the city, and especially in the countryside and smaller towns in the eastern end of El Salvador, the evangelists have been harassed.

Our hotel was a modest one in unfashionable downtown San Salvador, chosen for its reasonable prices and proximity to the marketplaces where the Criswell team would be evangelizing. At the time of the blackout, Keith Eitel and I were deep into one of the theological discussions I was habituated to. We had arrived at the concept of "providential," widely used by evangelicals (too widely, in Jim Parker's estimation). Eitel, like almost everyone else at Criswell, believed my presence at the school and in El Salvador to be providential. "I haven't heard of anything that isn't," I said, one of the very few times at Criswell I could be accused of anything approaching a sarcastic remark, but I thought I knew Eitel well enough to justify the teasing, not sarcastic, tone. Eitel responded quietly, "Only the Fall." And yet the Fall, too, or at least man's capacity for sin, must have been preordained, because Jesus Christ was ordained for his redemptive role "before the foundation of the world" (Eph. 1:4).

That first afternoon was devoted to paperwork and picture-taking at the main federal office building across town. We were shepherded over there in the Iglesia Bautista vans that we would use for the rest of our stay. The curious folks on the streets and sidewalks watched our passage through the clogged city. Stares followed us when we trooped through the front doors of the office building. Paperwork completed, we waited outside for our visas. I sat next to Lynn Crosslyn as he witnessed the woman sitting next to him. She graciously accepted the main tract our group handed out, *La Gran Pregunta*. The Big Question is, "If you had died the minute you started to read this, do you have the assurance that you would be in heaven?" Inside, the tract outlines a simple but sufficient means of salvation known as the Roman Road because it utilizes two passages from the book of Romans: "All have sinned and fall short of the glory of God . . ." (Rom. 3:23) and "For the wages of sin is death, but the free gift of God is eternal life in Christ Jesus our Lord" (Rom. 6:23).

Lynn and his wife Willetta, who accompanied him on the trip, had been to San Salvador before and fallen in love with the country. They seconded Eitel's remark that the people of El Salvador are much closer in spirit to the people Christ ministered to in his lifetime than are we Americans. It is not just that they are poorer. Their opportunities are also more limited, their world smaller. An irony of the situation, for me at least, is that these poorer people whose restricted circumstances might seem to mitigate any deep feeling of sin nevertheless, according to everything I was told and saw, are quick to acknowledge their sinfulness. As we moved around the city I would stand by as people in the most destitute sections of San Salvador quickly agreed with whoever was witnessing them that they were indeed sinners.

"But in America," Lynn pointed out to me, "tell people they're sinners and they don't like it." (A 1983 study at Notre Dame concluded the same thing about Catholic concern with sin. Confession is dying out: only 6 percent of Catholics go even once a month.)

"This is a more legitimate Christianity than in the United States," Lynn said. I agreed, if only intuitively and based on my long-held opinion that a great deal of American Christianity is perfunctory. I was ready to believe that the people in churches in El Salvador were there for good reason. Meanwhile, the sweet little lady to whom Lynn had handed the tract was still studying it. On their official forays into the plazas and barrios of San Salvador, the Criswell people would be accompanied by Iglesia Bautista staff or seminary students who functioned as translators when necessary. They were not with us this afternoon, so Lynn's conversation with this woman remained confused and inconclusive.

That evening I wandered around the corner from the hotel to buy some of the local, excellent, soft ice cream, and when I returned the vans and the evangelists had already left for the Soyapango area. I had no idea how to get there on my own, so I settled down on a stoop across from the hotel to await someone's return. Thirty minutes later—a quick thirty minutes, with the incessant street life for entertainment—I decided my absence hadn't been discovered until the vans were too far away. Right then a young fellow wearing a Christian T-shirt walked into the hotel. I was correct when I surmised that he, too, had missed the vans. His name was Victor and we teamed up because he knew the bus route to Soyapango.

Bus routes in San Salvador are individually owned franchises and the buses are brightly painted with their individual names. Most feature some form of silhouetted female painted on the front window. This was rush hour; we were jammed on. Thirty minutes later we found our group setting up in a vacant lot among the lanes and cinder block houses of Soyapango, one of the better of the hastily constructed earthquake refugee camps surrounding the city. The music was already in progress.

Our routine for every evening in San Salvador would be just about the same: drive to an area, set up the screen for the movie showing, begin the show with a singer or taped music, show the Christian movie, follow that with the preaching, and conclude with individual witnessing. People, mostly young, many with kids, began congregating the moment the local crew began erecting the portable screen. During the music segment the Criswell witnesses fanned out through the neighborhood looking for more people, passing out tracts, extending an invitation to the show. A car with a megaphone would cruise the roads calling people to the movie, which would be "in total color."

That night at Soyapango several hundred people had arrived by the time the movie started. This feature, titled *Thief in the Night,* was filmed years ago in Iowa. The story presents the Second Coming from a pretribulation point of view. A woman is awakened by her alarm radio to learn that the Rapture is taking place. As an unbeliever she is left behind; her subsequent fate is the focus of the narrative. However, that whole story turns out to be a dream: the woman wakes up in her bed as her alarm radio goes off. Moments later, the dramatic radio announcement of the Rapture begins again. This time it's for real.

The show lasted forty-five minutes. I skipped out toward the end and walked over to a ravine to look down at two utility line towers that had been recently bombed and toppled. I walked down the street to the local Assembly of God church, service in progress. About a dozen worshipers were listening to the sermon. A man leaned out the door to invite me in, but I declined. Most of the one million Salvadoran evangelicals are aligned with the Assembly of God denomination. There are about 1,200 of their churches in the country. The Baptists have only 26 churches in El Salvador, with the largest being Iglesia Bautista. Therefore, many if not most of the people who convert to born-again Christianity as a result of the Criswell/Iglesia campaign might not join that church itself, or even the Baptist denomination. But this is not the evangelists' concern.

The singer that night, and the preacher after the show, was Ed Lacy from New Orleans. Ed's preaching picked up on the theme of the movie. Are you ready if Jesus comes tonight? The Bible prophecied the first coming of Christ, and three times prophecied the Second Coming. The signs are present today: Israel, Russia, China—massive armies worldwide. Are you ready? Are you saved?

Ed preached in English, one clause, one sentence at a time; Joel Turcios, standing beside him, translated, and the two established a sharp give-and-take rhythm that riveted the crowd to the message. Ed told of his own battle with alcohol. He explained the distinction between a "religion" and a personal relationship with

Jesus Christ, without in any way imputing the derisive term religion to any specific faith, though he meant Catholicism. He concluded with the standard invitation to come forward and meet with a born-again Christian to learn more about the real message of Jesus Christ. People pressed in. Many more came forward than filtered away into the darkness. The Criswell people partnered with their Iglesia translators to evangelize one-on-one.

At times the conversations got fairly technical regarding means of salvation and other topics. These Salvadorans were definitely interested in the evangelical message and, as Steve Kern had said, they were familiar with the general terminology of Christian faith. Sometimes, but not that often, decisions for Christ are made on the spot during these campaigns. More often the local church people acquire the address of the potential convert and then follow up. The church has established Bible study groups in all of the neighborhoods we would visit, and their figures show that fully 60 percent of the people who say they'll attend a meeting do in fact show up—an extraordinarily high rate of return, I was told.

An hour after Ed's sermon there were still several dozen deep conversations in progress. The vacant lot was lighted only by a full moon and our three generator-powered lanterns. This was my first night out in El Salvador but I could already understand the sweet feeling enjoyed by the visitors from the United States. They were a totally committed minority bringing a message of salvation to a needy people with an antagonistic world waiting just beyond the borders of the light. It seemed to me that night in El Salvador that the political guerrillas on the left and the religious guerrillas on the right were operating out of the same psychological praxis, to borrow a favorite term of the liberation theologists. There's a romance to both movements, and it was easy to understand why the North Americans look forward to these mission trips back in time to first-century Christianity. Walking the blocks in Dallas is not quite the same.

The following morning a group of us returned to the airport for some of the luggage that hadn't arrived—or, as it turned out, had arrived but just hadn't been put out for collection following the flight. Waiting for the van in the hotel lobby Glenda Eitel and I discussed providence. Glenda has her own collection of episodes that are either remarkable coincidences or providential. Glenda's happened while the Eitels lived in Africa, and concerned the timely arrival of vital medicines, a tumor that mysteriously disappeared, and the like. My own first reaction to all such stories, and I hear them just as often from New-Agers as from Christians, is to think about all the times the world over when the medicine does not arrive in time, the tumors do not heal, fifty-four people aboard the flight are killed while the seventy-seven others survive by the grace of God. I get irritated at the logic of providence but this is *my* problem because Christians aren't talking about logic. They see miracles because with the way their fallen world operates, the medicine should never get there on time, all tumors should be fatal, and everyone on board should die. Unfairness means nothing to Christians. What God does, God does. He set man above beast, male above female, the Jews above all other ancient peoples.

That afternoon Leo Humphrey, the leader of the group from New Orleans, arrived in town. Humphrey is an old pal of Paige Patterson who spends many weeks every year in El Salvador and other Central American countries under the aegis of Good News in Action, Inc., of which he is the director. In New Orleans, Humphrey works a good deal of the time evangelizing among homosexuals and in the black neighborhoods. He and Paige Patterson were at New Orleans Theological Seminary together, and evangelized in the French Quarter. Everyone from Criswell had assured me that I would find Humphrey an entertaining, engaging fellow, and then some. They were right. He's a barrel-chested, gray-haired man with lots of energy spilling out into the world and green eyes that know the truth. He could be hard to handle one-on-one, that was obvious, but I'll say this for Leo Humphrey: in our several conversations he never once tried to strong-arm me, in part because, as he told me, when he sees the Christians on TV he knows why people reject the faith. He makes certain his own evangelizing is less offensive.

Humphrey is the kind of individual who would have stories to tell no matter what his line of work. He was on the TACA Airlines flight number 211 from San Salvador to New Orleans that belly-flopped onto a dike as it approached the airport in 1988.

"The prayers were flying," Leo said with a grin to a group of us. Winking at me he added, "Each in his own way, of course!"

That night Humphrey preached in Apopalan, a poor refugee area of dirt roads and unfinished cinder block flats, open to the air through doors and windows. There were thousands of kids in Apopalan. Before we fanned out for the premovie exercise Steve Kern warned us to beware the bands of young troublemakers. This area was a haven for cheap booze, drugs, and rebels. Whenever we heard sharp reports we thought—perhaps hoped—they were an exchange of gunfire, but they were probably firecrackers. That evening's film entertainment was *The Burning Hell,* a graphic depiction of the netherworld with worms in the eyes of the damned, searing flames, the works. Steve considers it the most effective of his movies for holding the attention of the crowd. Driving back to the hotel that evening our driver dimmed his lights as we crossed a high bridge, just in case the rebels had a bomb in place and would use headlights to time the detonation.

Thursday morning we went to the plaza. For the first week of the campaign Humphrey's crew from New Orleans was in charge of logistics for these morning revivals. A microphone, two portable speakers, and a sound board were all they needed. The plazas chosen were in the middle of hectic downtown activity. Hundreds of passersby would hear part or all of these messages, but the evangelists would not receive the focused attention of as many people as were attracted to the more isolated evening movies and preaching. It is also a lot hotter in San Salvador during the day.

Steve Kern had warned us to wear caps; he also advised us to take advantage of the afternoon breaks and get plenty of rest; after a few days, I knew why.

Instead of a movie, the daytime revival features a succession of preachers, translated on most days by Julio Contreras, seminary teacher and youth director at Iglesia Bautista. Another of the New Orleans evangelists, white-haired Eddie Martin, took the microphone first that morning. Martin said, "If this is the only life, there's too much misery. But there's another life, there's a heaven—and it's a place, not a state of mind, where every home is a mansion, and every road is paved with gold, where you'll have perfect health and live forever in the company of God. Why do people reject this offer? Why do people reject Christianity? They want to live in sin. They sell their soul for a beer.

"When I first came to El Salvador, I went to a travel agent. If you want to go to heaven, go to the only travel agent who can get you there: Jesus Christ. And the ticket is free, paid for by Christ on a cross."

Half a dozen people came forward after Martin's sermon to receive the free Bible and talk with one of the group. Next up was Ed Lacy, the musician with the group who told his crowd and me the story of one of the rock bands he used to play the drums with. One member of this group committed suicide, one was killed in a car crash after escaping from prison. These tragedies left Ed himself "driving on empty." He switched from rock to jazz and from pills to alcohol. One night eight years ago he saw a preacher on TV talking about the Second Coming: "God set me down in front of that TV and the Holy Spirit began speaking to me. He showed me Christianity. He showed me the Bible. I got down on my knees that night and asked Christ into my life. He gave me a taste of the everlasting drink of life."

Supporting a wife and four children, Ed hasn't had a paycheck in five and a half years. The Lord always provides by way of gifts from fellow Christians in thanks for his evangelical work. This was his twenty-eighth trip to El Salvador in the past four years.

He cited to the crowd Romans, chapter 3, the seminal verses that establish faith and faith alone as the road to salvation, the very verses that changed Martin Luther's life and, subsequently, the Western world: "Since all have sinned and fall short of the glory of God, they are justified by his grace as a gift, through the redemption which is in Jesus Christ . . ." (Rom. 3:23–24).

Ed called out, "If you can go to heaven by being a good person, or by doing good works, or by being 'religious,' then God *murdered* his Son on the cross. And God is not a murderer."

With that last illustration Ed was assuming a certain theological sophistication on the part of his audience, an appreciation of the faith-works dichotomy, which is an obsession with evangelicals but is probably not uppermost in the concerns of the audiences in the plazas of San Salvador. I hadn't heard that particular illustration before and I didn't believe that Ed was reciting it on his own authority. The juxtaposition of God and murder is not the kind of liberty a lay preacher is likely to take on his own.

I paused to analyze the argument: Jesus was crucified with his Father's knowledge and approval for the salvation of mankind. If any other means of salvation were available, then the crucifixion was not necessary and God is a murderer. But since God is not a murderer, by definition, it follows that the crucifixion *was* His only option and mankind's only salvation. I saw the point. It seemed ironclad to me. We only have to accept the assertion that Jesus was crucified according to the plan of God rather than by the autonomous hands of zealous men.

That night we went out to one of the marginal zones that are so marginal they don't even have official names. This was one called simply Colonia 10 de Octobre (a reference to the date of the earthquake). As primitive as it was, Steve Kern assured us that others are worse. Quite a few miles from the center of the city, this barrio was pressed up against the fog-shrouded mountains that ring San Salvador. As the crew set up their gear on a soccer field and thunder fired in the distance, we fanned out through the muddy lanes on the hillside. The shacks were constructed of tin or molded in mud, but electricity had been patched into the zone and some TV antennas were also apparent.

I accompanied Scottie and Judy Stice, with young Victor Hernandez doing the translating. In the water barrels outside the doorways I saw tiny, wriggling worms. Destitute people came to the doors and accepted our tracts and listened politely as Judy recited her own testimony of salvation. Her father is a retired Air Force man and Baptist Missionary Alliance preacher (the BMA is known for its conservatism), and she was nine when she realized she was a sinner and walked the aisle for salvation. Judy asked Lidia Zabalete if she could answer *La Gran Pregunta.* No. Judy asked her to join in a prayer of confession of sins and acceptance of Christ, and Lidia did so, kids hanging off her at every angle.

I was chagrined. This comparatively rich woman from the United States lecturing this pathetically poor Salvadoran mother about her sinful nature was too absurd. I say "lecturing" perhaps unfairly. Judy could not have been more gentle with her words, nor did the poverty witnessed by all of us dismay me alone. But I was surely alone in seeing the incongruity of the visionary hope offered by Christians and the overwhelming need of this family for its daily bread. Then again, the only reason I saw incongruity was that I did *not* see the visionary hope. If I did, I, too, would probably give it top priority.

A short while later, concluding a brief visit that didn't become an official witnessing session, Judy prayed with a man who was smiling stupidly the whole time—going along. Scottie then took over and witnessed to Ernesto Vasquez, who lived in one of the nicer shacks on Block A (#3), *lote* 3. This one had a concrete floor, and the man inside was working under dim light on electronics boards webbed with solder. Apparently the front room was his shop. He and whoever lived with him had another room in the back. A tiny puppy played at our feet. Vasquez listened very carefully as Scottie spoke and recited from the Gospel of John. He said he wanted to think about all this. Then his wife walked up and gave Judy the closest to a brush-off that I saw at any time in

San Salvador. Victor noted later that her shirt had the insignia of two crossed rifles, denoting, he thought, a possible rebel sympathizer.

The movie that night was about Barabbas but I didn't watch because Keith and Glenda Eitel were involved with a woman they had encountered who had four-month-old twins, both of whom were very ill; perhaps, Glenda thought, dying. When the Eitels had prayed for the babies the woman had broken into tears. Eitel had left transportation money for the woman to take the babies to the clinic operated in San Salvador by the Baptist church. After a discussion of the situation at base camp during the movie, the Eitels returned to the woman with the intention of taking her and the babies to the hospital immediately, but they found the babies doing better and settled for a promise that the woman would take the babies to the clinic the next morning. (She did arrive at the clinic the following afternoon, and the babies were better still.)

After the movie and preaching, sixty-four people, by official count, came forward to accept Bibles. The kids swarmed as we passed out the small "I Love Jesus" stickers that Leo Humphrey brings into the country by the thousands. The Eitels talked seriously with a young couple, husband and wife, and brought the man to a point of decision. The woman declined, graciously, stating that she wanted this decision to be made in her heart as well as in her head. Keith Eitel said he understood this and asked her to study with her husband and attend the Bible classes with him. As we rode away in our vans ten minutes later, we passed that couple walking hand in hand, conversing.

CHAPTER 21

~~~~~~~

Plaza Libertad in downtown San Salvador was the scene of the rally following the assassination of Archbishop Romero in 1980 that turned into carnage when bombs exploded on the four corners of the square. After the riot a thousand pairs of shoes were picked up. They had been stripped from their owners' feet in the flight of panic.

On Friday morning we set up shop for street preaching at Libertad, but I was drawn instead to the Rosario church nearby, the most striking church of any denomination I have ever seen. It's a concrete half-cylinder, unpainted, laid on its side. A series of stained-glass stripes runs the length of the structure, which must be almost two hundred feet long. From the outside the building gives no sense at all of celebration; it looks more like an edifice suitable for mourning, and this impact does not diminish as you walk through the poster-encrusted doorways into the dark and solemn vault of the interior. A semicircle of wood benches faces to the left, toward the altar, which is positioned under a canopy of exposed steel scaffolding. Above the steel run the narrow bands of abstractly shaped stained glass. The realistic Christ on the wood cross is the only note of tradition anywhere in the building.

Beyond the circle of benches is an area of freestanding sculptures—stone plinths supporting bronze figuration. In one vertical piece the stone has the shallow ripples that suggest the folds of a gown, from which a crude fretwork of arms and hands extend forth: harsh materials extending hope and comfort. In another piece the fretwork is shaped like a cowl, with hands covering the opening for the face.

The racket from the heavy traffic just beyond the walls was easily heard; small children played somewhere nearby; an old man swept the aisles; I was almost alone, sitting on a pew. Officially or otherwise, the architecture and the sculpture of that church are works of liberation theology, I realized, and here on that Friday morning I came closer than I ever had to sensing that there might be a Christian vision I might possibly understand in my head as well as in my heart, and then accept. Considering my mission on the trip and for this book, it's a shame this epiphany of sorts had to happen in a Catholic context but some of the people at Criswell, maybe most of them, maybe even all of them, will understand.

Officially, people come to Christianity because of their sinful nature: confess your sins and acknowledge Christ as He who has paid for them in substitutionary atonement. But in fact, people (adults) come to Christ out of suffering. They need help. Time and again at Criswell I heard the story of the man or woman born again when he or she could slog no longer through a life of drink, drugs, promiscuity, and guilt. That's one way of putting it. The other way is to say they were tired of suffering and, in many cases, tired of feeling the guilt from the pain they were inflicting on the people they loved. Occasionally the testimonies hardly bothered with the sin and moved straight to the suffering.

Evangelicals respond that the suffering results from the sinning. Perhaps it does, but I don't believe many Christians today really feel this. We all fail ourselves and others, certainly, but mankind in the twentieth century also has a picture of the world that sees many people as victims, too, and perhaps even as victims *first*. We're not focused on an inner-directed sinfulness and guilt. We can listen to Eddie Martin berate us for the rest of our lives and it won't penetrate, and not because we refuse to see. We do, but we also see something else. We see how God is implicated in this matter. *Gloria dei, vivens homo.* The glory of God is the living human being. Absolutely true, but the guilt of God is the suffering human being. People feel this way. Jim Parker said so: "A lot of people are just mad at the theistic God."

God is far away and the Fall was a long time ago. That Fall may have been self-motivated sin for Adam and Eve but it's unwarranted inheritance for you and me, and as such is not sin but suffering. Protestants sing about how sweet is the victory in Jesus, but Catholics hold high their truest symbol of the faith: Christ on the cross defeated. No cross in a Southern Baptist church will have on it the painted figure of the bleeding Christ so prominent in Catholic churches. Those figures are deemed idolatrous. Nor is the suffering of Jesus on the cross of immediate interest to these congregations. The idea behind their religion is the joy of the Resurrection and total faith in the meaning of that event for all believers: guaranteed salvation. Sitting on the pew that morning I had a better understanding why those few friends of mine who do turn or return to Christianity select one of the high manifestations. It's not only because they're more comfortable with the intellectual air, but also because these churches emphasize suffering over sin. Not officially, perhaps, but that's their import. The wages of sin may be death but the gift of *suffering* is eternal life through Jesus Christ our Lord: this, I believe, is the message of the Catholic church near Plaza Libertad in San Salvador.

A few weeks before the trip to El Salvador, I had mentioned to Danny Akin that I was beginning to glimpse the power that Christ on the cross holds for many people. And that was true. In the Rosario church I began to understand even more clearly the source of that power. Suffering calls forth love, the need to receive love, the wish to provide it (and the distinction between the two is probably arbitrary). "God is love" may be a meaningless tautology for evangelicals and logical positivists alike, insufficient for either salvation or semantic coherence, but this God of love is the one most people worship, dogma notwithstanding and if they're not too angry. This is the essence of the God whom the retired Methodist pastor Don Pevey beseeched when he dwelt on the spectacle of his alcoholic brother's ruined life. This is the God the Catholic author Andrew Greeley believes in. The Resurrection, the Atonement, prayer: all these dogmas of the Christian faith make sense, Greeley argues, if God is wholly, truly, and ineluctably love.

The finest sustained passage on Christian love in the Bible is the thirteenth chapter of First Corinthians. The previous chapter ends with Paul's reminding his audience that even if they are all apostles and prophets and teachers now, working miracles and speaking in tongues, they still "earnestly desire the higher gifts. And I will show you a still more excellent way." He continues:

If I speak in the tongues of men and of angels, but have not love, I am a noisy gong or a clanging cymbal. And if I have prophetic powers, and understand all mysteries and all knowledge, and if I have all faith, so as to remove mountains, but have not love, I am nothing. If I give away all I have, and if I deliver my body to be burned, but have not love, I gain nothing. . . .

Love bears all things, believes all things, hopes all things, endures all things.

Love never ends; as for prophecies, they will pass away; as for tongues, they will cease; as for knowledge, it will pass away. . . . Now we see in a mirror, dimly, but then [when with Christ], face to face. Now I know in part; then I shall understand fully, even as I have been fully understood. So faith, hope, love abide, these three; but the greatest of these is love (1 Corin. 13:1–13).

At Plaza Libertad Leo Humphrey had taken up the cudgels against the religion across the way. "Satan loves religious people," Leo was saying, "but he hates saved people." He followed this with a derogation of meditation, and he quoted the Christian sage who said that meditation is like praying in a room without doors. I could only believe the point to be irrelevant for this audience of young Salvadoran men, but perhaps I was wrong. At any rate, I understood how Humphrey's illustration applied to the Rothko Chapel in Houston, as just one example, and about which I have already made dissenting remarks. I compared the Rothko Chapel with the Catholic church I had just left. Both rooms are without doors, practically speaking, and without windows admitting bright light, but there is, even within the harsh modernity of that Catholic church, at least an *opportunity* for faith, hope, and love, all three, which is not present in the Rothko Chapel: the crucified Jew on the cross.

Three men responded to Leo Humphrey's invitation that morning. A few moved away. But most of the seventy-five or so men stood motionless as the sound equipment was stowed and the generator turned off.

The following evening, Saturday, we carried our wares to Colonia San Luis, a middle-class neighborhood within San Salvador that featured two-story brick flats separated by walkways, with tiny gardens front and back. In the distance loomed a volcano. Like everywhere we visited, most of the front doors were wide open and inside the television was on. Joel Turcios told me that most of these people would have been baptized Catholics, followed by a nominal observance in adult life. To them, he said, the announcement of a "Christian movie" might mean a Catholic movie.

These middle-class neighborhoods, generally speaking, produce smaller crowds than the barrios. This was certainly true at San Luis, where perhaps fifty or sixty people filtered onto the vacant lot and watched the movie projected onto a whitewashed wall. During the show Paul Carlisle and I talked about heaven and hell and other matters. We also had a long conversation one afternoon by the hotel pool. Carlisle is one of the two psychology professors at Criswell, teaching a heavy load that spring term: Marriage and Family Counseling, Counseling and Ministry in the Local Church, Theories of Personality (an introduction to Freud, Jung, and others; the first and in many cases the last such exposure to these thinkers that most of his students will ever have or want), and an evening course at a local church on Dynamics of Marriage and Family.

Carlisle had a straightforward Christian upbringing in the piney woods of East Texas. His first and only crisis occurred when he was sixteen, sitting in the back row in church and realizing he had been playing a game. From force of repetition I was beginning to understand that this is almost a standard rite of passage for teenage Christians—plausibly so. Who doesn't have a degree of posturing at that age? Carlisle was also wondering why almost all of the Christian testimonies he heard were from kids with drug and alcohol problems. Was this kind of bottom-dwelling a requirement for serious Christian faith? He decided no and went off to East Texas Baptist University in Marshall, where he majored in Religion, a Bible-oriented program that prepared the student for seminary work. Carlisle headed the Baptist Student Union. Back home his family was falling apart, his parents divorcing after thirty years.

Then Carlisle was out of school for a year and a half, working in his father's auto repair shop and counseling informally, confronting kids with *La Gran Pregunta*. Then he enrolled at East Texas State University for graduate work in Counseling and Marriage and Family. This was a strictly secular program, so for the first time in his life he was "alone," an experience similar to Jim Parker's secular baptism at Baylor a few years earlier and a hundred or so miles to the west. The "incongruities" between the material taught in that program—the secular presuppositions of a life without a God—and the personal lives of the teachers and students, which did not impress Carlisle with their stability or happiness, gave him sufficient reason to oppose that system of secular values. His Christian faith remained unscathed but not uninfluenced: when Carlisle explains his interest in counseling, he doesn't say something like "having a burden for people"; rather, he has a "knack" for it. When he talks about why he didn't enter pastoring he doesn't say he "never heard the call." He just wasn't interested.

With the movie playing in the background at San Luis, Carlisle freely acknowledged the difficulty that the modern, secular mind has with the ideas of heaven and hell, and he understands how unbelievers perceive Christian dogma and proselytizing as arrogance. "It's not arrogance," he said, "but deep concern. My purpose is to love *regardless.*" I believed him, as I believed it of almost everyone I met at Criswell.

Later Carlisle explained the three schools of Christian counseling: on one extreme, the Bible only; on the other, heavy psychology with little theology, and the middle ground occupied by the likes of him, espousing that every truth is God's truth, acknowledging that family background and dynamics are significant, taking what works from the secular psychologies and junking the rest. Bible-only counseling comes down hard, as it must, on sin. "Your problem is sin," begin these counselors. "Until you own up to this fact we can't even proceed." Carlisle's approach agrees that the problem is sin, certainly—yours *or* someone else's. However, as he explained, no Christian counselor can deviate from the final truth that only the blood of Christ can save you from sin, yours or someone else's.

～～～～～

The morning following the San Luis campaign we met with Hal Large, the pastor of Iglesia Bautista Miramonte. Large is an American from California, a graduate of Jerry Falwell's Liberty University, but he has been in El Salvador for eleven years and pastor of the church for the past five.

His financial needs are supported, in typical fashion, by about ten different churches or families in the United States, as well as by Iglesia Bautista, whose total budget is slightly less than $100,000. He is not a part of the cooperative program of any denomination in the States. In effect, he's a free-lancer. Large said, "There are advantages to being involved in cooperative programs, but the Lord provides." I was told elsewhere that a missionary family in El Salvador requires about $1,500 a month in order to live with reasonable but not excessive comfort. Just a few weeks before our visit an American family had sent Large $5,000 to help with the purchase of a house.

In Jacksonville, Homer Lindsay had cited the two things he believes any evangelical church needs: Jesus Christ and lost souls. Large agrees. His church really took off when it was invited into the hospitals of San Salvador, when the government, upset with the influence of liberation theology, kicked out the Catholic church. This opening was followed by access to social security hospitals, and then prisons: lost souls in abundance.

"This is first-generation Christianity," Large said. "It's inevitable when the second and third generations come along, things slack off." First generation, first century: these phrases connote just about the same thing, a raw enthusiasm for the faith. The secret of a thriving church, in Large's opinion, is to always have coming in another group of first-generation Christians—in the case of his church, the people reached through the plaza and evening revivals, who then attend the new outreach churches, of which there are six.

But despite the success of this outreach program, the rate of growth is slowing down at Iglesia Bautista. "Warfare, death, insecurity—the nation was coming apart, and the Catholic church turned against its own people," Large explained. "It all created a foxhole hunger for spirituality. But that revival growth of six, seven years ago could not be sustained."

An indication of the importance that Baptist churches place on overseas missionary work is that even Iglesia Bautista Miramonte sponsors a missionary, in Spain. After six years this man counts just twenty-five members in his church. The foxhole hunger in newly freed, economically booming Spain just isn't there. Large's opinion is that the most successful foreign missions for American evangelicals will be in the Arab nations.

He urged all missionaries to think in terms of the *local* church. The Campus Crusade wins people mainly to the Campus Crusade, which is not a church. Large doesn't believe this kind of evangelizing is biblical. Likewise, the missionary's goal cannot be "just going" in order to fulfill the Great Commission. They must establish churches. Large knows missionaries in Central America who are not even members of a local church.

"Terrible," he said.

The Criswell contingency was seated in one of the Miramonte classrooms, listening to Large, occasionally looking out at the activity in the apartment blocks just beyond the windows, when suddenly the pastor's mood changed, and so did his audience's.

"Fifty percent of missionaries go home after four years," he said quietly. "The first year is hell because too many missionaries are trying to do three things: learning to minister, learning to be married, and learning the local culture. Ideally, the first two should be out of the way before you go into the field."

If the first year is hell, subsequent ones will be merely difficult. Not everyone in the family, and that includes wives, may be as committed to Christ. Even after many years of established work in a country, the evangelist's life can be difficult. Perhaps it *should* be difficult. Large himself was leaving in a few days to join his wife and family, who were already in the States, for some much-needed rest and contacts with his local sponsors.

The following morning he led the Sunday service at Iglesia Bautista. The interior of the Miramonte church has a high ceiling, white walls, and lots of light from high, open windows—a stark contrast to the dark and solemn space of the Catholic cathedral. The Baptist church was spacious and friendly and so were the people and the service. This was Protestantism.

Music was provided by electronic keyboard, piano, violin, guitar, and a trio including Julio Contreras, one of our translator/ drivers, and his wife, who works in a bank. They sang hand-clapping gospels and hymns for twenty-five minutes and concluded with "Suprema Gracia." Large and his deacons wore coat and tie, but few others in the congregation did, and none of our group. The men wore their best short-sleeved cotton shirts and the women wore skirts or dresses. It was hot outside, warm inside; the fans were not totally effective.

Large spoke for fifty minutes on his text from Exodus, chapter 2, the travails of Moses and his people under Pharaoh in Egypt. A seven-minute prayer followed, and I noted with interest that it did not include the request for people to walk down the aisle in public commitment that is standard in the United States. Next was the offering, collected in red velvet bags suspended from ornate poles, which were extended down the pews by the deacons. Two hours in all, half an hour longer than normal for Miramonte, an hour longer than in the States. Parked out front as the congregation poured into the brilliant sunshine were taxis and ice-cream and sorbet vendors. In my sunglasses I must have looked like a North American strongman. (No one else I saw in El Salvador wore them, for reasons I never learned.)

That evening at the church Leo Humprhrey preached and Hal Large translated the sermon from Mark 10:17: "And as [Jesus] was setting out on his journey, a man ran up and knelt before him, and asked him, 'Good Teacher, what must I do to inherit eternal life?' "

The supplicant turned out to be the rich young man whom Jesus directed to go and sell all his possessions in order to have treasure in heaven. Leo preached on the subject of true and false conversions—a subject, indeed, I have wondered about many times, for there must be many false ones. The rich young man, to his credit, didn't even pretend. The Bible says his countenance fell when he heard the directive from Jesus, and he went away sorrowful.

"I am asked by people 'Am I saved?' " Humphrey called out.

"I used to say, 'I don't know.' Now I answer, 'No, I don't believe you are, because if you're truly saved you won't ask, "*Am* I saved?*" You'll proclaim, 'I am saved.' "

Many people are mentally converted, Humphrey continued, and perhaps even morally converted, but such mere conviction will not save your life. Leo told the story about the preacher from India (I had heard it before) who quipped to a visiting American missionary that about 1.5 percent of his country was Christian—"just about the same as in your country."

"If you don't know, you aren't saved," Leo continued. "I can't talk you *into* it because then someone could talk you *out* of it. The greatest definition of conversion? Conversion! Amen!"

That evening Humphrey did conduct the standard invitation following his sermon, and four people arrived at the front of the congregation. As in Jacksonville, once again I felt that all the Criswell eyes were on me. Once again, I failed them.

Bombs planted on utility poles exploded all night, some fairly close to the hotel. The air conditioner went off, came back on. Helicopters droned back and forth overhead. This was the closest we had been to the action.

~~~~~~~

Keith Eitel had joked when we arrived in the country that one day everyone might convert to Calvinism and go to the beach. They're saved or they're not saved—let's swim! It happened on Monday. The sand at La Libertad was black, the surf rugged, the undertow vicious. My Christian friends and I frolicked in the surf like a bunch of pagans in modest swim suits. (Joel Turcios noted that the Salvadorans favor extremely skimpy suits.) Dozens of bathers die in this surf every year, Joel said, but that statistic doesn't deter them. The traffic is so bad on weekends that the only highway from the capital is one-way to the shore in the mornings, one-way to the city in the evenings. (The day after our holiday a newspaper featured a picture of three *compesinos* slain on their way to La Libertad in their van—a random killing by the rebels, the government-sponsored caption hypothesized.)

We were back at work that evening, in one of the inner-city marginal areas not far from the hotel. Scottie Stice, Victor Hernandez, and I found four Mormons, and the husband of this family explained that his Mormon conversion had cured his drunkenness four years ago. He knows about demons; Jesus is the right way to be happy. Scottie left him with a copy of the Gospel of John, which he described as "the book of God, not the book of Joseph Smith." Then he said, "I won't argue with you whether the book of Joseph Smith is authoritative, but Joseph Smith didn't die on the cross. Christ did. The truth rests in Christ. I know this, Victor knows this, and we hope you know this."

Something must have been lost in translation because the man now said he'd never heard of Joseph Smith. We walked on. One flat was filled with American cheesecake posters. A feisty goat was tethered in the middle of another. As usual, the passage of the Americans and their translator passing out religious tracts was of universal interest. Even the dogs observed our progress.

During the movie screening two more bombs exploded just around the corner. The lights flickered off, then came back on. (All the electricity poles in San Salvador are equipped with movement sensors so that the transformer will shut down during an earthquake, and they function similarly when a bomb is exploded at the base.) While the bombs were exploding and the show was playing I had a final dialogue with Mark Graham, the young man who was not a Criswell student and sells ads for a radio station. He has already been divorced twice and was something of a boozer if not an alcoholic. He was convicted by Christ one night in church—or he *thought* he had been convicted—but nothing in his life changed, though the preacher had promised it would. Mark soon realized he had fallen prey to the lure of instant well-being, which some preachers play to. One night he went home from work, lay down on the floor, and cried his heart out. Then he felt the peace that came from realizing that God wants "not 80, 90, but one 100 percent of our lives."

That's the goal, Mark realizes, but he hasn't attained it. He even had a month-long adulterous episode with a Christian woman until both realized it was sinful. That revelation gave me pause.

Mark was under the impression that all reputable historians acknowledge the Resurrection of Christ as indisputably true. He didn't pick that up at Criswell, where the professors don't even claim that most Christian scholars believe a *physical* resurrection absolutely proven. However, I'm not certain I convinced Mark where matters stand. Mark said he had few friends now who weren't Christian because he had little to talk about other than this new subject. Nothing unusual here. Evangelical faith seems to require consistent reinforcement, but so what? Every belief system requires reinforcement, including the secular one. I don't see my friends *going* to church.

Regarding my failure to accept Christ, he said I had a hardened heart. I had been told this many times, usually not in so many words, and always with more finesse. Usually the problem was attributed to my "sin nature." Maybe I should have appreciated Mark's frankness but instead, for one of the few times at Criswell, I felt the anger rising. I don't believe I have a hardened heart. By most measures it's mushy. I almost told Mark that my heart was hard to whatever degree his head was soft.

~~~~~~~

Tuesday was my last day in El Salvador because I was returning to the States several days before the group. Over breakfast in the hotel, a small group of us discussed again the warmth and openness of these Salvadoran evangelical Christians, one of whom was serving us our meal that morning, compared with the "deadness" of Christianity in the States. John Ulrich quipped that evangelizing in the United States parallels the story of Jesus calling forth Lazarus from the dead. Some of the congregations in the States are dead. Ulrich's Christian testimony is unique among the people I met at Criswell, though certainly not unique among Christians as a whole. He came to Christ following a miracle. On August 5, 1976, his son, a young man, was taken to the hospital with no heartbeat and no brain waves. He had been found unconscious at a work site, and the cause of accident was unknown. He was in a coma for three days, and the doctors said there was nothing they could do. On the fourth day he awoke, stark-raving mad. John was in the room at the time. "I walked out of that room and I saw a sign for the chapel, and thought I might as well try that. I prayed. He was wild and crazy for three days. One night I picked up my wife and asked her to pray with me. We went to that chapel and I prayed all night. My shirt was soaking with sweat."

Ulrich promised God that he would give up smoking and drinking—he was an alcoholic—and his good job, which took him all over the globe, if only God would save his son. In the morning he went to his office, checked up on business, then returned to the hospital room. His son was sitting up in bed, talking calmly to his mother, who was stroking his hair. John sat down and questioned his son for two hours.

"He was perfect."

So John quit his high-paying job and took one at $140 a month. A year later he was offered a much better job and worked there while studying part time at Criswell. Then he realized he had to do more. He had promised God. His wife who had prayed about his alcoholism for many years went back to work to subsidize her husband's education and evangelism, which began with lay preaching at revivals. This was John's seventh trip to El Salvador; he had also been to Mexico, Chicago, and Cameroon. In the afternoons in San Salvador, while most of us read and rested, John usually passed out tracts. He threw tracts out the window of the van as we drove to our revivals, and people stopped to pick them up. John said, "I didn't come down here to pass the time."

That afternoon I sat in the dark dining room at the hotel (no power) for one last discussion with Keith Eitel, Leo Humphrey, and Steve Kern. I said, in reference to all proposed cosmic answers, "It's probably Christianity or nothing," and they all assented to this, Humphrey emphatically so. Then he added, "If Christianity isn't true, throw the Bible on the ground and stomp on it."

Radical, first-century, all-or-nothing Christianity, foolishness to Greeks and liberal Christians alike: that's what evangelicals practice and, in some cases, take pride in. Thinking of my experience in the Rosario church, I asked these men if they thought it necessary to suffer in order to become a Christian. "Absolutely not," Steve said, "and that's the beauty of the six-year-olds accepting Christ into their hearts."

I blurted out, "But, Steve, that kid was believing in Santa Claus a year or two earlier!"

I probably imagined this, but it seemed to me that was the only time that anything I said to the people of Criswell gave anyone pause or created the least little quaver in the straight line of their reflexive belief. There was a flutter behind the eyelids, I thought. If so, it was only fair, because I had felt any number of flutters, the last one in the Catholic church. But no one said anything.

I wanted to hear Steve's testimony. It turns out he was a classic searcher before he found Christianity. Thirty years old when I met him, he began searching in 1974, when his father, a navigator in the Air Force, moved to Sacramento. His mother had died two years earlier, when her son was thirteen, and her death had left Steve bereft. "I was very close to my mother, who was a sixties-type freethinker," he told us. "It brought home the reality of death. I cried for five or six days straight." He had hardly known his father, who was almost always away on duty, and he had no friends. His mother had been his emotional support.

He checked out the Mormons because he thought they were moral, but their teaching about blacks, which he considered de facto racism, put him off. He read encyclopedias and dictionaries. When he was sixteen he met some kids with Youth for Christ, and for the first time he heard about Moses, Noah, the incarnation, the Resurrection. He had not read a word of the Bible, he had not even been introduced to the terminology and main figures of Christianity, but somehow God had prepared Steve. He was convicted by the Holy Spirit on the spot.

He proceeded to get his degree in chemical engineering from the University of California at Davis, with no plans for pastoring. "I studied the Bible and went to church, but I wasn't seeking God's guidance." He met Pam, whom he would marry but who at that time was not a believer. "We talked about life for six hours at a time, for six months. She became a Christian in 1979, and we got married."

After graduation he got a job with Kaiser Aluminum and was sent to New Orleans. "Sports and adventure were our idolatries. I was an engineer and she was going to be a dentist and we'd be rich and go all over the world having fun." In New Orleans he couldn't find a church until he came across Leo Humphrey's Southern Baptist ministry. Steve had been attending Reformed churches, which are the equivalent of Presbyterian. Leo Humphrey taught the Bible and also emphasized evangelism—"real Christianity." One day Steve went out to one of the black projects with Humphrey and knew then that he had found his home. "This was what God wanted me to do."

Nineteen eighty-three. Moving up with Kaiser, earning a lot of money, giving a lot away. That December, Leo invited him to El Salvador, where he was impressed, as anyone is, by the receptivity of the people. "I didn't want to come here, but God was convicting me. When I'd pray, all God would say to me was, 'Go to El Salvador.' Finally I couldn't even sleep. It became hard to pray. I always said that Pam wouldn't want to go. I wasn't trusting in God."

Next August he finally surrendered. "I told Pam and she said God had been working with her, too, but about El Salvador specifically she still said 'No way.' I asked her to pray and two or three weeks later she said God had said she should do it. I loved my job, but I had no choice. It's not that you decide you hate everything you did before, but that you just love God more."

Steve could feel this way because his life hadn't been a wreck—far from it. He set their departure for August 1, 1985, giving himself a year to raise some "faith money," get his affairs in order, and sell his house. But following the oil bust, homes in New Orleans weren't selling. "I wasn't testing God, but I told Him I couldn't go if I didn't sell the house for at least $60,000. It's hard to explain but if you know God has called, you don't worry." He sold the house. He gave notice at Kaiser. "I had spent a lot of time with the think-tankers at work, and we'd go around in circles on all this, and when I decided to quit they started inviting me out. They were curious."

Another one of those stories: no money in the bank, no money coming in, and no worries. Unbelievers call these people fools. They call themselves Christians.

"You can't confuse Christianity with what you see on TV," Steve said. "A lot of ministers have never really been called. It's their *profession*. I believe God hates religion. Catholics see this conversion as 'changing religions,' not 'being saved.' Well, you *can* change religions, but if the Holy Spirit convicts you, you're beyond denominations. We raise up Christ, we never confront the Catholic church. Because of my love for God I'd do anything for Him. Six bombs have exploded within two hundred yards of my house within the past six years. But I'm not a poor suffering person. I love this. I'm fulfilling my purpose and I know it. I have peace. My friends from school don't have this peace. Everybody I told about my decision thought I was wasting my life. My dad, who has remarried, doesn't know what to say. He's afraid to talk to me. When I first told him I was saved, he got angry and told me never to bring up the subject again. I think people get angry out of pride. They don't want to humble themselves, intellectually. They call this a cop-out, but intellectual pride keeps them back. The phrase 'born again' is completely true. Now I know my purpose and my future—to live here and glorify God. You have to have a burden for people. I've picked up the newspaper and read about people dying, and had tears come to my eyes."

Steve and Pam Kern have three young children. Steve said missionary kids as a rule are "either totally rotten or really good people." The Kern family is supported by eight churches, and it has been a battle for Steve to receive money from people rather than give it away, as he used to when he worked for Kaiser. "I don't want to be a Jim Bakker. I don't want to do anything to excess." I asked Steve what's the difference, really, between him and me. Why are some saved and the vast majority not? The answer to that question I heard most often had been summarized neatly by Cheryl Baker when she said, "Because you want to live your own lives. You don't want to give anything up. You don't want to live for Jesus."

Steve Kern replied with a subtly different emphasis: "Some people need Him, and some don't. I love my friends who are lost, I pray for them, but when we talk, we're separated. It's not explainable. The need has to overwhelm the intellect." That overwhelming need has to be accompanied by courage, too. Secularism is the easy road today. Telling friends with Ph.D.'s you've become a born-again Christian takes nerve. I said to Steve it must be difficult to adopt a faith that threatens his mother with hell, and his father, too. He replied, "I can only hope that something happened in that last month for my mother. But it would be ignorance to reject a fact because it hurts someone. I couldn't reject the truth of Christianity because it endangers my mother."

A harsh statement, but right in line with Jesus' radical admonition in Matt. 10:34–38:

Do not think that I have come to bring peace on earth; I have not come to bring peace, but a sword. For I have come to set a man against his father, and a daughter against her mother, and a daughter-in-law against her mother-in-law; and a man's foes will be those of his own household. He who loves his father or mother more than me is not worthy of me; and he who loves his son or daughter more than me is not worthy of me; and he who does not take his cross and follow me is not worthy of me.

CHAPTER 22

———〜〜〜———

Most Criswell students will not end up in the exotic reaches of the Christian mission field; most will work in local churches like Craig Walker's South Mesquite Baptist Church east of Dallas, about as far from first-century Christianity as it is possible to get. Craig represents the main goal of Criswell College, 70 percent of whose students are men who will wind up as Southern Baptist pastors (including some who don't graduate), with many of them starting their pastoring before they graduate from college. Small churches in or near Dallas know that Criswell is a source of apprentice pastors, men who will happily take on the chores of running a small church. These churches are the training ground, although nothing says that Craig Walker won't remain at South Mesquite for twenty years. The odds are, however, that he will not. Pastors have career ambitions, too. A church that averages fewer than one hundred people at Sunday services, like South Mesquite, will not hold some of them for very long.

The church itself is a small A-frame facility with exposed beams, cinder block walls, and wood paneling. A small choir of nine or ten folks, an upright piano, and sometimes taped orchestration provide the worship music. One Sunday when I was in attendance the speaker on the left was giving out static. Three ceiling fans stirred the air. A handful of Baptist churches are like First Baptist Jacksonville or First Baptist Dallas—grand affairs at which the worship service sometimes has the trappings of a Broadway show—but most are like South Mesquite, featuring down-home Christianity in which neither the pastor nor his people can rely on professional music, brilliant elocution, and the excitement generated by the mere presence of several thousand people to fan the flames of religious ardor.

Preceding me into the church on Sunday morning was a man who stubbed out his cigarette before entering. Southern Baptists as a rule don't smoke. Criswell people verified what I suspected: no one at First Baptist Dallas is likely to approach the auditorium smoking a cigarette. Not done. But it is done at South Mesquite, every week. The crowd that morning was variously dressed, some in coats and ties, some in blue jeans. Most of the women wore dresses. Kids were crawling everywhere. In the middle of the pews was one little black girl all by herself.

The service began with announcements and a hymn, "Victory in Jesus," and then the invocation prayer for which the men in the congregation were invited to come to the altar—a tradition often observed in Baptist churches. There will not be an equivalent invitation to the women.

Then one of Craig's deacons told a story. The man's daughter lives in Houston and she does not, as a matter of course, stop to help stranded motorists. It's too dangerous. But on this day she saw a woman sitting in a car at the side of the road. Some impulse made her look in her rearview mirror. She thought about stopping just this once, but drove on. Finally she did stop and turned around and for the first time in her life drove back to the scene of a stranded motorist. The woman in the car was pregnant, as it turned out, and the car had a broken drive shaft. As the deacon's daughter assisted this woman with her car problem, she also led her to the Lord.

These episodes do not "just happen," the deacon assured the congregation. The hand of the Lord is working. He then sang, in excellent voice and to an upbeat taped accompaniment, "My God Is Real."

Craig Walker, dressed in a gray suit, then delivered the Message from God's Word—the sermon. His text was from Paul's letter to the Philippians, 3:7–11, beginning, "But whatever gain I had, I counted as loss for the sake of Christ. Indeed I count everything as loss because of the surpassing worth of knowing Christ Jesus my Lord. . . ."

Craig asked everyone to close their eyes. "Those of you who know Jesus, raise your hand. Now, those who didn't raise their hand, can you say that you are seeking Jesus? If you're seeking Jesus and want to find Jesus, raise your hand."

I didn't raise my hand at either point, and I felt Craig's eyes on me. Maybe he didn't even look in my direction, but in such a small space, with fewer than one hundred people present, I was pretty sure he must have. I never asked him and he never said anything but I think I somehow hurt his feelings. What was I doing there if I wasn't even *seeking* to know the truth? Why wouldn't anyone do that?

Craig continued with his message. We cannot be born into salvation. If anyone believes so, he is lost. "I say this not to shame you," Craig explained, "but to alert you."

You cannot count on anything but Jesus. You must come empty to the cross. Your righteousness is as filthy rags. You cannot serve two masters. Socrates said the unexamined life is not worth living. For the believer, there is no neutral ground: your life is pleasing to God, or to Mammon. Do you really want to know Jesus? If so, you must die unto yourself. Do you know Jesus better today than yesterday? Than last week? Than last year? If not, you're stagnating. In softball, would you hit a home run but refuse to run? How then could you be born again in Christ, and refuse to grow?

Craig pronounced his clipped cadences in a high voice—slightly too high, technically. His message didn't have the polish of Adrian Rogers's address at the convocation in Jacksonville, but who would expect it? Rogers is a master with vast experience, and Craig is a beginner. His sermon was well crafted and the analogy with softball was apt. He told me later that the Thursday and Friday night softball games are by far the most popular activities at the church. In conclusion, Craig asked us again to bow our heads and close our eyes. "Do you know Christ? Do you want to? Believers, I see some of you at every ballgame but not on Tuesday visitation or Wednesday prayer meeting."

He stepped down to the front of the congregation for the traditional invitation. Craig stood there alone. No one came forward. He mentioned parents, boys and girls. Now I was feeling bad for him. I wanted someone to make the move.

"If you reject Him now, will He call you again? Will He call you before it's too late?" No one came forward, so we all joined hands for what was, given the result of the invitation, the bittersweet final hymn, "I Have Decided." Craig then moved to the door to greet everyone as they filed out. Then he locked up and we drove the few blocks to his home for supper.

Yes, he told me on the way, those services when no one comes forward during the invitation, and they are not uncommon at South Mesquite Baptist, were difficult. The power of preaching to move people is impressed on all conservative pastors. If their folks are not moved, pastors take it personally.

Not long before my visit in East Dallas I had joined young Philip Martin at a Wednesday night service at First Baptist Dallas, W. A. Criswell presiding. The pastor was in a pensive, even vulnerable mood as he told us about a trip to India with his wife, where they observed an apparently infertile woman wailing in a temple, and he had thought about the story of Rachel in the thirtieth chapter of Genesis. Rachel, both cousin and wife of Jacob, was barren and certainly Jacob wasn't the problem because he fathered six sons and a daughter with Rachel's younger sister Leah, two sons with Leah's maid Zilpah, and two sons with Rachel's maid Bilhah. In the twenty-second verse of the chapter, God remembers Rachel and opens her womb and she bears a son and names him Joseph.

Criswell marvels at the story of Rachel. He has nothing but compassion for the people of India, trapped in their "barren idolatry," and he also weeps for the lost in his own culture.

"There are over one thousand churches in Dallas," he told us, "and most of these are poorly attended. And this is the Bible Belt!" He related the story of driving for hours in the Northeast one Sunday evening, looking for a church that was even open. He talked about the previous Sunday's service at First Baptist Dallas—a "powerful and dynamic service, and not one person saved. Not one."

He almost collapsed as he delivered those last words. This is the evangelist's curse: the lost seem to multiply, to number as the sands of the sea. I wanted to go forward just to help the kind old man. I've seen a lot of crocodile tears shed by the televangelists. Criswell wasn't faking. I thought about the lovely line in one of Vincent Van Gogh's letters to his brother Theo, a reference to their failure to sell any paintings: "There may be a great fire in my soul, but no one comes to warm himself."

But at least W. A. Criswell is buffered somewhat by the sheer size of his establishment. Rare is the service at which no one at all comes forward, for any reason. Craig Walker's small church leaves nowhere for the pastor to hide. "Begin where they are," said the leader of the evangelism workshop in Jacksonville. It occurred to me sitting in Craig's church that many pastors might have murmured at that point, "And then begin again, years later, where they still are." The outsider might believe that each of the thirty to sixty million Americans who will assent to the label fundamentalist or evangelical or charismatic Christian is a zealous firebrand for the faith. I might have believed this before I went to Dallas, but I learned otherwise. The statistician's bell curve with the large middle ground and quickly tapering ends describes conservative Christian behavior just as it does many other phenomena. There's a small percentage of Green Berets, an equal number of deadbeats, with the large majority in the middle, people who seem to be, judging by their actions, just about as interested in softball as in salvation. As my distant Methodist pastor Don Pevey said to me in San Antonio about many of his Methodists, "They see the decent, fine, honorable people of the world going to church, so they go to church. There's a lot of that in all denominations."

This is tough on pastors like Craig Walker. It's tough to be so convinced of a truth and not be able to convince others or, almost worse, to see people going through the motions in a matter of such vital importance. Eight years before I met him, when he was twenty-five, he was earning $50,000 a year working at the new General Motors plant in Matamoros, Mexico, right across the river from his home in Brownsville. The total budget for South Mesquite, including his salary, is $92,000. In the Valley he owned a two-story house, boat, car, and plane. Now he and his wife Debby and their three kids live in the modest one-story pastorium provided by the church. His mainly working-class congregation is primarily involved with the tasks and difficulties of daily life. Craig knows their concerns well: he knows all about being obsessed with the house, boat, car, and plane (although there weren't any planes parked on the streets of Mesquite, I have never seen as many cars and pickups—at least three per household seemed about average—parked in garages, driveways, streets, and yards). But Craig was called away from all this. Why isn't everyone else?

Based on nothing that Craig said to me, based only on what I saw in his and other church services in Dallas, I understood why many of the sermons at the pastors conference in Jacksonville stressed the importance of hanging in despite the difficulties, and why the laughter was so nervous at evangelist Junior Hill's joke about the pastor who said things were going pretty good because this church was dying more slowly than any of his others had. The same guest pastor who had told us in chapel about the preacher's fall from grace after seeing the lewd image on television told the story of another preacher. This man had been a powerful pastor, and after quitting he went on to be quite successful in another field. One day a young associate asked him if he knew Jesus Christ. After the ex-pastor told the man his story he was asked, "Do you ever miss it?" He replied with a description of how medieval soldiers were summoned to battle in the early morning by the call of trumpets.

"Yes," he concluded, "I miss the call of trumpets every morning."

The subject of another message in chapel was "Count It All Joy," from James 1:2: "Count it all joy, my brethren, when you meet various trials, for you know that the testing of your faith produces steadfastness."

John Burns, Criswell's librarian, brought this message to the students. If God is with me, who is against me? Be not weary in well-doing, because in due course ye shall reap what ye sow. "Patience, my friends," Burns advised the students. "How long will I be in Dallas? How long will I be in school? How long till my wife becomes as spiritual as I am?"

Laughter here.

"Count it all joy."

CHAPTER 23

$\approx$

A
nd after some days Paul said to Barnabas, "Come, let us return
and visit the brethren in every city where we proclaimed the
word of the Lord, and see how they are." And Barnabas wanted to take
with them John called Mark. But Paul thought best not to take with them
one who had withdrawn from them in Pamphylia, and had not gone with
them to the work. And there arose a sharp contention, so that they
separated from each other; Barnabas took Mark with him and sailed
away to Cyprus, but Paul chose Silas and departed, being commended
by the brethren to the grace of the Lord. And he went through Syria and
Cilicia, strengthening the churches. (Acts 15:36–41)

Early in the term at Criswell, Danny Akin cited this passage to
prove that Christians, good Christians, can have honest differences
of opinion about denominational matters and still go their separate
ways in accomplishing the good work. I wondered about this as I
was flying to Las Vegas for the Southern Baptist Convention in

June. For a decade now bitter fights have been waged for control of the denominational bureaucracy, focused on the question of inerrancy and, beyond that, enforcement of inerrancy within the bureaucracy and the seminaries. Recall W. A. Criswell's remark in 1988: "We're trying to rescue the convention from the leprous hands of the liberals! Don't believe a word of the lying liberals! They call themselves moderates—but a skunk by any other name still stinks!"

Other Southern Baptists take to heart the idea that theirs is indeed a "priesthood of the believer" (as opposed to a priesthood of the priesthood) and all politics be damned, politics being by definition an attempt to enforce belief. Baptists have always sought and revered independence. First comes the sanctity of the individual conscience, then the independence of the local church. The Southern Baptist Convention is a voluntary collection of 38,000 like-minded local churches. A church can withdraw at any time and join one of the other Baptist conventions, or be independent. There's no Southern Baptist priesthood or the equivalent; anyone can be a Baptist minister; each church hires and fires pastors as it wishes. Each church gives as much money as it desires to the denomination's Cooperative Program, which funds the seminaries and missionaries and other programs.

A lot of Southern Baptists have been turned off by the fighting. John Bisagno, one of the more respected of their preachers, head of the First Baptist Church in Houston, said of the battle, "Today, in what may be the twilight years of world history, the greatest evangelist and missionary tool in the history of the kingdom of God stands like a crazed animal, chewing itself to death."

I hesitate to go into all this too deeply. It's politics as well as theology, and as such you have to be involved for it to mean much. Paige Patterson may be, along with Judge Paul Pressler, one of the two masterminds behind the conservative movement in the denomination, but some others at Criswell don't care a great deal. Nor is Southern Baptist business inherently more interesting than whatever's going on in, say, the inner circles of the AFL-CIO.

It was about thirty years ago that the Southern Baptist denomination began to show signs, belatedly, of the classic liberal/conservative debate about the Bible that had been resolved decades before by most of the other main Protestant denominations. The year was 1961. Conservatives in the denomination were shocked when a professor at Midwestern Seminary espoused a nonhistorical interpretation of the first eleven chapters of Genesis. This professor would no more call himself a liberal than I would call myself a conservative, but his belief was the standard liberal line that the Creation account doesn't have to be historically and scientifically true in order to be spiritually and heuristically true.

There were signs that other seminary professors did not adhere to a strict inerrancy. In 1969 Criswell published *Why I Preach that the Bible Is Literally True,* and a group of seminary professors criticized his work. That same year a British scholar and popular visiting pastor in Southern Baptist pulpits suggested that God might not in fact have directed Abraham to slay Isaac (Genesis 22). Another seminarian confessed his doubts about the Old Testament episode in which Elisha breathes life into a young boy (2 Kings 4:30–35).

Conservatives, led by the attorney Paul Pressler of Houston, Patterson's good friend who now sits on Texas's 14th Court of Appeals, began to counterattack. Pressler was educated at Phillips Exeter, Princeton, and the University of Texas Law School. Count back on his family tree quite a few generations in any direction and you will find Southern Baptists. At Exeter, founded for the purpose of training men in the Word of God, Pressler had to inform his Baptist pastor what it meant to be saved. At Princeton he found secularism and liberalism rife, and throughout the Northeast he "found out the extremely negative impact that [liberalism] had had on culture and society and presentation of the gospel." Then he discovered signs of liberalism in Texas, even at Baylor, the theoretically Baptist college that also strained Jim Parker's patience—but Parker was mainly upset that Baylor's accommodation with secularism was *unacknowledged.*

Pressler and other conservatives argued that there should be some basic tenets of belief, and that in fact they already existed in the Baptist Faith and Message, adopted in 1963, which states that the Bible is "truth, without any mixture of error, for its matter." Simply put: believe the Bible, teach the Bible, and save souls. If you can't accept this doctrine, fine, these activists said, but you shouldn't be teaching in Southern Baptist seminaries, disseminating your thinking in Southern Baptist publications, or preaching from Southern Baptist pulpits. Do it somewhere else. They argued that the idea of a priesthood of the believer implies the responsibilities of right belief, not the rights of dissident belief. Hal Lindsell, the best-selling Christian author of *The Battle for the Bible* and other books, publicly invited the estimated 500,000 "liberals" in the convention to leave it for another denomination.

Writing in 1985, Paige Patterson described the genesis of the dispute: "The present controversy would have occurred sooner or later. Had there been no Martin Luther, there would still have been a Reformation. . . . The conditions existing in sixteenth-century Europe made the Reformation inevitable. Similarly, conditions in the Southern Baptist Convention in the last quarter of the twentieth century dictated the inevitability of such a confrontation. Too many contemporary Southern Baptists sat through classes in Baptist colleges or seminaries in which alternatives to the faith of their homes and churches were presented as certainties. . . . Some of the doctrinal truths that I had been taught to hold precious were not only debunked but also ridiculed. On occasion my precious pastor Dr. Criswell was held in derision. The fires of evangelism and fervency of heart were often doused with the condescending remark of the lofty academe."

And this from Patterson: "I found incongruous the apparent anomaly of professors who accepted their wages from churches whose positions they proceeded to undermine."

All Southern Baptists will assure you that they "believe the Bible." But what exactly does this assertion mean? Conservatives say it means their doctrine of inerrancy. The opponents of the conservatives—call them moderates or liberals; they call themselves moderates—accuse the conservatives of advocating a "creeping credalism," and Southern Baptists have always opposed creeds. A professor of Christianity at Mercer University, in Macon, Georgia, wrote, "On any Sunday morning in any Sunday school class in the Southern Baptist Convention you can find ordinary Baptists who do not agree on what the Bible says." He urged that the denomination fall back on the usage in a famous little book, *The Axioms of Religion,* which decrees the Bible to be cherished as "sufficient, certain, and authoritative." If any Christian approaches the Scripture with this reverence and with "the competency of the soul," his interpretation must be accepted as within the confines of the faith. In the Father's house are many mansions.

Criswell College was founded in 1970 for the expressed purpose of defending the conservative, inerrantist position within the convention. Then the conservatives decided to gain control of the other seminaries and the denomination bureaucracy in general. The organization of the convention provides a way to accomplish this: election of the convention president, who has enormous appointive powers. Hold the presidency for enough years and any faction can eventually dominate the various boards of directors. Ronald Reagan was in office for eight years; he appointed 50 percent of all currently sitting federal judges. Going to Las Vegas, the conservatives had controlled the presidency of their convention for ten years.

They made their first assault on the presidency in 1979, when the convention was held in Houston. By this time Paige Patterson was Pressler's co-conspirator in the palace coup. Conservative groups caucused all across the convention and decided on Adrian Rogers from Memphis, Tennessee, as their candidate. (Ten years later I had heard Rogers deliver the fine sermon in Jacksonville about Abraham and Isaac.)

Folklore holds that Pressler ramrodded the show from one of the sky boxes in the Astrodome. Buses loaded with conservative "messengers," as the voting delegates are called, rolled into the

Astrodome parking lots the morning of the election. Churches can send only so many messengers as voting delegates, and the conservatives cheated in this regard. That's what the moderates said, and the registration secretary for the convention acknowledged "irregularities." Pressler himself was accused of voting as a member of a church of which he was not a member; later he explained his membership was honorary. Rogers was elected with 54 percent of the vote, the results were declared official, and the conservatives were rolling. In 1980, Pressler was quoted as saying his faction was "going for the jugular." Paige Patterson named names as "liberals," and he was censured, mildly, by W. A. Criswell following a meeting with some of the deacons of First Baptist Dallas.

The conservative Adrian Rogers served one term. Three other conservative, inerrantist presidents were elected over the next six years, then Rogers again in 1986 and 1987. In 1988, Jerry Vines from First Baptist Jacksonville was elected.

The losing moderates in the convention accuse the conservatives of turning the denomination into a papal state and crowning their president as its pope. A Southern Baptist can't say anything nastier than that. The conservatives had always said they would not fire people who were doing a good job, but they are now being accused of reneging on this promise by employing pressure that amounts to firing. The president of one of the six Southern Baptist seminaries has resigned, and another clings to his job while calling the fundamentalist group "satanic." A seminary professor obtained an appointment from Princeton (tantamount to signing a confession, from the perspective of his enemies) and wrote somewhat hysterically about the conservatives, "They want to bludgeon dissidents into submission. Southern Baptists didn't believe this could happen. It's not unlike Germany in the 1930s. People saw German trains carrying Jews away and still didn't believe it."

The candidate the moderates run for president always claims to be just as theologically conservative as any inerrantist. Where they differ, these losing candidates say, is in their "philosophy of leadership," their willingness to include among the flock anyone who wants to be there, their refusal to establish litmus tests for membership or employment. Jerry Vines referred to this thinking as a neoorthodoxy in which the opponents "use our vocabulary but not our dictionary."

Vines was up for reelection in Las Vegas, and before all this started the second one-year term was considered automatic. Not anymore. There was even some thought that the reelection of Vines could be in some jeopardy in 1989 because of the Las Vegas venue. Some ultraconservatives might not even come to the city, which is, after all, the very triumph of the secular values they decry, where one of the nightclub acts is billed as the "Hallelujah Chorus" and where a local Catholic church, for one, accepts casino chips in the offering plate. One of the assurances the fundamentalists received before they agreed to the Vegas site was a great evangelism effort before and during the convention, and this in fact took place. Photocopies of the Las Vegas phone book were sent all over the country, and every name in it was prayed for by a squad of volunteers. Southern Baptists went door-to-door in Las Vegas for two weeks prior to the convention. On the Sunday beforehand, a thousand messengers fanned out across the city. During the convention, evangelist Arthur Blessit, who has made a reputation by bearing a wooden cross on his shoulder at many of his appearances throughout the world, led hundreds of messengers on a campaign down the strip, and he had his cross with him. (Since then Blessit has divorced his wife, married the proverbial younger woman, and announced publicly that God has granted him "the dispensation of David," thus allowing him to continue in his work; this audacity made Paige Patterson furious.) The last figures I heard in Las Vegas reported 1,500 good prospects, with 360 decisions for Christ.

~~~~~~~

A friend of mine, an amateur gambler who lives in New York, works in the movie business, and usually stops off in Vegas on his transcontinental flights, had informed me that the Hilton, convention headquarters and also my hotel, has the best—least sleazy—casino in town. I had never been in one and budgeted $200 in losses—exactly $200 more than any legitimate Southern Baptist would leave at the tables.

The fact that this was a convention and not a prayer meeting was immediately evident. The knots of people gathered in lobbies and hallways, talking and gesticulating, could have been politically minded delegates to any convention except that none of them smoked or drank. These 24,000 Southern Baptists had come for politics, though they believe and contend that the politics of the convention has a great influence on worship back in the churches. Las Vegas was far from San Salvador, and it would seem that the politics here were also a long way from the first-century Christianity that attracted the Criswell evangelists to El Salvador, but maybe not. The history of Christianity is rife with doctrinal conflict, accusations of heresy, and witch-hunts of one form or another, beginning with the disputes related by Luke in Acts and continuing to this day in the Christian denominations that still have the stomach for it—that still believe Christianity requires a claim to exclusive truth.

The press room at the convention center was an efficient operation in every respect, managed by pros and staffed by volunteers who knew what they were doing. I was presented a massive folder of material, all of it separated, labeled, and well written: advance stories, advance speeches, newspaper clippings, committee reports, agendas. Nearby tables were stacked with the partisan publications. I saw a group of reporters seated around a sharply dressed, handsome-preacher type (not a Paige Patterson type, in other words). Thinking that this man must be a principal in the proceedings, I pulled up a chair on the fringe.

"Would you dismiss a professor who . . . ?"

"Should there be an official two-party system?"

"Do you hold to your statement that votes have been 'stolen'?"

"What do you believe are the grass-roots beliefs of Southern Baptists?"

"What do you think about Southeastern Seminary students being advised to go see *The Last Temptation of Christ*?"

I moved in closer. These questions sounded like those directed at a candidate. I had met Jerry Vines in Jacksonville, so I surmised this must be Vines's opponent, the moderate Daniel Vestal. I was right. Vestal handled all these questions well, as a seasoned public performer would.

"In the past few weeks I've learned of incredible disenchantment . . . a lot of churches are quitting the convention . . . most of us are conservative but we don't want stuff rammed down our throats . . . one person, one conscience . . . priesthood of the believer . . . look at the leading contributors to Baptist programs: quiet, middle-of-the-road centrists . . . all this talk about 'theological purity' and 'low morals' at Southeastern and Southern seminaries, but the faculties are the same as they've been, just about . . . yes, there should be more inerrantists on the faculties, but how should it be done? That's what Paige is always asking me—'How?', and I answer through the power of prayer, preaching, and persuasion. These things can work."

This last attitude struck me as either remarkably ingenuous or shrewdly disingenuous, but then Vestal added, "To think that the nature of Southern Seminary will be changed in one year or ten is either naïve or dishonest. . . . This political movement may be used by God, but it has too many lies in it . . . students at Southeastern are refusing to shake hands with the president.

" 'How can I be a front man for the liberals?' they ask me. I'm not. I'm for a free convention. Thank you, ladies and gentlemen. I hope to see you at six o'clock tomorrow night."

That was the appointed hour for the victor's news conference. Vestal wasn't going to be there and he knew it. I headed back down the long series of corridors from the convention center to the hotel and casino proper. By this time in my Criswell odyssey—almost six months—I was overdosed with Christian theology and doctrine and politics. I knew the opposing positions in the presidential election, I knew who was going to win, I thought I knew these people as well as I ever would. I was going to Las Vegas mainly to see the place. And I wanted to gamble some.

I had made no plans for meeting with Paige Patterson or anyone else from Criswell. I knew Patterson would be too busy, and the others I would see around. Sure enough, here was Danny Akin in the lobby, wanting to know if I had been in the casino yet. Akin would want to know how I did. He was already getting into the spirit of any political convention—denying rumors. He had come over on the plane with a delegate from North Carolina, where they tend to be liberal, and this man had asked whether it was true that W. A. Criswell hands out little statues of himself as mementos of visits and interviews.

"Can you believe that?" Akin exclaimed.

Sure. He invited me to a banquet that evening at the Riviera, for Criswell alumni. Walking through the livelier, gaudier, and much smokier casino at the Riviera I understood why my friend recommended the Hilton. These dealers wore pink shirts; at the Hilton they dressed in black and white. The Riviera pit bosses fit the seedy stereotype perfectly, while their equivalents at the Hilton casino could have passed, almost, for Southern Baptist messengers.

The Criswell occasion was a high-spirited affair, and why not? They would win the election, their cause was booming, these graduates were well placed and rising. I found myself next to Mrs. Patterson's parents, wonderful folks. Her father is a retired mortician and he and his wife still live in Beaumont. Every place setting featured a fresh silver dollar, which Patterson urged each alumnus to return to the college in the manner of Matt. 13:8, which concludes Jesus' parable about the sower and his seeds, some of which will fall on rocky soil, some on thorns: "Other seeds fell upon good soil and brought forth grain, some a hundred-fold, some sixty, some thirty."

"So with your checks," Patterson called out, "let us know how you're doing!"

Then he caught me off-guard and introduced me from the dais.

"Mike's an atheist"—momentarily ashamed, I called out "Agnostic!" by way of correction, and he accepted that—"and I know he won't mind when we pray for him. He's a dear person, and many of us have come to love him."

I was annoyed—with myself. Patterson had caught me off-guard with his "atheist" designation and induced me into that semantic emendation, but he was right. We're *functional* atheists, no matter what the polls show. And his sally convinced me of one thing. I'd never attempt to put one over on Paige Patterson. I had always assumed that his unfailing kindness to me during my term at his college was to some extent political. I was writing a book about Criswell College, after all, for a partially secular audience, presumably. Why would he want to antagonize me? But I had never taken his generous and undoctrinaire attitude, shared by almost everyone else at the school, as *mainly* calculated. It was a Christian attitude, and it was real. I give myself credit for knowing the difference. I took his introduction of me as the pet atheist at Criswell to be another mark of his irrepressible mischievousness and genuine interest in all folks and their diverse ways—a mark of his personality, not his faith. The same holds true for Danny Akin, Jim Parker, Keith Eitel, and just about everyone else I've mentioned in this narrative. One thing I had learned at Criswell: theological dogmatism can be passionately espoused by personalities who are not in the least doctrinaire.

This had puzzled me. I had asked several people at the school why, if they believed I was so wrong in my beliefs I am going to hell, I didn't feel this condemnation on anything but an intellectual level. Why wouldn't it interrupt a friendship and, for that matter, the whole flow of living in the wide world in which most of the people encountered would also be going to hell.

Patterson answered me this way: "While there is a clear divide, as far as we are concerned, between those who are saved and those who are lost, the clear divide is purely the grace of God. It is no matter of character within us that makes us superior to anybody. We just don't see any big difference, we really don't. We are both sinners who have rebelled against God, and just by His precious grace I happen to be forgiven. I have *accepted* His forgiveness.

"Also, and however falteringly we follow the faith we claim to believe, we do believe that every individual, lost or saved, is the handiwork of God—to get technical, he is the *imago dei*—the image of God. And as such this person is the object of God's most intense love, and that being the case, for me to be anything other than totally accepting, not to reach out to him with every fiber of my own being, would be to deny the faith. It would be a failure to extend to others the same kindness and love that God has extended to me.

"One of the things that happens to you in conversion is that there's a fundamental change in your attitude toward people when the Lord moves into your life. You don't any longer see them as the girl who sells you the hamburger or the guy who changes your tires. You see each of them as very precious people, each of whom has a fascinating personal story. You get to where it's fun to be with them, see what makes them tick."

Patterson then told me about his rabbi friend with whom he exchanges letters. "Bless his heart, he is under so much conviction he can hardly see straight. God's conviction. He knows deep down in his heart that Jesus is the fulfillment of Old Testament prophecy. He wouldn't admit this in ten million millennia, but God's dealing with him. The hound of heaven's after him. He's miserable, bless his heart. But if he were to die tonight, he would unfortunately be in hell, as far as I'm concerned. This grieves my soul."

Riding back to the Hilton in the Pattersons' rented car I suggested that I play the slots with my dollar and give all the pot to Criswell. Fine, Patterson said, but I crapped out. At the convention proper I didn't pay much attention. I did have an interesting conversation with the official Catholic observer, whom I recognized by his collar. He had been attending these conventions for quite some time, and related them to the growing charismatic wing of his own denomination. There are an estimated two and a half million foot-stomping Catholics. I assumed the cleric understood that Southern Baptist evangelicals don't want to be confused with charismatics of the Jimmy Swaggart variety, with a lot of speaking in tongues.

At my first session at the gaming tables I made about fifty dollars and walked away, then turned back and lost that fifty and fifty more. So I learned quickly how the casinos make their money. I was also keeping my eye out for convention messengers who might be gambling. I never saw one. Someone mentioned that two or three had been spotted playing in other casinos, and this made sense. I don't believe anyone would risk playing right there in the headquarters hotel.

One evening I noticed a Japanese player at the roulette wheels who seemed to have an interesting system. He had in front of him a dozen or more wobbly stacks of pink chips, each worth five hundred dollars. When the ball was dropped, he grabbed the stacks and shoved them randomly on the betting form—hundreds of thousands of dollars, by my astonished reckoning, on each spin. Within half a dozen games he had multiplied his stacks, not the biblical thirtyfold, but at least threefold, I'd say. He scooped up what he could, directed his associates who were gathered around to get the rest, and walked over to the baccarat pit, an exclusive domain separated from the rest of the casino by steps, ropes, and a guard. But we could stand outside and watch. A couple of Southern Baptist messengers were next to me, talking quietly about all the good that could be accomplished with just one stack of those chips. One asked the other as they walked off, "But what *would* you do if you had it?"

I struck up a conversation with one of the high, high rollers' henchmen, who was also standing outside the pit. His boss is named Mori, and he is one of the wealthiest men in the world. He comes to Las Vegas two or three times a year and wins or loses about that many million dollars each time. I was feeling bad about the three hundred dollars I was down, and more so when I reported this to my wife, who wasn't happy. I had gone out to Vegas with a limit and hadn't been able to hold to it. I'd been suckered.

Jerry Vines was reelected with 57 percent of the vote, a wider margin than his victory a year earlier. Paul Pressler declared, "The course correction is complete in the Southern Baptist Convention. Praise God for what's happened in the SBC. We've returned to our biblical roots." I had seen Pressler in the elevator of the hotel but didn't introduce myself because he was surrounded by well-wishers. I was supposing the Paige Patterson connection would have assured me a few special words.

In his speech to the convention messengers, Vines sought to heal any wounds. He emphasized the common bond that unites all good Christians, certainly all Southern Baptists: evangelism on behalf of lost souls. "If there is anything that Southern Baptist pastors and people agree on, it is our mandate to let every person know about the gospel of Jesus Christ." Holding aloft his Bible he said, "This is the only book I know that can change a human life."

Then he held up another book, a small red one with the names of everyone he had brought to the Lord in the preceding twelve months. He cited a few examples. Then he said, "I'm not going to tell you how many names are in that book, because to be perfectly honest, I'm ashamed." He told his audience about the illiterate man in his congregation in Jacksonville who has won forty people to God by handing them a tract and asking if they would please read it aloud to him.

I asked a cab driver in Las Vegas if any of the delegates had tried to convert him. "A lot better than them has tried," the man replied cheerfully. He was about my age. "But nothing wrong with it. Just trying to get away from reality. Hell, look at this"—he gestured wildly out the open window with his free arm—"this whole place is just a Disneyland for adults. Same thing."

In the cabbie's opinion, if we all believed alike it would be an awfully dull world. It would be dull for Christians, too, because the lost are their raison d'être. In various newspaper stories during the convention, messengers expressed surprise that Las Vegas was as interesting and its people as friendly as they turned out to be. My driver returned the compliment about the Southern Baptists.

"They're supernice people," he said. "And I know some in Texas, too, and they treat me like family. The Mormons are nice, too. But just don't try to convert me. I'll come to you."

My last evening in town I walked the strip, watched the high-wire act at Circus Circus, compared the all-you-can-eat deals at the restaurants and the smoke level in the casinos. The Hilton rated superior in regard to smoke, but perhaps that was because of the crowd, or lack of it, that the casino was drawing during the convention. I scrutinized the people who come to Las Vegas for a vacation and wished the Baptist evangelizers sincere good luck. Some of those folks on the strip clearly needed help. Then again, I had enjoyed the Hilton casino. I was even mulling a return trip to try out a system that had come to me lying on my bed, tapped out. Why not double the bet at the blackjack table every time I lost? Bet the $5 minimum, lose that, bet ten, lose that, bet twenty, lose that, bet forty, lose that, bet eighty—by now, the odds are pretty good you're going to win. You will have lost 5 plus 10 plus 20 plus 40—$75. But then you win the $80. Start over $5 to the good. Working it out in my head it seemed too good to be true. I grabbed the pencil and pad and did the math again. No doubt about it. You cannot lose if you just keep doubling your bet. Of course, you won't win much, $5 every series of bets, but you can sit there all night, nurse a Christianity-and-water, and earn some all-you-can-eat money.

I didn't understand how the casino could tolerate consistent losses, even small ones, to the players who had stumbled across this obvious system. What's the catch? I called my gambler friend in New York. At first he was stumped but then came up with a possible explanation. Every table has a minimum *and* a maximum limit. At the $5 minimum table at the Hilton, the maximum was $1,000. So extending my series of bets, say I lost the $80, too, then $160, $320, and $640. The next double, $1,280, is too high. I can't bet that. I've lost $1,275 and can't continue with the doubling scheme that would assure my eventually getting back to that measly $5 profit.

But, I argued with my friend, what are the odds of losing eight straight blackjack hands?!

"Try it and find out," he said darkly.

Well, I didn't, I couldn't, but when I got home I went to the library to check it out. Indeed, I *had* discovered an ancient, sure-fire, obvious gambling scheme—if there's no maximum limit. But there is, and the doubling system is the reason for it. The casino will gladly dole out the $5 losses to anyone playing that system, because, long though the odds are, eventually the player will have that unlikely series of eight consecutive losses that total $1,275. The house will win in the end.

I had never before had the least interest in gambling, but I got into those numbers in a serious way, and I know the reason why. In contrast to Criswell College and the Southern Baptist Convention, they were the secular world, the relativist world, the free world—my world. This flirtation with gambling was the same craving I had felt on arrival back in Dallas from the bus trip to the preachers conference, when I remarked to friends that what I wanted was to drink frozen margaritas and to see an R-rated movie—at the same time, if possible. Nor was I, with that remark, putting down the people on the trip. I was simply stating the truth that in essence they have their world and we have ours; the two overlap, but they don't coincide.

~~~~~

When I walked into Paige Patterson's office for the first time I didn't believe the truth claim of biblical Christianity, without having thought about it a great deal. Many months later, and after thinking about that claim a great deal, I left Criswell College still rejecting it. Others who can't dismiss or explain the sense of the miraculous they encounter in the world and in their lives are able to make a modest leap of faith by accepting the life and message of Jesus of Nazareth as the true Christian miracle, by attesting that his is an earthbound divinity that may well serve, in the language of Paul Tillich, as the ground of our being.

"Who can explain Jesus Christ?!" Don Pevey exclaimed to me in the restaurant in San Antonio. The retired Methodist pastor who has no firm doctrine of hell lacks any explanation whatsoever for the phenomenon of Jesus' career and legacy on earth, and he has no definitive assessment of what it means for mankind. Yet Pevey is profoundly moved by that saga. I came to think of him as something of a go-between for the evangelicals and me.

"The Atonement? I've *never* understood the shedding of the blood. Robert Schuller tells the beautiful story about Princess May, the granddaughter of Queen Victoria, who became ill with diptheria. The doctors told the child's mother Princess Alice that she couldn't go near her daughter. But after days of hearing the child, stricken with a high fever, calling out 'Why doesn't my mother come and hold me?' Princess Alice couldn't take it any longer and rushed in and kissed her daughter on the lips. They both died thirty days later—on the same day—and were buried together. Schuller says this is a picture of the Atonement. Humanity cried out in its sickness, and the Incarnate One came and risked death to show His love. That's a pretty good story."

Actually, several of the details of that story are incorrect, but the point is accurate: while nursing her children during their illness, Alice did contract diptheria, and died. In any event, this kind of analogy is about as close to an Atonement theory as liberal Christians get today. Any sort of doctrine along the lines of the evangelicals' "washed in the blood of Jesus" is set aside as the embarrassing residue of an ancient "slaughterhouse religion."

Pevey followed that story with yet another one, Ray Bradbury's tale of the space traveler who encountered on every planet he visited the localized tale of the man who came and told them to love one another. "That story satisfies something in me," Pevey said quietly. "The creator of it all is just as concerned with whatever is out there as with us on earth. I believe there's life everywhere. The souls cremated in the gas chambers rise up and encounter the same redemptive God the Christian encounters."

Pevey is not an inerrantist: "The Methodist thinks we're kidding ourselves if we believe we can read a book, memorize the words, and solve the problems of the 1990s. This is where the Methodists and the Baptists part ways. We can get along on most things, but not that. Methodists want to keep the words and check ourselves by them. Here's a story: Admiral Byrd decreed that his explorers could go out from base camp as far as they wanted to if they erected a post when they were just about out of sight of the base camp. Then they could go until they were just about out of sight of that pole, when they should stop and erect a second pole. That's the way they explored the white continent. So we Methodists say that you can go as far as you like so long as you keep scriptural tradition in sight. If you lose sight of it, then you can get lost in humanism and the like."

I asked him whether Paul Tillich, say, had wandered too far from the scriptural signpost.

"No, no, no. I don't think Tillich got lost at all. I do think he wandered a lot farther than most of us can or will. But there were always with Tillich a few fundamentals: the incarnation of God in Jesus, the atoning work of Jesus as a deep mystery."

Pevey might be an exception in his interpretation of how far Tillich's theology wandered from the norm. Some Christian commentators believe the theologian strayed into pantheism late in life.

I asked Pevey about the claim to exclusive truth expressed by orthodox Christianity. He replied, "Every religion claims to have the truth; in a way, they must. The whole missionary movement is based on the certainty of truth. But Methodists are disturbed by this. I am often asked, 'What kind of judgment is there upon a person born as an Arab, reared as a Muslim, who prays to Mecca three times a day?' With the Methodists I know, something tells them this judgment wouldn't be fair. Most Methodists say the Jews will be saved. I think most would also say that the devout Muslim also goes to heaven. Most Methodists aren't preoccupied with whether His name *must be* Jesus."

What about Jesus' assertion to be the way, the truth, and the life?

"That statement is true, but it isn't exclusive. Jesus is the redemptive quality of a God *determined* not to lose His creation. God is determined. He put up with Samuel: 'Do the best you can, Samuel.' Then he brought along Isaiah, and *then* Jesus Christ: 'Now you guys have it!' And then, though God was determined to save His world, men said, 'Like hell you are,' and they crucified the incarnate God. And this is our humanity, so perverted from what we were originally created to be. Nothing irritates me more than when someone says, 'That's man's inhumanity to man.' No! It's man's *humanity* to man."

We paused and sipped our coffee. Then Pevey reminded me that perhaps he's not the average Methodist, maybe not even the average Methodist preacher. He thinks the new preachers coming up might actually be a bit more conservative than he is. "I'm a heretic, basically," he sighed, and launched into his own concept of the world beyond, a complicated edifice in which all time is now and he and Abraham confront the redemptive power of God at the same instant. "I know it's screwy, but it satisfies me."

That last phrase—"it satisfies me"—is often the telltale mark of some kind of unorthodox Christianity, but Pevey said, "I must be true to what I believe. I pray I won't lead anyone astray. That's the reason I didn't preach about many of these things. The average preacher lays awake at night pondering the mysteries of God, but knowing very well that if he started talking about these things openly, he would be nothing but harmful. Most people will reflect whatever their pastor preaches, if he's at all persuasive. Whatever he says, the congregation will say, 'Well, probably so, he's a pretty nice guy.' Then they come up and say, 'Hey, that was a nice sermon . . . when do the Cowboys come on this afternoon?' "

Our laughter distracted the other diners. I asked Pevey about the average Methodist's beliefs concerning various Christian doctrines that are vital to the evangelicals at Criswell College.

The virgin birth: "The virgin birth is part of the Methodist doctrine but wise is the preacher who keeps his mouth shut about it, because there's a wide spectrum of what that concept really means. Generally it is not considered essential to belief, but a couple of years ago at a church here in town a guy came up to me and said, 'I've got to talk to you.'

" 'Well, what is it? Is it an emergency?'

" 'I feel like it is. Do you know that our preacher does not believe in the virgin birth?' "

"*No!* Well, in this conservative person's mind taking away the virgin birth takes away the divinity of Jesus Christ. And unless you have a divine Jesus Christ, you don't have anything but a *philosophy*"—the evangelical position exactly. "The mistake that preacher—a young guy—made was to talk about what he *didn't* believe rather than about what he *did* believe."

The physical resurrection of Jesus: "Most Methodists believe in the physical resurrection. A lot believe in the so-called spiritual resurrection. But all say that on the third day something happened that caused the frightened disciples to become courageous disciples. What was it exactly? You don't want to get too tied down with flesh and blood walking through doors."

The Fall and original sin: "The average Methodist would assert a literal picture of Adam and Eve but with a lot of questions indicating they don't really believe it. People used to love to ask me, 'Who did Cain go off and marry if there was nobody but Adam and Eve and Cain and Abel?' And I told them not to get stuck on myth—a good word that's considered a bad one. Myths can be true without being totally true."

The Second Coming: "That's not thought about much, nor preached about much, either. There *is* a lot of preaching about an encounter with the redemptive quality of Christ—liberal-sounding stuff!—but I wouldn't get up and preach that kind of thing. It confuses people. Most Methodists believe in the end of the world, the trumpet will sound, He will come. They believe this because it's all they know. They're not going to worry about it too doggone much. It's not going to happen in their lifetime."

Heaven and hell: "A lot believe heaven and hell are here and now." Or, as my mother put it, "It's today, not tomorrow." Pevey noted the new popularity of cremation, and added, "No Methodist years ago would have dreamed of such a thing. They thought the body had to be kept ready because there would come the time when something was going to zap them."

Then Pevey's wife arrived to pick him up. I would like to have spent hours with this man whose Christianity doesn't claim to be definitive, much less exclusive, who simply finds in the faith and communicates very effectively to anyone who cares to hear one deep and beautiful mystery: God incarnate determined to save His children from themselves.

Some of these children reject this salvation, preferring to go it alone. I suppose I must be included in their number even though I still can't answer with any confidence Criswell professor Jim Parker's *Tres Gran Preguntas*. As Parker suggested, voguish skepticism may indeed be logically flawed and may lead to, if not a pure nihilism, a vaguely perceived but still pernicious limbo. A look around lends some credence to that hypothesis. But here we unchosen are and perhaps here we are meant to be, destined to participate in the sufferings of God at the hands of His godless world. In the conversation between Sartre and de Beauvoir related earlier, in which the philosopher confesses to the feeling that he is "a being that could, it seems, come only from a creator," de Beauvoir follows up by asking Sartre what is the benefit of nevertheless *not* having believed in God, of having lived a life apart from Him.

Sartre answers: "It has strengthened my freedom and made it sounder: at the present time this freedom is not there to give God what he asks me for; it is there for the discovery of myself and to give me what I ask of myself. That's essential. And then my relations with others are direct: they no longer pass through the intermediary of the Omnipotent; I don't need God in order to love my neighbor. . . . This life owes nothing to God; it was what I wanted it to be. . . . And when now I reflect upon it, it satisfies me; and I do not need to pass by God for that. You and I, for example, have lived without paying attention to the problem. I don't think many of our conversations have been concerned with it."

"No, none."

"And yet we've lived; we feel that we've taken an interest in our world and that we've tried to see and understand it."

The modern world, including liberal Christianity, suggests that you can't ask for more than that, but evangelical Christians, in the name of the Bible, do.

AFTERWORD

~~~~~~

Two prominent individuals in this narrative hit the national head-lines in 1991. In the summer, the dynamic speaker Darrell Gilyard admitted to a series of extra-marital liaisons after he had been confronted by his mentor, Criswell College president Paige Patterson, and other Baptist leaders. Some newspaper stories charged that Patterson had previously participated in a cover-up of the scandal. Patterson acknowledged that he had heard rumors about Gilyard and had even conducted interviews with some of the women allegedly involved, but he said he had been unable to come up with actual proof. Gilyard maintained his innocence throughout that period. After the public revelation, Gilyard resigned from his church and immediately began a new one, at which he now preaches to small congregations. He accused Paige Patterson and others at Criswell College of racism.

Then, in the fall, the trustees of Criswell College summarily removed Patterson from his position as president. Press accounts were crowded with various conspiracy theories, but the trustees held to their original assertion that Patterson had been devoting too much time to Convention affairs, too little to the interests of the college. They said they wanted him to take a different position at the school. W. A. Criswell, pastor emeritus at First Baptist Dallas and founder of the college, said he would follow the judgment of the trustees. Faculty, staff, students, and Patterson supporters throughout the Southern Baptist Convention raised an outcry. A group of prominent pastors from around the country confronted the trustees in a hastily convened meeting at the Dallas–Ft. Worth airport and threatened to withdraw all support from the school unless Patterson returned to his post. Ten days after the removal, following a meeting with the trustees at which he agreed to focus more on the concerns of the school, Patterson was indeed reinstated as president.

Finally, just days after the resolution of that crisis, the delegates to the Southern Baptist Convention of Texas, meeting in Waco, voted to uphold the move by the trustees of Baylor University to sever the historic relationship between that school and the Southern Baptist Convention. This was the final act, perhaps, in the struggle for control of Baylor between the "moderates," led by the Baylor trustees, and the conservatives, led by, among others, Paige Patterson. In May 1992, Patterson accepted the appointment as president of Southeastern Seminary in Wake Forest, North Carolina. Six members of the Criswell College faculty, including Danny Akin and Keith Eitel, accompanied Patterson to Southeastern. Jim Parker turned down his invitation to move, choosing to stay in Texas to run the Trinity Institute. His contract at Criswell College was not renewed.

ACKNOWLEDGMENTS

First, of course, I must thank everyone in and around Criswell College. The definitive list of teachers, students, staff, and unaffiliated spouses who gave generously of their time and energy to help with this book would be a long one indeed, and would include many dozens of people I met in Dallas, Jacksonville, Las Vegas, San Antonio, and El Salvador. Not a soul among them gave me anything but 100 percent cooperation— and more: they gave this skeptic their total trust, and I devoutly hope I have not betrayed it in any way. I'm tempted to single out three or four or five for special recognition, and perhaps I should, but I'm also afraid of hurting someone else's feelings, a fate none deserve. So I will settle for just one special word of appreciation to the president of Criswell College, Dr. Paige Patterson, whose invitation to the school made this book possible and whose infectious wit and bonhomie are largely responsible, I believe, for making Criswell an enjoyable place to study and, yes, to worship.

I thank the Henrich family, my hosts in Dallas for quite some time: Bill, Emily, John, and Mary (in alphabetical order).

As always, I thank my wife Patty and my agent Joe Spieler for their great work with the various drafts of this manuscript. (I owe them for a lot of other stuff, too.) Finally, I thank my editors David Rosenthal (Random House) and Caroline White (Penguin), and all the women and men at those two houses whom I never met, and without whom the book could not be published or read.